JUNG AND EASTERN THOUGHT

In *Jung and Eastern Thought* J.J. Clarke seeks to uncover the seriousness and relevance of Jung's dialogue with the philosophical ideas of the East, arising from the various forms of Buddhism, from Chinese Taoism, and from Indian Yoga. Through his commentaries on such books as the *I Ching* and *The Tibetan Book of the Dead*, and various essays on Zen, Eastern meditation, and the symbolism of the mandala, Jung attempted to build a bridge of understanding between Western psychology and the practices and beliefs of Asian religions, and thereby to relate traditional Eastern thought to contemporary Western concerns.

This book offers a critical examination of this remarkable piece of intellectual bridge-building: first, by assessing its role in the development of Jung's own thinking on the human psyche; secondly, by discussing its relationship to the wider dialogue between East and West; and, thirdly, by examining it in the light of urgent contemporary concerns and debates about inter-cultural understanding.

J.J. Clarke has taught philosophy at McGill University, Montreal, and at the University of Singapore. He is currently Senior Lecturer at Kingston University, UK, where he is director of the degree programme in the history of ideas. His book *In Search of Jung* has recently been published by Routledge.

Also available from Routledge

In Search of Jung
J.J. Clarke

Jung and Searles
David Sedgwick

Analysis Analysed
Fred Plaut

Jung and Phenomenology
Roger Brooke

Jung and the Monotheisms
Edited by Joel Ryce-Menuhin

Shame and the Origins of Self-Esteem
Mario Jacoby

JUNG AND EASTERN THOUGHT

A dialogue with the Orient

J.J. Clarke

London and New York

First published 1994
by Routledge
11 New Fetter Lane, London EC4P 4EE

Simultaneously published in the USA and Canada
by Routledge
29 West 35th Street, New York, NY 10001

© 1994 J.J. Clarke

Typeset in Times by LaserScript, Mitcham, Surrey
Printed and bound in Great Britain by
Mackays of Chatham PLC, Chatham, Kent

British Library Cataloguing in Publication Data
A catalogue record for this book is available from the British Library.

Library of Congress Cataloging in Publication Data
Clarke, J.J. (John James), 1937–
Jung and Eastern Thought: A dialogue with the Orient/J.J. Clarke.
p. cm.
Includes bibliographical references and index.
1. Jung, C.G. (Carl Gustav), 1875–1961 – Philosophy.
2. Jung, C.G. (Carl Gustav), 1875–1961 – Religion.
3. Psychoanalysis and philosophy – History.
4. Psychoanalysis and religion – History.
5. Philosophy, Oriental – Psychological aspects – History – 20th century.
6. Asia – Religion. 7. East and West. I. Title.
BF109.J8C54   1993
150.19′54 – dc20   93-8078
CIP

ISBN 0–415–07640–4 (hbk)
ISBN 0–415–10419–X (pbk)

CONTENTS

ACKNOWLEDGEMENTS

I wish to express my thanks to: Routledge, London, and to Princeton University Press, Princeton, for permission to quote from *The Collected Works of C.G. Jung*, and from the two volumes of Jung's *Letters*; to Routledge, London, for permission to quote from *Modern Man in Search of a Soul* by C.G. Jung; to Collins and to Random House for permission to quote from *Memories, Dreams, Reflections* by C.G. Jung; and to Sheed and Ward, London, for permission to quote from *Truth and Method* by H.-G. Gadamer.

I am very grateful to the many friends and colleagues who have given me invaluable encouragement and criticisms in the writing of this book. Special thanks are due to Michael Barnes SJ, Andrew Burniston, Jill Boezalt, Jane Chamberlain, Beryl Hartley, John Ibbett, Mary Anne Perkins, Jonathan Rée, and Andrew Samuels who read and commented on the text at various stages in its evolution.

My thanks are also due to the Faculty of Human Sciences at Kingston University who provided financial support during the academic year 1992–3 which gave me some remission from teaching duties in order to complete the book.

ABBREVIATIONS

Abbreviations employed in the text are as follows:

CW   *The Collected Works of C.G. Jung*. The first digits refer to the volume number, the second to the paragraph number. Thus CW8.243 refers to *Collected Works*, Volume 8, Paragraph 243.

MDR   *Memories, Dreams, Reflections*

MM   *Modern Man in Search of a Soul*

SY   *Synchronicity*

US   *The Undiscovered Self*

Full details of the above works, and all other works cited in the text, are given in the *Bibliography* at the end of this work.

Jung's writings on the East have been collected together in one paperback volume entitled *Psychology and the East*, published by Routledge, 1982.

Part I

PROLOGUE

1

INTRODUCTION

WHAT THIS BOOK IS ABOUT

Enthusiasm for the ways and ideas of ancient China and India, especially for Buddhism, Taoism, and Yoga, has flourished in the West since Carl Gustav Jung was first drawn to the East in the early decades of the century. Western fascination with the ways of the East has indeed been growing ever since Jesuit missionaries first went to Asia in the sixteenth century, and the love affair with the East, which has been such a remarkable feature of the cultural life of our century, would certainly have occurred without Jung's help. Nevertheless, he was in many ways a pioneer in this field, one of the first psychotherapists to recognise the possibility of a fruitful relationship between Western and Eastern concepts of the mind, and his early championing of some of the strange and elusive texts such as the *I Ching*, which were beginning to appear in the West after the First World War, helped to encourage serious interest in Eastern thought. Furthermore, in his approach to the reading of Eastern texts he showed a considerable degree of awareness of the philosophical issues provoked thereby. His writings in this field displayed an understanding of many of the issues involved in the field of inter-cultural communication, and helped to initiate critical reflection on the whole question of the West's intellectual and ideological relationship with that great mysterious 'other' – the Orient.

This book, then, is about Jung's contribution to the East–West dialogue. But it is more than that, for his attempt to extend his psychological endeavours beyond the boundaries of Western cultural traditions raises many intriguing and controversial questions, and so the book will also address wider issues concerning the whole relationship between the Western and Eastern intellectual traditions. On the one hand, this approach will help to place Jung's contribution in a more ample historical and intellectual context, thereby opening up new perspectives on the development of his own thinking. It will also enable us to raise important questions about the nature of dialogue itself, about whether and how a real meeting of minds between East and West is possible, and indeed about whether we should even continue to speak of 'East' and 'West' in this way.

Jung's attempt to engage in a dialogue with Eastern philosophies has frequently been misunderstood. His efforts to make sense of ideas from Eastern religious and philosophical traditions have seemed marginal to his central work in the field of analytical psychology. To his detractors they have represented an example of his bizarre interest in the occult, to be judged alongside his incursions into the realms of astrology, alchemy and flying saucers. To his admirers his efforts have often been an embarrassment, at best a peripheral interest, at worst a regrettable deviation from his true scientific path.[1] When a critic, Edward Glover, sought to belittle Jung's psychology he described it as 'a mishmash of oriental philosophy and bowdlerised psycho-biology' (1950: 134). Hearnshaw, in a more recent book on the history of psychology, spoke patronisingly of Jung's 'flirtation with Oriental cults' (1987: 166), and the Orientalist Girardot ascribed Jung's Eastern interest to his 'mania for scrap-collecting' (1983: 15). His popularity amongst the followers of New Age philosophy has only added to the suspicions of serious scholars, and has helped to confirm them in the belief that Jung's Oriental interests are examples of his notorious mystical bent.[2]

In an earlier book, *In Search of Jung* (1992), I sought to rescue Jung from facile dismissals of this kind by locating him within the broad sweep of Western thought and by attempting to show that, despite a wayward style and an unorthodox range of interests, he deserved as a thinker a secure place in the history of the ideas and intellectual debates of the twentieth century. I pointed out that, while Freud's work has become a focus of debate in many academic fields, a test-bed for ideas in areas ranging from Logical Positivism to post-structuralism and feminism, Jung remained largely ignored by the academic establishment. This may have been excusable at a time when reductionism and scientism ruled, and when interest in metaphysical matters was regarded as the mark of a scoundrel. But the intellectual climate has changed. Jung's central concern with the structure and dynamics of the psyche, though distinctly unorthodox in the context of the intellectual climate in which Freud worked, can now be seen as part of a much wider endeavour to shift the centre of gravity away from positivism and mechanism, a shift which has become associated with fundamental changes within the physical sciences themselves. There has also emerged in recent decades a serious attempt to grapple with ideas from non-European traditions, and to revive interest in conceptual structures which were at one time thought to have been consigned irretrievably to the scrap-heap. In particular, the growing dialogue with the East, a dialogue which has moved from the backstreets of San Francisco into the mainstream of academic life, means that Jung's own work in this field needs to be re-examined and reassessed.

My chief aim in the present study, then, is to focus on one specific aspect of Jung's work, and to attempt in a similar spirit to the earlier study to uncover in a critical way the seriousness and relevance of his excursions into the philosophical and religious territories of the East. I aim to show that these excursions, far from deserving epithets such as 'flirtation' and 'scrap-collecting', played a substantial role in the shaping of his overall method and psychological viewpoint. Eastern

4

ideas represented in his intellectual development, not exotic distractions from his more serious work, the mere hobbies of a man of wide sympathies, but rather an essential ingredient of the leaven from which his most important ideas were fermented, a transforming influence that permeates the whole of his creative output. A secondary aim will be to trace the connections between Jung's work in this context and the whole historical development of the East–West dialogue. Here too it will become evident that his Oriental interests, far from being the passing fad of a maverick, represent an intellectual endeavour which is part of a long, though sometimes obscured, tradition. They have also foreshadowed in remarkable ways the emergence in recent decades of communication at all cultural levels between East and West. A third aim will be to draw out from Jung's writings in this field an account of his methodology, and to reflect on the way in which he perceived and carried out his own project. This will not only enable us to gain a better perspective on his own thinking, but will provide a platform on which to raise and debate wider philosophical and ideological issues concerning the appropriation of the ideas of one culture by another.

Emphasising the germinative role of Eastern thought will also enable us to gain a fresh perspective on Jung's attitude to Western culture in general and to Christianity in particular. It will become evident in our close examination of his writings in this field that, while he remained firmly attached to his cultural and religious roots, he deemed it necessary to re-examine some of the fundamental assumptions of the Western tradition with the aid of ideas drawn from Oriental philosophy. We shall see that, far from giving succour to those who seek to place Christianity in a unique and superior position in relation to other religions, he frequently expressed the exact contrary view, and maintained that in certain respects Christianity had much to learn from the religious ideas of the East. Seeking to stand outside the cultural traditions of Europe gave Jung a vantage point from which to view, in a fresh light, not only the philosophical assumptions of Christianity, but also the foundational beliefs of his own culture as a whole, and to broaden the perspective from which we are able to criticise our own civilisation. Certainly, as will become evident in what follows, Jung did not manage to shake off his Western prejudices in his treatment of the Orient, but unlike many Westerners who have turned to the East to confirm their own beliefs, Jung actively sought there a platform from which to engage in self-analysis and self-criticism.

JUNG'S INTEREST IN THE EAST

What drew Jung Eastwards? On the face of it there is an obvious affinity between his own thought and the ways of thinking of Eastern philosophers, and even if he had never written a word on this subject it would be possible to draw clear parallels between them. Here are some examples of places in his thinking where this is most apparent: (1) The emphasis in Jung's writings on the primacy of inner experience and on the reality of the psychic world. (2) His insistence that a certain kind of numinous experience, rather than creeds or faith, is the essence of religion. (3) The quest for an amplified notion of selfhood which goes beyond the narrow confines of the conscious ego. (4) The belief in the possibility of self-transformation by one's own efforts. (5) His endeavour to overcome the intransigent opposition of matter and mind, in particular with the concept of the psychoid archetype. (6) Above all, the quest for wholeness based on creative interaction between complementary opposites within the psyche. All of these ideas and concerns of Jung can be linked to some degree with philosophical and religious ideas and concerns that originated in China or India.

At an intellectual level, this affinity may be traced to Jung's early reading of the German idealist philosophers of the Romantic period such as Schelling and Schopenhauer, philosophers who, along with other writers of the time, had themselves absorbed much of the spirit of the East into their own thinking. They were crucial in the shaping of Jung's own outlook, and, contrary to the standard view that Jung derived most of his inspiration from Freud, his concept of the unconscious and of the transformative nature of the psyche, even though brought down from the metaphysical heights to the level of empirical psychology, can more plausibly be traced to these philosophers.

On a more personal level, Jung was by nature something of a Taoist. This is evident from his autobiography and from the personal memoirs of his friends, and can be seen in the strong bond he felt with the natural world, expressed in his love of water, of stones, and of mountains, as well as in the closeness he experienced at his hermitage-like Tower at Bollingen to the basic demands and accoutrements of living. This bond appeared early in life when he often preferred to immerse himself in the experiences of nature rather than in human society, and carried through to his old age where he found evident solace in the simple unadorned environment of his Tower. According to his close friends he had the Taoist facility for 'going with the current of life', and seemed to be most at ease with the world and with himself when engaged in simple activities such as gardening, cooking, sailing, and stone-carving. In the final paragraph of his autobiography, he gave eloquent expression to a deep 'feeling of kinship with all things', with 'plants, animals, clouds, day and night'. In this moving valedictory to the world, he quoted Lao-tzu's saying: 'All are clear, I alone am clouded', a remark which reflects, too, the undogmatic, even relativistic, tenor of his thinking, a further link with the outlook of the Taoist sages. His capacity, too, to confront his own unconscious, and to tackle the painful aspects of his psyche which he called the 'shadow', had clear parallels with Eastern spiritual traditions, especially those of Buddhism where the path to enlightenment, far from being a serendipitous swoon into a blissful state, demands the most rigorous self-examination, the heroic struggle with uglier aspects of human experience, and the uncompromising rooting out of delusions and misconceptions. In his own personal life he recognised, too, the importance of the worlds of dream and fantasy, and of what might loosely be called the non-rational dimensions of his personality, even to the point of admitting the existence within himself of a shadowy 'Number 2' personality

6

which was in tune with a world beyond the reach of everyday consciousness and convention. He never went as far along the road of irrationalism as some hostile critics have suggested, but like many Oriental thinkers he was aware of the need to draw the irrational and the paradoxical into his thinking, and of the need to balance the rational function, so finely tuned in the West, with its opposite.

THE WIDER CONTEXT

I write as an historian of ideas, however, which means doing more than drawing parallels and outlining affinities, intriguing though these may be. It means, in the first place, tracing the development of Jung's dialogue with Eastern thought, and seeking to explain the shaping of his thought in relation to Oriental ideas. But it also means relating them to the wider historical context. I shall argue that Jung's work in this regard represents, not an idiosyncratic and wayward endeavour, but a continuation and fruition of the work of dialogue with the East that has been developing in Europe since the Age of Enlightenment. His vision of the East was in many ways unique, arising out of his own psychological preoccupations, and I shall be at pains to emphasise the pioneering nature of Jung's endeavours in this field. As Mokusen Miyuki has expressed it: 'C.G. Jung's Analytical Psychology has provided the West with the first meaningful psychological avenue to approach Buddhism and other Asian religious experience' (Spiegelman and Miyuki, 1985: 172). A number of other eminent psychoanalysts have also made Eastern excursions in order to illuminate their theories and practices; the list includes Erich Fromm, Karen Horney, Medard Boss, and R.D. Laing. Jung, however, must be acknowledged as one of the first twentieth-century psycho-logists to recognise the possible contributions of the East to this discipline.[3] Nevertheless, his work can also be seen as part of a tradition of intellectual and cultural interaction with the East that goes back through nineteenth-century figures such as Schopenhauer and Schlegel, to Voltaire and Leibniz in the previous century. To borrow a phrase used by Newton, he was himself standing on the shoulders of giants.

It is often supposed that the meeting of East and West, with the exception of a few freakish episodes like the travels of Marco Polo, is of relatively recent origin, dating at the very earliest perhaps from the period of rapid imperial expansion in the nineteenth century. Even then it is usually seen to be not so much a dialogue as a confrontation between mutually uncomprehending cultures, epitomised in the oft-quoted lines of Kipling, 'Oh East is East and West is West / and never the twain shall meet'. (Though we do not always remember the lines which almost immediately follow: 'But there is neither East nor West, Border, nor Breed, nor Birth, / When two strong men stand face to face, though they come from the ends of the earth!') Some have even been led to imagine that the dialogue was the product of the colourful, exotic 'sixties, when gurus came from India to teach Westerners the arts of yoga and meditation, and Westerners turned to the *I Ching* and to *The Tibetan Book of the Dead* for inspiration.

Scholarly guardians of our culture have tended to perpetuate this misconception by treating Western culture – its thought, and philosophy – as if it were an encapsulated entity, something that can be treated entirely separately from the thought and philosophy of the Orient. Even at the present time, when in the post-Second World War climate there has been an evident and wide-ranging cultural interchange, an inter-penetration of lives and ideas between East and West, students in the field of humanities are often educated solely within a closed cultural world that is confined by and large to Europe and North America. Histories of ideas, which should be in the business of opening, not confining, minds, still tend to ignore Eastern thought, and most histories of philosophy, if they address the matter at all, dismiss it as not strictly speaking 'philosophy', or at best politely but firmly put it on one side as being outside the professional competence of the author.[4] Allied to this is the perpetuation of an overly-simplistic division between 'East' and 'West' which, while undoubtedly a useful fiction for expository purposes, is often employed in an uncritical manner, thereby tending to promote an innocent abstraction to the status of a dangerous myth.[5]

There is, however, a different view, namely that our 'two cultures', though in many respect separate, with separate traditions and distinct historical lines of development, actually do overlap at certain crucial points, and that an exchange of ideas has been taking place, albeit at the margins, for a very long time. Joseph Needham, the author of the monumental study, *Science and Civilization in China*, who has been conspicuous in his attempts to open up our cultural vision to wider horizons, expressed this view forcibly when he remarked that 'For three thousand years a dialogue has been going on between the two ends of the world. Greatly have they influenced each other' (1969: 11). The full story of this long dialogue is not for telling here, though in Chapter 3 I shall give an historical outline of the conversation 'between the two ends of the world' as a context for my main task of recounting and analysing Jung's own contribution to this story.

This alternative perspective on our history points to the need to rewrite the history of Western thought and culture within a wider framework, to rethink it in terms of what Heidegger has described as a 'world civilization', a 'house of words' in which all human beings dwell and communicate.[6] It must be written, not as if East and West are alien beings who have on a few occasions come into uneasy contact, but as a single narrative, albeit with many sub-themes and sub-plots. To quote the philosopher Jaspers: 'We can no longer ignore the immense worlds of Asia as nations of eternal stagnation with no history. The scope of world history is universal. Our picture of mankind is incomplete if this scope is restricted.' This rewriting of history, furthermore, is not merely a matter of narrow scholarly interest, but has a much wider significance, for, as the philosopher N.P. Jacobson points out, 'Nowhere is provincialism and cultural hypnotism more disastrous, perhaps, and linked more intimately with continued ignorance, mutual suspicion, and hostility . . . than in our ethnocentric histories' (1969: 36). The reader need hardly be reminded that in the nineteen nineties many of the narrow sectarianisms and xenophobic nationalisms that liberal-minded people believed to be in reteat, have regrouped their forces and have mounted a fearful and destructive counter-attack. Even after the end of the Cold War the ideal of a world order in which all nations and cultures can live in peace and mutual toleration seems as elusive as ever. The – literal! – reorientation of our histories could hardly of itself assuage the inter-cultural tensions and communal conflicts which beset our world, but at the very least historians and philosophers have an obligation to help lower the fences that divide peoples from each other, and to contribute towards the construction of a global 'house of words' in which diatribe will be replaced by dialogue, hatred by toleration.

DOMINATION OR DIALOGUE?

The attitudes of tolerance and the method of dialogue, though no doubt admirable in themselves, are not virtues easily acquired. No one could imagine nowadays that the writing of history is a neutral, disinterested pursuit, for it is always carried out from within history itself, and historians inevitably carry with them the assumptions and prejudices of their epoch. In writing a history of ideas, therefore, we cannot claim possession of an Archimedean point with which to get leverage on absolute, objective, prejudice-free knowledge, and there is no sense in working towards a universal history in which all cultural mind-sets have been removed. However, at the very least we need to become more aware of the assumptions and prejudices that we inherit from our intellectual traditions, and nowhere are these more evident than in our approach to the East. Here Western attitudes of superiority and cultural hegemony, amounting often to more or less blatant racism, have seriously distorted our perception of that culture and our relationship to it, and it will be one of our major tasks in what follows to draw out and examine these assumptions. It will be our task, too, to recognise and to address some of those almost intractable philosophical questions that arise when we seek to engage with and to make sense of ideas from a non-Western culture. This issue of inter-cultural understanding, as an epistemological rather than as an ideological question, is one which has preoccupied the minds of philosophers in recent years, and must therefore enter into any discussion of the nature and validity of the East–West dialogue.

The Western interest in the East has certainly been the product of mixed motivation, and has been of mixed blessing to the objects of its attention. On its darker side it has sprung from and given expression to Western imperialism, and the West's approach to the East has often, in the words of one scholar, been 'one of political domination, economic exploitation, [and] religious proselytism'. On the other hand, he continues, it has also been 'the goal and referent of Utopian projections, of searching for identity and the origins of Europe, of European self-questioning and self-criticism' (Halbfass, 1988: 369). Edward Said, a trenchant critic of what he calls 'Orientalism', namely the ambivalent fascination for the East that accompanied the imperial expansion eastwards of the European powers in the nineteenth century, sees this fascination as an extension of the

West's sense of its own cultural and racial superiority, and as involving the projection of crass stereotypes and myths. Orientalism is, for Said, more than just a body of neutral knowledge concerning a particular segment of the human race; it is a mode of discourse that presents, expresses, and serves to perpetuate a certain view that the European powers have of themselves, and constitutes 'a Western style for dominating, restructuring, and having authority over the Orient' (1978: 3).[7]

Yet at the same time, as a qualification to these unsettling views, and as a compensation for the narrowness of the West's historical outlook, it is necessary to remind ourselves of the extent, however limited, of the East's influence on the West, and of the many-sided nature of that influence. It must be noted that there has persisted, from the time of Leibniz and Voltaire in the eighteenth century to the time of Jung and beyond, an intellectual relationship with the East of a quite different kind from that characterised by Said. This relationship has displayed an earnest respect for Eastern peoples and their cultures, and, far from consciously denigrating or belittling the East, has frequently elevated it to a position of moral and philosophical superiority, holding it up as a tool of cultural self-criticism and as a model for self-improvement for the West. In many ways it can be seen as typifying the West's capacity for self-analysis, and as constituting a sort of cultural anxiety in which the 'strange', the 'foreign', the 'other' is held up as a mirror for self-examination and self-correction.

This two-sided approach will help us to place Jung's own dialogue with Eastern philosophies in better perspective, and in particular it will enable us to assess its weaknesses as well as its strengths. On the one hand, in reading Jung at the close of this century, three decades after his death, we are often struck by a certain political naivety and historical obliviousness that pervades his thinking on this matter, and one of our tasks will be to address to Jung the sort of ideological and philosophical questions broached by Said and other critics, and to confront the difficulties and deficiencies in Jung's whole approach. Although – as will be evident in the text which follows – I find myself in sympathy with many facets of Jung's thinking, I shall also be investigating the weaknesses in his approach, and shall draw attention to some of the arguments brought to bear on him by critics. On the other hand, I shall try to convince the reader that his interest in the East was consciously motivated, not out of any sense of cultural superiority, but out of the need, as he saw it, to diagnose and to rectify profound deficiencies at the heart of Western culture – a motivation which he shared with many previous generations of Oriental enthusiasts. At one level his Eastern studies provided 'the indispensable basis for a critique of Western psychology' (CW18.1483), at another nothing less than the means for confronting 'the spiritual change we are passing through today' (MM: 250).

Furthermore, in the pages that follow I hope it will become clear that Jung's dialogue with the East has nothing to do with the tired retreat to 'outworn creeds' or to world-denying mysticisms which are often associated with enthusiasm for the religions of Asia. His work in this field is clearly addressed to the needs, as he saw them, of our own times, and like that of many engaged in this dialogue, from Leibniz to our own day, he saw his work in this context, not as a purely theoretical exercise, but as a matter of urgent moral concern. His exploration of traditional philosophies, therefore, was not a matter of regression, let alone of nostalgia, but was motivated by a desire to reconcile and integrate traditional thought with modern perspectives.[8] He would surely have agreed with the philosopher Radhakrishnan that such a dialogue represents 'the supreme task of our generation', for it seeks nothing less than the reconciliation of cultural antagonisms and the building of a new commonwealth of ideas and practices.

Jung's task was self-evidently ambitious, and he was aware that in human affairs utopian ideals and high-minded enterprises can never yield the sort of perfection and completion that philosophers and mystics have often dreamed of. Unlike some who have trodden the same path, he saw no possibility of, or even desirability in, a merging of cultures and the construction of a single unified world-view which would reconcile all opposites within a total synthesis. What he sought rather was to participate in what Michael Oakeshott has called 'the conversation of mankind', a dialogue with the philosophies of the East, in particular those of China and India, thereby 'to build a bridge of psychological understanding between East and West' (CW13.83). This meant, for him, not an attempt to assimilate or to identify with these cultures – a goal which, as we shall see, he deemed to be impossible – but rather the understanding of common themes and the recognition of common tasks. It was an overlapping, not a merging, of conceptual horizons – an activity of mutual engagement of the kind we enjoy in a fruitful, if challenging, conversation.

HERMENEUTICS

This dialogical approach could properly be called *hermeneutical*, a term that will play an important part in our bid to understand Jung's relationship with Eastern thought. Hermeneutics may be defined as the art of interpreting texts, in particular texts from the past whose meaning may seem to be elusive. The term arose in the context of the need of biblical scholars to interpret the Bible – a text which was constructed in a language and in a culture remote from our own and whose meaning therefore required some form of mediation. It has recently acquired a more general philosophical sense, and in the work of the contemporary German philosopher Hans-Georg Gadamer it has been used as a way of redefining human understanding as such, by way of contrast with the empiricist and positivist approaches that have been associated with the physical sciences. A fuller account of Gadamer's philosophical hermeneutics, and how I propose to apply it to Jung, will be given in Chapter 3. I shall argue that Jung's dialogue with Eastern philosophies involved implicitly many of the features of a hermeneutical understanding, and that applying this term – with reservations – to Jung illuminates not only his own unique style and method, but also his relationship with those other Western thinkers who have sought some kind of accommodation with Oriental ideas.

Chapter 3, therefore, represents an attempt to set up a framework for the examination of Jung's dialogue with the East. In Chapter 2 the broader scene is set: under the heading of 'Orientalism' some of the attitudes, prejudices, and stereotypes which have helped to shape our attitude towards the East are discussed, and this is followed by a thumbnail sketch of the history of the East–West dialogue prior to Jung. That completes *Prologue*, the introductory section of the book. For some readers this may be overlong and they may wish to move straight to the central section of the book. Nevertheless, I need to underline the fact that one of the major themes of this book is the claim that Jung's interest in the East is not at all quixotic and bizarre, but is part of an historically much older interest, one which has flourished in this century only after a long period of maturation that reaches back many centuries. And, as we have just noted, this interest also raises important philosophical and cultural questions, questions which will recur throughout the book. It should also be stressed that Jung himself sought to place his theories within a broad intellectual and historical context, drawing attention to their 'wide significance and application' (CW6.xi) and to their 'relevance to philosophy and the history of ideas' (CW18.1739). It is hoped, then, that for these reasons, this section will provide a useful background to the central section of the book, *Dialogue*, which narrates and analyses Jung's own dialogue with the East. Chapter 4 traces out the main paths of Jung's intellectual journey to the East, and Chapters 5–7 deal with specific texts and concepts, such as the *I Ching* and the mandala, ranging through the major historical traditions of Taoism, Yoga and Buddhism. In the final section, *Epilogue*, Chapter 8 looks at the doubts and reservations arising from Jung's own reflections on his task, examining on the one hand his attempt to separate off his psychological approach from the metaphysical assumptions of the East, and on the other his warnings concerning the adoption of Eastern spiritual techniques by Westerners. Chapter 9 examines varieties of criticisms that have been or might be levelled against Jung's views on this question, and here I shall discuss some of the evident limitations that are to be found in Jung's hermeneutical approach. The concluding chapter offers an overall appraisal of the contemporary relevance of his endeavour to 'build a bridge of understanding' between East and West, and asks how we might read Jung today on the issue of East–West understanding.

This method of exposition serves to underline my own approach which I would also describe as hermeneutical. I see myself as engaging in a dialogue with Jung, and through him with the texts and ideas he wrote about. The precise nature of the hermeneutical approach will be set out in more detail below, but for the moment it will suffice to say that the notion of dialogue implies an ability to listen to other people and to respect their otherness, while at the same time being aware of one's own situation and one's own point of view and prejudices. I have therefore endeavoured to allow Jung to speak for himself in the middle section of the book, reserving critical discussion for the final section, where it will be made clear that we cannot now 'read' the East in the way that Jung did. In doing things this way I want to avoid the impression that I believe myself to be offering anything like a final definitive interpretation, or to be standing magisterially in judgement over Jung, for my own reading of Jung, as indeed his of Oriental texts, is as much a creation of me and my times as a reproduction of Jung's.

In the course of pursuing this study I have become increasingly aware that even the notion of dialogue, with its bipolar implications, is misleading, for the processes of listening, interpreting, and assessing, which are the integuments of the dialogical activity, lead one endlessly back and forth without any final or secure resting place. Jung himself was writing for different purposes over a long span of years, for different audiences and in different contexts, so it would be a mistake to imagine that there is a single simple Jungian viewpoint awaiting discovery. Indeed, as I shall indicate in what follows, Jung was highly ambivalent himself towards his Eastern 'discoveries', hedging them round with what I characterise in Chapter 8 as 'reservations and qualifications', and often seeming to be debating with himself the value of the whole enterprise. Furthermore, Jung's own contact with Eastern thought was thoroughly mediated, and depended on translations and interpretations which, as we shall see in Chapter 9, were in some respects highly problematical. In addition, the interpretations of Jung put forward in this book not only arise out of my own ever-shifting viewpoint, and are shaped by my own personal prejudices and my European standpoint, but are informed and conditioned by a whole range of critics who, during the decades following Jung's death in 1961, have contributed to the 'dialogue'. In the final chapter I raise the question of how we might read Jung's commentaries from our *fin de siècle* standpoint, but do so with the full realisation that the end is also a beginning and that dialogue promises no final agreement. Perhaps the best way to approach the task of making sense of Jung's encounter with the East is to quote his own words in the *Prologue* to his autobiography: 'the only question is whether what I tell is *my* fable, *my* myth' (MDR: 17).

2

ORIENTALISM

What is the Orient? The East? It is not a fact of nature, it is an *idea* – precisely a *Western* idea – which has a history and a pathology, and is infused with myth and hidden meaning. In the words of Edward Said: 'The Orient was almost a European invention, and had been since antiquity a place of romance, exotic beings, haunting memories and landscapes, remarkable experiences' (1978: 1). It constitutes the 'other', that which stands opposite to us as strange and alien, and it is this very otherness which confirms our own self-image and defines our own self-identity.

Though Said was speaking more specifically of Islam and the Middle East, his remark could equally apply to the Orient that relates to the present study, namely the lands and cultures of India and China. The lumping together of these two highly individual civilisations, along with several other Asian cultures as well, under the general category of 'The East' is as much a construct of Western consciousness as the 'Orient' of the Islamic Middle East. Indeed, the whole idea of cultures as entities which have distinct characteristics and which in some sense stand opposed and alien to one another is a European invention. No doubt most societies in human history have developed a sense of their own identity and hence their difference from other societies, and have formulated, if only implicitly, an idea of 'us' and 'them', evincing thereby varying degrees of incomprehension and animosity towards the 'other'. But for Europe the question of the 'other' has seemed especially problematic, whether that 'other' be outside or within. And it is in Europe that we have refined into a philosophy the notion that cultures are quasi-entities which are in some fundamental sense sealed off from each other, and which therefore require some special effort, perhaps impossible to achieve, in order to communicate with each other.

I shall refer to this attitude as *enclavism* ('enclave' means literally 'locked in'), by which I mean the more or less conscious and systematic tendency to erect obstacles to inter-cultural communication. Before examining Jung's own attempt to communicate with the East we need to know something about those barriers which, successfully or unsuccessfully, he sought to transcend. As we shall see,

Jung's own dialogue with the East was beset with many of the prejudices and enclavist assumptions which run deep in the Western psyche. We shall see that, in his endeavour to 'build a bridge of psychological understanding between East and West', he was running up against, and sometimes even rehashing, stereotypes, fantasies, and even full-blown philosophies which for hundreds of years have posed as a barrier to East–West understanding. But we shall also discover that there is another considerably more edifying side to the story. While the West's attitude to the East has often been that of an imperialist power seeking to affirm its distance from, and more especially its distance above, the 'other', there has prevailed since the Renaissance a counter-movement characterised by the desire to overcome differences, to penetrate the supposed impenetrabilities of Oriental thought, and to draw the philosophies of the East into the orbit of the West's own self-reflection. It is in the tension between these two positions – that which distances and that which draws together – that we shall be able to come to some understanding and judgement concerning Jung's own enterprise.[1]

CULTURAL ENCLAVISM

'Enclavism' is more than just the common breed of xenophobia which we share with most other cultures on the globe: it amounts to a family of more or less articulated attitudes and responses. It is sometimes evident in our way of writing and thinking about history. History as it is commonly written in Western cultures is set within a story, told and repeated in various forms, which portrays *our* history as the history of the peoples of Europe, as essentially that of the children and heirs of Greece and Rome and of Judaeo-Christianity.[2] The history of other peoples to the East and to the South is essentially a different story, *their* history. This does not mean that we ignore the history of other peoples, only that we locate it on the margins as 'not ours'. There are many myths woven into this story. Some of the most influential are: first, the idea of *Progress*, the belief, implicit or explicit, that the history of the West, by contrast with other traditional cultures such as those of India and China, has an inherently progressive tendency that culminates in the Modern World, the world of science, technology, individualism, and enlightened rationalism. This myth received its most powerful impetus and authority from Hegel who imagined that the World Spirit advances in a Westerly direction, leaving the East ossified at an earlier stage of development. His dialectical view of history implied, furthermore, that the spirit of the East was taken up and included in the Western synthesis which has 'gone beyond the East' and in so doing the West can understand the East in a way that the East cannot understand itself. More recently it has found voice in the writings of Teilhard de Chardin who speaks of traditional China as lacking in impetus for renovation, and of India as having got lost in a fog of obscuring metaphysics, leaving to the Christian West the honour of being 'the principal axis of anthropogenesis' (1959: 211). In both these cases, not only is the West seen as advancing beyond the East, but it is also endowed with a kind of epistemic authority over it.

15

The West is therefore not simply one culture amongst many but has a unique global mission, namely that of providing a universal framework in which all other cultures can be included.

A second influential myth is the belief that 'our' religion, Christianity (we tend to ignore its Asian origins), represents a unique vehicle of divine revelation and hence is superior to all other religions. This 'scandal of particularity', as it is sometimes called, is certainly not unique to Christianity, but it has undoubtedly played an important role in the shaping of our attitudes to non-Christian and non-European cultures. The cumulative effect of such myths is to set on our mental noses a pair of spectacles through which we see our culture as something both essentially different from and inherently superior to others.

Enclavism is also a product of modern post-Cartesian philosophy. It has become widely accepted, in a variety of versions – some more explicit than others – that human understanding can only operate properly within certain methodological limits or boundaries, beyond which there are epistemological monsters – things that cannot be known or cannot be spoken of coherently or meaningfully. It is as if human thought were laid out on topographical lines, with space-like discriminations between what can and what cannot properly be said or thought.[3] In the Cartesian Rationalist tradition it is evident in the emphasis on the role of rational method in determining unequivocally and exclusively what can be known. The empiricist tradition has emphasised experience as a criterion of demarcation, with the natural sciences taking on the role of border guards. In the twentieth century, Logical Positivism, which is in a sense the culmination of both these traditions, set the frontiers of meaningfulness in terms of verifiability, a criterion applicable without regard to local cultural differences.

In recent anglophone philosophy it has taken a more pluralistic, more relativistic, form, with such notions as 'conceptual schemes', 'conceptual frameworks', 'paradigms', and 'language games', which have tended to underscore the holistic assumption that knowledge is embedded within specific conceptual or linguistic matrices, which in turn are embedded in what Wittgenstein called 'forms of life'. Concepts are seen as acquiring meaning, not singly and in paired isomorphism with entities in the world, but as inextricable components of a framework of interrelated concepts. These notions have inevitably encouraged the view that there is a factor of essential incommensurabilty or untranslatability between different cultures. Wittgenstein's idea of a 'language game' perfectly summarises this way of thinking, for it sees words or concepts as being like pieces or moves within a game which lose their sense when removed from that context. Furthermore, by showing the absurdity of comparing moves in one game with moves within another, the game model tends to reinforce the picture of languages as enclaves, hermetically sealed from one another, thereby rendering futile any attempts at comparisons between them.[4]

It is not surprising that these philosophical notions have, deliberately or inadvertently, intruded on the territory of social anthropology. A good example is that of Peter Winch (1958) who, making use of Wittgenstein's notion of a 'language game', has argued that all thought and experience is culturally mediated, and hence there is no neutral ground from which to establish the criterion of rationality within any given culture, or on which science can claim a higher rationality than primitive witchcraft. This conclusion, while combating any inclination towards cultural imperialism, at the same time could be seen as implying the impossibility of any inter-cultural communication at all; if human experience cannot transcend the limits of a particular culture, then no sense can be made of inter-cultural comparisons. An earlier example of this is to be found in the writings of the influential philosopher and anthropologist Lucien Lévy-Bruhl (1922), who helped to shape Jung's own thinking, and who claimed that there is a radical difference between primitive and modern mentalities. Another anthropologist, Benjamin Lee Whorf (1956), is well known for his argument that the structure of a language determines the thought-structure of those who use that language, and hence shapes the way they experience the world.

This attitude is frequently echoed within the discipline of the history of ideas. Here it is commonly maintained that the sense of a text, belief, or idea can only be given within a specific historical context, a view which has at various times been called either 'historicism' or 'contextualism'. The word 'historicism' has many meanings, but here it is intended to convey the belief that all meanings are contingent upon the historical context within which they arise. It is not only philosophy but all the humanities disciplines that have undergone in recent years, especially since Kuhn's seminal work *The Structure of Scientific Revolutions*, an 'historical turn' whereby they have come to see the human mind in its various aspects as caught inexorably within the web of language which in turn is embedded in the matrices of history. Such a view could also be described as 'relativist' insofar as sense can be made of any term only from within a specific cultural context; there are no 'sky-hooks', as Richard Rorty has called them, which enable us to lift ourselves clear of our cultural and historical entanglements.[5]

ORIENTALISM

Enclavism as a general attitude stands behind and gives implicit support to what Said has called *Orientalism*, providing ideological justification for the sense of alienation and inflated fantasy that has characterised the West's attitudes to the peoples and cultures of the East. It encourages the belief that East and West represent radically disengaged mentalities between which lie deep epistemological chasms. Raghavan Iyer has spoken of a 'glass curtain' that has been erected over the centuries between East and West (rather like the Iron Curtain of Cold War days) through which Asians and Europeans see each other 'as through a glass darkly', a psychological barrier which contains 'a mixture of mythical and tangible differences wherein it is difficult to disentangle the myths from the facts' (1965: 4). Much earlier an American historian, N.D. Harris, spoke of a 'wall of exclusion' giving rise to the feeling of separateness, seclusion, and suspicion between Asians and Europeans (1928: 8). More recently Richard Bernstein has

17

referred to the pervasive fallacy that 'there are essential determinate characteristics that distinguish the Western and the Eastern "mind"' (in Deutsch, 1991: 93). Furthermore, this 'glass curtain', or 'wall of exclusion', has not only helped to secure our boundaries with other cultures, keeping those inside 'pure' and those outside at a safe distance, it has also helped to provide a convenient justification for our belief in our inherent superiority.[6] Other cultures have provided similar techniques, the Chinese being a conspicuous example. But it is probably only within Western European culture that this notion has been elevated into a general theory of history, one in which European culture is seen as enjoying an especially privileged place.

Of course, there is an obvious sense in which the peoples and cultures of the Orient, as indeed of the West, exist entirely independently of our prejudices, and are hardly European inventions. But Said's argument runs deep here. He is not merely stating the obvious fact that the concept of the East was invented in the West, and that the peoples of, say, India and China had until the Europeans came along no conception of a common Oriental identity. His point is that the creation of the concept of the Orient, along with the whole baggage of images and prejudices which that contains, was a means towards the self-definition of Europe and played a crucial role in affirming Europe's cultural 'hegemony', namely the sense of our special and superior role in the order of things, and hence our right to trade, convert, and conquer. The Orient, Said writes, 'has a special place in European Western experience . . . [It] has helped to define Europe (or the West) as its contrasting image, idea, personality, experience' (1978: 1–2), and far from being just a 'structure of lies or of myths which, were the truth about them to be told, would simply blow away', it is 'a sign of European-Atlantic power over the Orient', a form of discourse closely tied 'to the enabling socio-economic and political institutions', and whose role is 'direct domination' (pp. 6–7). In brief, Orientalism is 'a kind of Western projection onto and will to govern over the Orient' (p. 95). It is true that in the twentieth century a consciousness of Asian identity has emerged in the East itself, but this has been largely in response to Western imperialism, and is to a great extent a reverse image of Western self-perception.

A similar view is expressed by P.C. Almond in his book *The British Discovery of Buddhism*. He draws our attention to the fact that during the second half of the nineteenth century 'there was an enormous upsurge in awareness of, and interest in, Buddhism' (1988: 1). This upsurge was by no means confined to scholars, for the teachings of the Buddha attracted wide popular interest through such publications as Edwin Arnold's *The Light of Asia*, and through organisations like the Theosophical Society. Attitudes were polarised. On the one side there was widespread sympathy for these teachings, some seizing upon them as a weapon with which to subvert Christianity. But on the other hand there were many who proclaimed these teachings as incoherent, even wicked, and Almond documents in some detail the Victorian habit of denigrating Buddhist ideas and practices in order to demonstrate supposed Western superiority and to justify the imposition of the Christian faith on the East. He quotes as typical the declaration in an article on Buddhism in Ceylon in the *London Quarterly Review* for 1854–5 that 'we have been raised up to civilize the savage, to colonize the uninhabited, but habitable portions of the globe, and to diffuse the blessings of the Gospel amongst mankind' (1988: 42). Like Said, he views Buddhism in nineteenth-century Britain as a construct, a creation: 'It *becomes* an object, is constituted as such; it takes form as an entity that "exists" over against the various cultures which can now be perceived as instancing it, manifesting it' (p. 12). He sees this process as a kind of conceptual filter through which we are able to see 'two qualitatively different modes of being human, the oriental and the occidental, the latter of which was essentially other, and which was in most instances perceived as inferior' (p. 140).

There is also, indeed, what Said calls the 'Orient of the academy', the systematic study of Eastern languages and cultures, a rigorous body of knowledge in which Western scholars have since the middle of the nineteenth century invested much industry and talent. It might be argued that the sort of projections by the West onto the East that we have been alluding to are actually the product of popular ignorance and political wishful thinking, and could therefore be removed by the careful application of a more independently minded methodology. But according to Said the scholars are themselves caught in the same ideological trap as everyone else. Their knowledge, well constructed and appropriately documented though it may be, is in effect 'an accepted grid for filtering through the Orient into Western consciousness . . . for display in the museum', and as such is 'shot through with doctrines of European superiority, various kinds of racism, imperialism, and the like' (1978: 6–8).

Let us now look more closely at the kinds of prejudices and stereotypes that the West has projected onto the Orient, whether from the popular or the scholarly ends of the spectrum. Almost any schoolchild is familiar with such stereotypes, which range from blatant racism to seemingly harmless comparisons and categorisations. Oriental 'splendour', 'cruelty', 'cunning', 'sensuality' are good representative examples to begin with, though perhaps the most notorious and long-lived epithet is 'Oriental despotism', coined in the eighteenth century by Montesquieu, elaborated in the nineteenth by James Mill who used it as virtually an indictment of the whole Indian culture, and enjoying wide popular currency in the twentieth. Another common sterotype is contained in the phrase 'the mysterious Orient', the idea that the mind of the Oriental is inherently unfathomable, in a way that inspires either fear and suspicion or contemptuous dismissal. The latter is well exemplified in a remark by one of Kipling's characters in *Our Viceroy Resigns*: 'You'll never plumb the Oriental mind. And if you did, it isn't worth the toil.'

It is a two-way game, of course, which Asians play as well, tossing back epithets in the European direction such as 'decadent', 'hypocritical', and 'aggressive'. For example in the nineteenth century the Hindu philosopher Vivekenanda popularised the idea of 'Western materialism', portraying Europeans as wild beasts, drenched in liquor, and addicted to the exclusive satisfying of sensual appetites. Even prior to the arrival of the Europeans, the Chinese could be equally inventive in creating fanciful caricatures of the peoples beyond the borders of the Middle Kingdom.

A favourite stereotyping sport consists in drawing sweeping contrasts between Eastern and Western thought, values and society, sharp polarities which are seen as summing up essential differences. A commonplace example of such polarities is to be found in the contrast between Western materialism and rationalism on the one hand, and Eastern spirituality and mysticism on the other. Pairs of epithets such as these are part of what Iyer has described as the myth of perennial conflict between East and West, a myth which depicts the relationship between them as one of eternal embattlement, whether between peoples or ideas. This myth can, he believes, be traced back to the Ancient Greeks, and in particular to the historian Herodotus who saw the conflict between Hellenes and Persians in the fifth century BC as an epic struggle between opposing civilisations, though he adds that Herodotus drew no racist conclusions from his account of the Persian wars, and ridiculed the notion that there are any essential differences within the human race (1965: 13). In fairness to Herodotus it must also be stressed that the image of the Persian wars as an archetypal contest between the freedom-loving Greeks and the despot-prone Orientals was actually more the creation of modern than of ancient historians. Iyer argues that it was Hegel, in particular, who has played an important role in shaping our attitudes in this regard by elaborating the mythical contrast between the heroic, liberty-loving, creative, and dynamic West with the aggressive, despotic, stagnant, and unchanging East, seeing them as constituting quite distinct moments in the evolution of self-consciousness and freedom (see 1965: 14).

A whole series of scholars and thinkers in this century have sought to understand the Orient in terms of such polarities. The great French sinologist Marcel Granet, for example, in his book *La Pensée Chinoise* (1934) characterised the Chinese way of thinking as 'anti-causal' and 'anti-conceptual', by contrast with Western rationalist modes of thought. Granet, who has had a considerable influence on the development of classical Chinese studies, was himself influenced by Lévy-Bruhl who, as we saw earlier, drew a distinction between the mystical, pre-logical thinking of primitives and the analytical, scientific mentality of modern man. Jung himself, who was influenced by Lévy-Bruhl's thinking, elaborated in considerable detail a psychological theory concerning East/West differences which he conceived in terms of the introvert/extravert distinction; we shall return to this later. Lily Abegg, building on Jung's ideas, claimed in her book *The Mind of East-Asia* that 'the entire East-Asia character could be reduced to a single denominator', and that this could be demonstrated by showing that 'the East-Asian and the Westerner are entirely different, particularly in their psychological constitution' (1952: 3–7); in brief, the Westerner is typically extraverted, giving expression to dynamic and aggressive psychological characteristics, whereas East-Asia, in her view, is typically introverted, defensive, and resistant to change (p. 316). In *The Meeting of East and West* (1946) the philosopher F.S.C. Northrop argued that there is an incommensurability between the two cultures due to the Asian tendency towards an aesthetic attitude, which favours 'concepts by intuition', and the European tendency towards a theoretic one, which favours 'concepts by postulation'. Albert Schweitzer, too, made a contribution to this genre in his book *Indian Thought and its Development* (1936). Drawing on a distinction made by Nietzsche, he contrasted two opposing attitudes, typical of India and Europe respectively, which he called 'world and life negation' on the one hand and 'world and life affirmation' on the other (see Radhakrishnan, 1939: 64–114).

The creation of Eastern stereotypes is evident also in the writing of histories of philosophy. Hegel may have consigned Eastern philosophy to the childhood phase of mankind's spiritual development, but at least he sought to integrate it within a universal history. His example was rarely followed in the subsequent century. Throughout the nineteenth century and well into the twentieth, histories of philosophy written in Germany, England, and France tended largely to exclude India and China, either ignoring them completely or justifying the exclusion on the grounds that philosophy is a peculiarly European phenomenon, a Western tradition that took its rise in Ancient Greece. An example of a more explicit attempt to drive a wedge between Asian and Western thought is to be found in W.K.C. Guthrie's *History of Greek Philosophy*, where he states that 'The motives and methods of the Indian schools, and the theological and mystical background of their thought, are so utterly different from those of the Greeks that there is little profit in the comparison' (1971: 53). In similar fashion Anthony Flew in his *Introduction to Western Philosophy* sought to exclude from his study any source 'east of Suez' on the grounds that Western philosophy is concerned 'first, last, and all the time with arguments, [whereas] most of what is labelled Eastern philosophy is not so concerned' (1971: 36).[7] This attitude is magisterially and succinctly confirmed by Bertrand Russell – a philosopher by no means ill-disposed to the Orient – with the statement in his *History of Western Philosophy* that 'Philosophy begins with Thales'. With equal authority Heidegger, who was no stranger to Oriental writings, proclaims that '"philosophy" is in essence Greek'.

A more even-handed approach is evident amongst those who attempt to see the relationship between East and West as a *complementary* one, whereby each, while expressing a one-sided attitude or psychological characteristic, needs the other in order to aspire to some kind of wholeness. A good example of this is to be found in R.E. Allinson's recent book, *Understanding the Chinese Mind*, where he argues that there are evident differences of emphasis as between Chinese and Western thought, more practical in the case of the former, more theoretical with the latter, though there is no *essential* difference between the two mentalities since they merely represent different but complementary realisations of human potential. Another example comes from the Catholic theologian Raimundo Panikkar, son of an Indian father and a Spanish mother, with a deep concern for inter-cultural and inter-religious understanding, who suggests that 'In every human being there is an East and a West, just as any human being is in a certain way androgynous, but normally one of the two aspects of the human

21

predominates' (1979: 310). Bede Griffiths, a Christian monk who holds Eastern religions in high esteem, argues in a similar vein that West and East represent 'two fundamental dimensions of human nature: the male and the female', and that the masculine, rational outlook of the West is disastrously unbalanced without the complementary virtues of the East (1982: 151). Some have even suggested that this complementarity is connected to the bi-hemispherical structure of the brain, a conception which can be traced back to the nineteenth-century Belgian poet, Maeterlinck, who drew a distinction between the 'Western lobe' and the 'Eastern lobe' of the brain, arguing the need of each to find its complement in the other if world catastrophe was to be avoided (see Radhakrishnan, 1939: 249).

As we shall see later, the complementary approach is in essence the view adopted by Jung. He did, it is true, recognise the dangers of *projection* in such a procedure, the danger that the East simply becomes the shadowy 'other', that uncomfortable part of ourselves which we do not care to be identified with: 'Because the European does not know his own unconscious', he warned, 'he does not understand the East and projects into it everything he fears and despises in himself' (CW18.1253). In this regard his thinking comes close to that of Said. But in spite of this qualification, Jung's discussion of the relationship between Eastern and Western mentalities is pervaded by the assumption that each represented a distinct and opposite, though complementary, psychological type. This view clearly lays itself open to the charge of over-simplifying what is a complex historical and cultural phenomenon. It also lays itself open to the sort of objection we have been considering in the last few pages, namely that, in spite of its good intentions, it stereotypes, and thereby belittles, the religious and philosophical thought of the East. These criticisms will be examined more fully in Chapter 10, and it remains to be seen whether they seriously weaken my claim that Jung's dialogue with the East has been an essentially fruitful one.

THE EAST–WEST ENCOUNTER OF IDEAS

Up to this point in the chapter, the argument has largely been couched in terms which give support to Said's notion of 'Orientalism'. I have laid out for consideration a range of examples of the manner in which certain ways of conceptualising the East have the effect of perpetuating myths and prejudices – a procedure which frequently serves to flatter our self-image and to confirm our belief in our inherent superiority. Even in the case of complementarity it could be argued that the very imposition of broad binary categories, however benign in intention, serves to emphasise Western power over the East – putting the latter in its place, as it were. These attitudes have also had the effect of seeming to place the West in a mental enclave which is at an impossible distance from the East, and to render unprofitable any attempts at mutual intellectual exchange.

However, in spite of the undoubted existence of hidden agendas behind the West's attitude towards the East, it would be a mistake to place exclusive emphasis on the West's will-to-power and its exploitative intentions. Such a

one-sided assessment would ignore the profound and subtle cultural and intellectual interaction that has taken place between Europe and Asia over the past four
hundred years. It is true that the West's perception of the East has often been
clouded by the mists of fantasy, and has typically made use of simplistic dicho-
tomies, but these have often had benign rather than sinister intentions, and have
frequently idealised the East, even to the point of elevating it to a moral position
high above that of the West. The function of the 'other' in Western discourse,
therefore, has been not merely to reinforce our self-perception, to exalt and
apotheosise it, but also to call it into question. The 'discovery' of the ideas of the
East by Western thinkers has not been merely the extension of Western hegemony by other than military or commercial means, but also has represented a
prolonged and quite remarkable exercise in self-criticism and self-renewal on the
West's part.

Said's concept of 'Orientalism' as a product of the West's hegemonic tendencies has certainly been salutary in its challenge to certain established Western
attitudes, and in uncovering some of the hidden strata in Western discourse
concerning the East. But it must be remembered that Said's concern is primarily
with the *Middle* East, with the world of Islam which has historically represented
a very real threat to the survival of Christendom. It has inflicted on the West a
number of humiliating defeats, and it is therefore not surprising that it has
provoked in the West a need to assert its superiority. But when we pass beyond
Cairo, Baghdad, and the old Persian Empire we meet with cultural worlds which
have burdened us with no such baleful memories, but which, quite on the
contrary, have roused the West at the deepest levels of its mental and spiritual life
in ways which cannot simply be reduced to political or ideological factors. It is
not my intention to whitewash the history of Europe's encounter with the civilisations of India and China, which is in many of its aspects a deeply depressing story
of Western greed and aggrandisement, but rather to draw attention to its positive
aspects, those which, at least from the West's point of view, have been im-
measurably enriching and transforming.

In the remainder of this chapter, then, I shall begin to sketch out an alternative
to Said's picture of Orientalism, specifically with regard to the dialogue with the
civilisations of East Asia. I shall do this by drawing attention to two characteristics of this dialogue which have played an important role in the evolution of
Western thought over the past few centuries. These are concerned with the part
that the East has played, first, in the critical self-awareness of the West, as a
mirror in which to examine its own shortcomings, and to inspire renewal; and,
secondly, in the emergence of a sense of universalism, a conception of the unity
of mankind that transcends all its local and historical variations. Some preliminary words need to be said about each of these as preparation for fuller
treatment later.

The West has needed the East, and welcomed its ideas, in ways that have not
always been reciprocated by the East. As the historian Richard Halbfass notes:
'India has not reached out for Europe, has not searched for it, has not historically

prepared the encounter with it' (1988: 369). The East has not been driven 'by the zeal of proselytisation and discovery, and by the urge to understand and master foreign cultures' (p. 172), and has at no time prior to this century sought to define itself in relation to an 'other'. It is true that the history of Modern India and China can only be understood adequately with reference to their struggle with Western political and cultural ideas – with what is nowadays summed up somewhat vaguely in the term 'Modernity' – but this struggle has been forced upon the nations of the East by Western imperialism, and has not arisen spontaneously from within their own traditions.[8]

Europe, on the other hand, has greedily sought knowledge of the philosophies and religions of the East, often, as I suggested above, as a means to bolster its own sense of superiority, and to justify religious conquest, *but also as an instrument of self-questioning and self-renewal.* From the time of the first Jesuit missions to India and China in the sixteenth century, the information flowing back into Europe about these strange cultures has been incorporated into the prevailing debates about the status of knowledge, belief, and values which, from that time onwards, have continued to occupy the minds of European thinkers. The sixteenth century was a crucial period in European history, a major turning point in which the old religious, moral, and epistemological certainties were beginning to crack and break under the impact of new knowledge and new methods. The confident consensus of the fifteenth-century Renaissance, in which the authority of the Roman Church and its philosophical traditions was beginning to be reconciled with seemingly alien traditions, such as Hermetic magic, astrology, alchemy, and Cabalistic mysticism, was violently shattered in the following century by a combination of historical forces. These included: the Protestant Reformation with its destruction of the universality of the Roman Church, the revival of ancient sceptical philosophies which called all claims to knowledge into question, and the emergence of a powerful new natural philosophy that owed little to either Aristotle or the Roman Church. Another important factor was the exploration of the globe by European adventurers, and the consequent inflow of ideas from cultures at least as ancient and as mature as those of Christendom. Taken together these events constituted a traumatic break with the cultural and philosophical traditions that had bound European Christendom together for a thousand years, and presented a powerful challenge to its sense of identity.

The uncertainties engendered by this rupture have continued to preoccupy the European mind, and have set the agenda for many of the debates that have constituted the modern intellectual tradition of the West. The consensus that held together the hearts and minds of mediaeval Europe gave way more or less rapidly to a culture of dissent and uncertainty, and above all of self-doubt; as John Donne expressed it in 1611 in his poem *An Anatomie of the World*: ''T'is all in peeces, all cohaerence gone'. The philosophy of Descartes, who sought to stem the tide of scepticism by means of a new method for the attainment of truth, served only to clarify the nature and extent of the new uncertainties, and to engender what in recent years the philosopher Richard Bernstein has termed the 'Cartesian

anxiety', the fear that, without a way of achieving unqualified rational certifi-
cation of our beliefs, everything falls into madness and chaos (1983: 16ff). Much
of modern philosophy may be seen as a response to and a perpetuation of this
anxiety. But it was by no means just a problem for philosophers, for the story of
Western culture as a whole since that time can be viewed as a series of more or
less unsuccessful attempts to recover something of the lost myth of the mediaeval
pax Romana, a unifying culture in which a fully human life is possible for all. The
'Cartesian anxiety' is therefore but one aspect of a widespread *'cultural* anxiety',
a paranoid self-doubt that has plagued the West for the last four centuries.

It is in this context that we must seek to understand the prolonged dialogue
with the East that has been taking place since that time, and beyond that to make
sense of Jung's own Eastward excursions. In the years following the Second
World War the West has become increasingly concerned to challenge its own
cultural past and to engage in dialogue with other cultures and traditions, but this
should not blind us to the fact that accommodation to the ideas of the East has
been taking place, albeit at the margins, for a long time.[9] We are accustomed to
the idea that the epic voyages by European mariners in the fifteenth and sixteenth
centuries had a profound impact on the future course of European political and
economic history. What is less commonly appreciated is the parallel impact of
these voyages and their aftermath on its *intellectual* history, and the extent to
which the opening up of the passage to the East also opened up new opportunities
in the West for self-examination and self-criticism. Nietzsche once commented
that 'to understand history . . . we have to travel . . . to other nations . . . and
especially to where man has taken off the garb of Europe or has not yet put it on'
(1986, 2.1:223). It was precisely the 'discovery' of the philosophies of China and
India in the centuries of economic and political expansion that enabled Europe to,
as it were, step outside of its history and direct the light of inquiry onto its own
beliefs. As we shall see in the next chapter, even a cursory examination of the
history of the dialogue between East and West reveals again and again the quest
for self-understanding and the desperate search for a way of recovering something that the West believes it has lost – a search in which Jung, far from being
an isolated and idiosyncratic example, may be seen as a distinguished modern
representative.[10]

Many twentieth-century thinkers have expressed the view that the value of the
East–West dialogue lies in its potential for European, and also Asian, self-
analysis. Albert Schweitzer, for example, believed that 'In Indian thought we
learn to understand better what is going on in our own thought', and that the real
significance of the dialogue between what he saw as complementary opposites
'lies in the fact that each becomes aware of what constitutes the inadequacy of
both, and is thereby stimulated to turn in the direction of what is more complete'
(1936: 17 and x). Radhakrishnan was even more explicit and ascribed the
Western attraction to Indian thought to a 'failure of nerve' on the part of
European culture which had fallen into a state of deep self-doubt and which
sought in the East inspiration for renewal (1939: 252). And Abegg, as we saw

earlier, viewed the dialogue with the East as providing the opportunity to see our own culture in a new light, redeeming it thereby from its narrowness and helping us 'towards the discovery and rediscovery of things in our own tradition of which we had already lost sight' (1952: 336–7). We shall later discover a similar view in Jung's writings. As a psychiatrist who saw his role as extending far beyond the consulting room, he too approached the East in a therapeutic spirit, his aim being nothing less than the rediscovery by Europe of its lost soul.

This sort of cultural criticism is often linked to the belief that the importance of the West's contact with the East lies in the need to transcend what Abegg called the 'narrowness' of our tradition, and to develop a truly universal culture. Again and again we find that what has fascinated Western thinkers is not so much Eastern ideas as such, or the specific content of Eastern philosophies, but rather the vision of mankind reunited into a single family, the vision of a global culture in which the conflicts, communal and political as well as intellectual, which have divided mankind, have some possibility of being transcended. The attraction of the East lies in the anticipation that, though it may at first sight appear strange and 'other', our engagement with it eventually seems to promise the way out of and beyond our ethnocentric provincialness. The one-sidedness of the West is therefore something that can only be overcome through an active engagement with its opposite. The philosopher Max Scheler spoke for many when he wrote:

> We have never before seriously faced the question whether the entire development of Western civilisation [has been a] one-sided and overactive process of expansion outward. . . . We must learn anew to envisage the great, invisible solidarity of all living beings in universal life, of all minds in the eternal spirit – and at the same time the mutual solidarity of the world process and the destiny of its supreme principle.
>
> (Quoted in Dumoulin, 1976: 321)

This universalist aspiration has taken many forms in modern history. In Leibniz it was driven by the need to reconcile the religious and political antagonisms that, in his time, were tearing Europe apart. With the Romantics it took a more metaphysical form, and centred on their desire to reunite humanity and nature into a single spiritual whole, where, in Schiller's words, immortalised by Beethoven in the Ninth Symphony, 'all men will be brothers'. In the nineteenth century it frequently took a more explicitly religious form, most conspicuous perhaps in the shape of the Theosophical Society which believed that, through the discovery of the ancient religions of India, it had found the key to a universal religion, a universal truth that underlay all religions' varied manifestations in different times and places. The search for underlying identities which transcend cultural relativities has in these and all kinds of other ways been a feature, too, of the twentieth century's dialogue with the East, in theology, philosophy, and many other fields. These range from calls for mutual understanding which, according to E.A. Burtt, 'must be cultivated at the philosophical level if man is to progress successfully towards stable co-existence and peaceful growth in a world community' (1967: 253), and according to Ninian Smart presents the planet with 'unparalleled opportunities of mutual fecundation and challenge', perhaps even leading towards a 'global city' (1981: 21ff), to Huxley's ideal of a renewed *philosophia perennis*, and Heidegger's vision of a 'planetary thinking'.

The many forms that universalism takes have behind them a moral imperative, namely that in order to live together in peace we must seek a measure of mutual understanding. For some – we shall call them the 'utopians' – this arouses inspiring images of a single global belief system, a sort of Hegelian reconciliation of all opposites in which harmony is achieved through the assuagement of cultural and religious tensions. In this vision we all come to see the world in the same way by discovering that beneath all the historical differences there lies a unity of vision; a universal religion of mankind, such as that envisaged by some Theosophists, would be the appropriate vehicle for the achievement and main- tenance of such a goal. For other rather less utopian minds – whom we shall call 'pluralists' – it implies the ability to live with and to honour differences, a goal to be worked at, not through the overcoming of these differences but through the unending conversation of mankind in which differences are retained and res- pected; in this vision, East and West are not sublimated into some higher synthesis, but work through dialogue towards shared understandings. The appro- priate vehicle for the pursuit of this goal is dialogue.

To sum up, then, the meeting of East and West, in spite of the strictures of Said and others, has provoked a powerful challenge to the Western sense of its own superiority. It confronts that sense of hegemony we spoke of earlier, which, in both Christian and scientific-rationalist forms, has encouraged the belief that the tradition that was the joint product of Jerusalem, Athens, and Rome represented something special, exclusive, and privileged in the story of mankind. It has at the same time, by way of compensation, offered to the West a unique way of addressing fundamental questions concerning its own identity and destiny, and urgent issues concerning the very future of mankind. Jung's writings on Eastern philosophies represent, as we shall see, a significant contribution to this dis- course. He was an example of a Western thinker whose engagement with the East was impelled, not by any great pretensions to scholarly objectivity or neutrality, nor by any Romantic desire to escape from the modern world and all its troubles, but by the sort of moral imperative of which we have just spoken. Like the utopians he was convinced that underlying the strangeness and the alien surface of Eastern philosophies could be found universal strata, collective, though un- conscious, archetypal characteristics which are common to the human mind as such. But like the pluralists he pursued this imperative, not through the con- struction of a system built out of the dismantled components of both cultures, to which he hoped all would eventually subscribe, but rather through engaging in a dialogue with the philosophical texts and ideas of the East. He was in fact typical of many thinkers, from Leibniz up to the present time, whose study of the mind of the East has arisen from the conviction that only by placing itself within this wider context can the West be saved from itself.

27

These themes will emerge more clearly in the next section where we briefly trace the story of the East–West dialogue, and where we shall set the scene for the narration of Jung's endeavours.

EAST COMES WEST

The claim made by Joseph Needham that 'for three thousand years there has been a dialogue going on between the two ends of the world' is a necessary counter-balance to the Eurocentrism of standard intellectual histories, and the enclavist attitudes that have often prevailed in the West. But it is of course an exaggeration. In the first place it represents too extended a time-span: the best historical evidence to hand would suggest the subtraction of half a millennium from Needham's estimate. In the second place the dialogue is for much of the time subdued, often little more than a whisper, and from the fall of Rome to the High Middle Ages there is virtual silence. The two ends of the earth have often engaged in the dialogue of the deaf, and have systematically and perversely misunderstood each other. Furthermore, the historical evidence of real cultural exchange prior to the Enlightenment period is often flimsy and circumstantial, and in general it is not always easy to distinguish between direct influence and happy coincidence. Nevertheless, something of this story, with all these qualifications entered, needs to be recounted here, if only in outline, in order that we can make sense of Jung's own voice in this conversation. What we need to see is that Jung's attempt to build a bridge of understanding, though unique in its own way, was in certain crucial respects part of a tradition – perhaps more acurately a sub-tradition – that goes back a long way, perhaps even to the ancient world.

We could begin around 400 BCE with Plato, or even further back with Pythagoras in the sixth century BCE, for it is often said that the ideas about the soul and the cosmos that are common to these two thinkers, and which were to have such an important influence on subsequent European thought, bear a striking resemblance to concepts within Indian metaphysical systems. Or we could begin with the invasion of India by Alexander the Great in 327 BCE, an event which is historically well documented, and which saw the opening up of some kind of dialogue between the Hellenic intellectual world and the gymnosophists – the naked philosophers as the Greeks called them – of India. Or even with the reign of another 'enlightened' emperor, Ashoka, who established an empire in India in the fourth century BCE, who widely propagated Buddhism within his territories, and who sent monks westwards to preach the Buddhist *Dharma*. These and many other considerations have provoked intriguing speculations concerning the contributions of the Orient to the Greek and Christian culture of Europe, and have even suggested to some the need to rethink the very identity of Western Christendom. But it would be more relevant to our present task to begin the story in the modern period, where hard evidence is more forthcoming, and light cast on Jung's part in the story more illuminating.[11]

Mythical images of the fabulous East had abounded in Europe since the time of Marco Polo's journey to China in the thirteenth century, but the opening up of the modern mind to the ideas of the East really began with the missionary work in China and India of the Jesuits, the shock-troops of the Catholic Counter-Reformation, in the latter half of the sixteenth century. Prominent amongst them was the figure of Matteo Ricci who, in the light of his heroic but doomed attempts to accommodate Christian concepts and practices to Confucianism, must surely deserve the title of 'Patron Saint' of the East–West dialogue. The ultimate aim of Ricci and his companions was indeed the conversion of the heathen peoples of the East to the 'true' gospel of Christ, but the priests of the Order of Jesus were no bigoted, narrow-minded evangelists but highly educated and cultured men who had in their long education absorbed the mind-expanding ideas of Renaissance humanism, and in the course of their work they sent back to Europe detailed and sympathetic accounts of the beliefs and practices of the people they sought to convert, and translated some of the classical texts of Confucianism into Latin. The ideas they brought back from the East were eagerly received and discussed by the philosophers of the day and were to have a profound influence on the formation of the ideas of the Enlightenment – an influence which is often not adequately acknowledged.[12]

The popular image of Oriental influence in the age of Enlightenment is usually confined to the decorative arts. What is not always appreciated is the extent to which ideas brought over from China, and to a lesser extent from India, by the Jesuit missionaries entered deeply into the arguments and debates of that period. 'In the late seventeenth and eighteenth centuries, Europe became', as one historian puts it, 'infatuated with a vision of Cathay' (Edwardes, 1971: 103). The list of Enlightenment thinkers who professed a more than passing interest in Eastern philosophy is impressive and includes: Malebranche, Bayle, Wolff, Leibniz, Voltaire, Montesquieu, Diderot, Helvetius, and Quesnay (the list does not include Rousseau, however, who remained unimpressed by the current images of Cathay). Confucian China was the chief object of interest, and while Hindu notions were also debated in the same period, the ideas of India did not really capture the imagination of Europe until later during the Romantic age.

Three related aspects of Confucian thought, ethical, political, and cosmological respectively, were the chief sources of this infatuation. What the Enlightenment philosophers believed they had found in China was a highly successful civilisation built on principles of conduct and good order, which were not only without benefit of Christian revelation but were believed to be based on a purely rational foundation. The admirably well-regulated conduct of the state and the disciplined private conduct of its citizens were thought to be the product of a system of ethics that arose out of a purely philosophical source with no trace of mysticism or religious dogma. Moreover, this philosophical source in its turn was seen to connect with cosmological principles that were purely abstract and impersonal, and which presupposed no notions of worship or accompanying notions of sin, guilt, or salvation.

Voltaire was undoubtedly the leader of the sinophiles. In his *Essai sur les Mœurs*, first published in 1746, he wrote that 'If as a philosopher one wishes to instruct oneself about what has taken place on the globe, one must first of all turn one's eyes to the East, the cradle of all the arts, to which the West owes everything'. Voltaire's whole life was devoted to the task of subverting, with all the considerable powers of his intellect and wit, and expressed with the matchless fluency of his pen, the establshed order of Christendom as embodied in Church and State. Just as he used the England of Newton and Locke to attack French institutions, so he conscripted Confucian China, as portrayed by the Jesuits, in his battle against the bigotry and superstition of the old European order. Confucius was perceived as an ideal philosopher-statesman, an archetypal rationalist who not only propounded a political philosophy that was free from religious dogma, but whose ideals were supposedly the foundation of the tranquil and harmonious political order that was imagined to prevail in China. A similar weapon was used by Voltaire with which to assault the established religious order, the Roman Catholic Church. China, and India too, represented in his eyes a deistic state, namely a religious order based, as was the political order, on the natural light of reason. Furthermore, the very antiquity of Chinese civilisation seemed in his view to contradict biblical chronology, and the antiquity of Indian religions suggested they were actually the source of Christianity itself, perhaps even the root from which all religions had sprouted. He certainly had no liking for what he described as the 'polytheistic rubbish' to be found in the East, but Oriental religions in their higher manifestations demonstrated to him, and to his fellow Enlighteners' satisfaction, the possibility of a religion based on reason alone.

The use that Voltaire made of his Jesuit-filtered image of China to attack and undermine the established order was repeated and refined by many of his contemporaries. In the powerful urge towards self-criticism during a period in which all the traditions of Western Christendom were called into doubt, the East was held up as a mirror in which Europeans were invited to review and to criticise themselves. Idealised images of the East were used by many writers during that period as a way of casting unfavourable light on conditions at home, and indeed this whole episode of sinophilia could be seen as part of the agonising process of self-doubt and utopian reconstruction that has been such a characteristic feature of modern Western thought.

Much of this self-doubt was inevitably negative and destructive in its implications, since for many the old order had to be swept away completely before a new order could replace it. The positive side of this process was perhaps best represented by the great German philosopher Leibniz, a thinker, incidentally, for whom Jung had great admiration. More of an establishment figure than Voltaire, Leibniz's life-task was not so much the destruction of the status quo as a search for principles of harmony whereby the warring religious and political factions of Europe could be reconciled with each other. This search, which began as a reaction to the continuing conflicts between Catholics and Protestants, took on a universal dimension, for he was deeply committed to an ecumenical outlook which embraced not only Catholics and Protestants but also the religions and intellectual beliefs and practices of non-Westerners, such as the Chinese (see Mungello, 1977). In this context he conceived the idea of a universal language, modelled on the Chinese ideographic script, which would facilitate the reconciliation of disputes between warring religious and philosophical factions. The inspiration he derived from China, moreover, came not so much from its moral and political philosophy as from its metaphysics, and more from what we would now identify as Taoism rather than Confucianism, with its concept of universal harmony based on the reconciliation of opposites. He found especially fascinating the binary symbolism of the *I Ching*, a text which, as we shall see later, Jung also studied with great interest.[13]

We can detect a similar enthusiasm for the East when we come to the Romantic period towards the end of the eighteenth century, but whereas China was the chief object of interest for the philosophers of the Enlightenment, it was India that captured the minds and imagination of the Romantics.[14] The interest in Indian ideas during the Romantic period was as pervasive as was the interest in China during the earlier epoch, and it was the extent of this interest that led the Orientalist Raymond Schwab to revive the idea of an 'Oriental Renaissance'. He believed that the introduction of Indian thought into Europe from the late eighteenth century onwards and its integration into the cultural and philosophical concerns of the period amounted to a cultural transformation of the same order as that of the Renaissance of fifteenth-century Italy, that 'the revival of an atmosphere in the nineteenth century brought about by the arrival of Sanskrit texts in Europe . . . produced an effect equal to that produced in the fifteenth century by the arrival of Greek manuscripts and Byzantine commentators after the fall of Constantinople' (1984: 11).

As in the Enlightenment period the springboard for the new Orientalism lay in the perceived need for renewal, for a revival of what the poets and philosophers of the period felt the age had lost, namely a oneness with mankind and a oneness with nature. Where the earlier Oriental interest had sprung largely from ethical and political demands, the new version arose from what can only be described as a metaphysical thirst, a need to escape the icy blasts of Rationalism. As the historian A.L. Willson puts it, in the Romantic period India became for Europe a 'magnetic image [which] attracted the fancifulness and inventiveness of Romantic culture', which became 'absorbed into the style and metaphor of Romantic poetry and prose . . . [and] gave direction and contour to Romantic philosophy' (1964: 239–40)

It was amongst the German Romantics that the new Oriental enthusiasm first flourished. There the Romantic sensibility found fertile soil, not only amongst the poets, playwrights, artists and musicians, but also amongst the remarkable family of philosophers and thinkers who flourished at the end of the eighteenth and the beginning of the nineteenth centuries, running from Herder and Goethe through Hegel and Schelling to the Schlegel brothers, and Schopenhauer. They were all coloured in one way or another by what Schwab has called 'an Indian tint', and were infected by what Said describes more luridly as 'the virtual epidemic of Orientalia affecting every major poet, essayist, and philosopher of the period' (1978: 50). Herder, who in many ways set the agenda for Romanticism, also set the tone for Indophilia with such comments as: 'O holy land [of India], I salute thee, thou source of all music, thou voice of the heart', and 'Behold the East – cradle of the human race, of human emotion, of all religion'.

What then was the point of contact between the Romantics and India? To what problems did it appear to provide the answers? In the first place there appeared to many to be a remarkable parallel between the broad lines of idealist philosophy and the ancient metaphysical beliefs of India. There seemed to the Romantics to be a form of monistic pantheism at the heart of Indian thought which tallied with their own way of thinking about God and nature, and in general a mystical temper which matched their own need for an alternative to the materialism and empiricism of Bacon and Locke. The second point of contact between the two cultures lay in the Romantics' obsessive quest for origins that are older than Homer and the Ancient Greeks. The 'discovery' of Ossian, a fictitious Gaelic bard invented by a Scotsman, James Macpherson, in order to satisfy this quest, was more than matched by the discovery of Sanskrit and of a poetic literature, the *Vedas*, which not only pre-dated Homer, but might even go back beyond the times of the Bible itself.

Herder was the intellectual power behind this movement, and was responsible for drafting in the Orient in order to pursue the strategy of outflanking the traditionally accepted sources of European culture. He was perhaps the first to claim that the source of all civilisation lay, not in the Mediterranean, but in India, and that India was not only the cradle of all civilisations, but the source of human language as such. In so doing he helped to propagate the Rousseauean picture of a decadent Europe contrasted with an ancient idyllic society.[15] Other eloquent voices responded to his call to arms. Perhaps the most significant was Goethe who, along with Herder, had inspired the proto-Romantic *Sturm und Drang* (Storm and Stress) movement of the 1770s, and who is usually seen as the great champion of Greek civilisation. In the Preface to his set of poems, *East–West Divan*, a work which was to have an important influence on a whole generation of poets, he wrote that he wished 'to penetrate to the first origin of human races, when they still received celestial mandates from God in terrestrial languages' (quoted in Schwab, 1984: 211). Schelling, a crucial figure in the development of German idealist and nature philosophy, found in the Vedic poems a source of myth that was clearly not a product of the Mediterranean. And Schlegel saw India as 'the real source of all tongues . . . the primary source of all ideas' (quoted in Iyer, 1965: 194 and 200), and was especially concerned to trace Germanic culture directly back to the Indus valley without passing through Athens.[16]

Out of the quest for non-European origins arose a third point of contact, a matter of perhaps greater significance for the future, and one which will be of importance when we come to consider Jung, namely the concept of a universal humanity that transcends all surface local and historical differences. The

Romantics were deeply worried by what they saw as the fragmented nature of European thought and culture, and of mankind in general, and the Indian connection offered to them the clue to a universal religion. Thus Schelling, as a result of his mythological studies, came to the conclusion that 'thanks to research [on] the *Vedas*, the primitive unity of the human race was becoming a historical truth rather than a theological hypothesis' (quoted in Schwab, 1984: 218). Even the Protestant theologican Schleiermacher speculated that there was a single source for all religions, and that was to be found in the Orient. For Friedrich Schlegel, 'Asiatics and Europeans form a single great family; as Asia and Europe together make up a single indivisible whole, so we should strive the more to see the literatures of all cultured peoples as one continuous development, as a single closely knit structure, as a unique unity' (quoted in Iyer, 1965: 200). Behind all of these lay the belief that the great religions of mankind derived from a 'universal revelation'; as Schwab puts it, the universal 'myths and mysteries were assumed to hold secrets common to the faithful of all nations' (pp. 216–17), a single truth veiled beneath the clothing of local legends and faiths, 'a single God for all mankind' in Schelling's words.

Something of this attitude, namely the demand of the Romantics for a global concept of the human spirit and of human history, is to be found in the writings of Hegel, who was of course in many respects critical of the Romantic outlook. He certainly did not share their unbridled enthusiasm for the East. He detested the 'wild excesses of fantasy', the 'unrestrained frenzy' and the chaos of myths and icons which he detected in Indian culture (see Halbfass, 1988: 89), and generally perceived the East as stagnant, frozen in its past, and incapable of resuscitation. But despite his failure to do justice to Indian philosophy, seeing it merely as a rather confused childish precursor to the 'real philosophy' which, as far as he was concerned, 'begins only in Greece', he spent a lot of time expounding its views in detail, and sought to locate these within a universal history of the human spirit. He was not, indeed, the first to include Eastern thought within a history of philosophy, but he was the first to subject it to systematic treatment and to attempt to see the development of mankind as a single totality. His study of the Orient represented in many ways a unique enterprise in the history of ideas, and though his interpretation was later taken as a justification for dismissing India entirely from the historiography of philosophy, it nevertheless, as Halbfass suggests, 'exemplifies once and for all one basic possibility of dealing with a foreign tradition' (1988: 98).

Schopenhauer's interest in Indian philosophy is better known than Hegel's, and exemplifies to an even greater degree the extent to which the East had penetrated the philosophical discourse of the age. Unlike Hegel, his attitude towards the philosophies of India was one of almost unreserved admiration. While denying that his philosophical system was influenced in its basic structures by the East – Kant is clearly the major influence – he nevertheless had been acquainted with the ideas of the Upanishads for several years prior to the publication in 1818 of his major work, *The World as Will and Idea*. He drew close

33

parallels between his own philosophy and that of Hinduism, and suggested that an understanding of the Upanishads would not only help towards an under-standing of his own philosophy, but would bring about a fundamental change in European thought. According to Halbfass 'he showed an unprecedented readi-ness to integrate Indian ideas into his own European thinking and self-understanding, and to utilize them for the illustration, articulation, and clarification of his own teachings and problems', and furthermore combined with this 'a radical critique of some of the most fundamental presuppositions of the Judaeo-Christian tradition such as the notion of a personal God, the uniqueness of the human individual and the meaning of history, as well as the modern Western belief in the powers of the intellect, rationality, planning and progress' (1988: 120).

The discovery of Buddhism, and its dissemination by Schopenhauer amongst others, in the middle years of the nineteenth century, initiated a further phase of the Oriental Renaissance after the Romantic period, and represented a further phase of the dialogue between West and East. Amongst those deeply affected not only by Schopenhauer's work in general but also his by Oriental leanings were two giants of nineteenth-century culture: Wagner and Nietzsche. Wagner for a period actually described himself as a Buddhist, announcing that 'I have un-consciously become a Buddhist. It is a world-view compared with which every other dogma must appear small and narrow'.

Nietzsche's relationship with Buddhism was more complex and ambivalent, but nonetheless more important than it is usually perceived to be. It is difficult to judge the degree of influence that Eastern thought had over his intellectual development, but what is certain is that the ideas of the East, especially those of Buddhism, weave their way in and out of the dialectical to-and-fro of his arguments, providing, as with earlier thinkers such as Leibniz and Voltaire, an instrument with which to develop a critique of Western philosophy and Christian values, a weapon to lay bare the bankruptcy of the Judaeo-Christian tradition. While he remained critical of what he perceived as the more negative 'nay-saying' aspects of Buddhist philosophy, and in this regard associated it with the Christian outlook, he believed that Buddhism lacked Christianity's bitterness, guilt, and resentment, and represented a more psychologically honest and far more realistic account of human suffering, based on a strictly atheistic and pragmatic outlook, and avoiding all metaphysical consolations. It was, he thought, the only genuinely positivistic religion, a system of 'mental hygiene' rather than of theological doctrine, perhaps even the religion of the future: 'a European Buddhism may prove indispensable', he speculated, and even suggested that he himself 'could be the Buddha of Europe'![17]

During the course of the second half of the nineteenth century Buddhism entered deeply, not only into the popular imagination, fed by works such as Edwin Arnold's *Light of Asia,* but into the intellectual debates of the period. Attitudes towards Buddhism were decidedly ambivalent. Its teachings certainly posed considerable problems for Christian clergy and theologians who were already having to contend with assaults from Higher Criticism, Positivism, and Darwinism. Indeed the newly discovered Buddhist teachings had a great appeal to many seeking a religious alternative to the Christian tradition, and became a veritable battleground in that 'age of doubt' between Christianity on the one hand and the forces of atheism and secularisation on the other.

As with Hinduism during the Romantic period, there was the question of origins. This was sparked off by the evidently pre-Christian source of Buddhist teaching, which, along with the remarkable parallels between their ethical teachings, was used by some critics hostile to Christian orthodoxy to suggest that Buddhism might be a source, independent of Judaism, of Christian belief and practice. And as with Confucianism in the eighteenth-century, there was excited admiration for the lofty nature of Buddhist ethical teaching, which of course did not have the benefit of Christian revelation. It was inevitable, therefore, that Buddhism should be exploited by the advocates of agnosticism and secularism, who, like their eighteenth-century counterparts in relation to Confucianism, saw in Buddhist ideas a model of a purely rationalistic morality, even of a non-metaphysical religion. Thus, A.O. Lovejoy, writing at the turn of the century, spoke for many intellectuals when he described Buddhism as 'essentially a system of spiritual discipline based, not upon metaphysics, but upon a psychology of sensation [which] knows nothing of any ontological absolute' (quoted in Welbon, 1968: 219), and Richard Armstrong, writing in 1870 in defence of the idea of an atheistic culture, pointed out that three hundred million Buddhists were sufficient refutation of the claim that the idea of God is naturally revealed to all men (see Almond, 1988: 100).

Enough has been said to indicate the scope of the intellectual relationship between East and West up to the end of the nineteenth century, and to illustrate the manner in which this singularly underestimated aspect of European discourse was conducted. This relationship flourished and diversified in all sorts of ways during the early decades of the twentieth century, not least in the fields of Oriental scholarship. As we shall see in a later chapter, Jung's developing interest in the East in the inter-war years reflected both a continuing fascination with Buddhist and Hindu philosophies within the European-American cultural world, and also the emergence of two new objects of interest: Taoism and Zen. These in a way complete, in broad outline at any rate, the Eastern voices with which the West has engaged in dialogue since the Jesuits first went to China and India. Partly under the influence of Jung himself, they, along with the older voices, have continued to speak urgently and persuasively to the ever-increasing number of Western minds ready to listen and to respond. As with the earlier transmissions of Eastern ideas they were received, not only in the spirit of disinterested scholarship, but also with the deliberate aim of subjecting to criticism, even of subverting, the very foundations of Western culture. From a broad historical perspective it is hardly suprising that in the 1960s, when so many young people gave voice to their disillusionment with the values of Western Christendom, they found expression for these disillusionments in a new Oriental turn. At a more scholarly level, the Oriental turn can be witnessed in a number of disciplines, including philosophy, theology, and psychology, where in parallel fashion the study of the East has proved a catalyst in the process of self-criticism which has become almost a salient characteristic of our 'post-Christian', 'post-modern' age.

In conclusion, we can detect two themes which have threaded their way through the relationship between East and West, and which have continued into the twentieth century. The first theme is the search for parallels between Eastern and Western thought, leading to the postulation of a universal religion or philosophy underlying all cultural differences, which in turn can be linked to the concept of the oneness of mankind. The second theme concerns the critique of Western civilisation, of its decadence and narrowness, and the mounting of a challenge to the uniqueness of the Christian message, of the belief in progress and in European superiority. The East has, as I have indicated, provided the West with a mirror with which to scrutinise itself, an external point of reference with which to conduct its agonising obsession with self-examination and self-criticism. This phenomenon has been observed in various forms from the time of Voltaire onwards, and is even more conspicuous in the twentieth century where doubts about the intrinsic value of modernity and of European civilisation have often been given expression by means of a turning towards the East. Sometimes, perhaps, as in the popular movements of the sixties, this has be viewed as a form of escapism, a tendency of which Jung himself was, as we shall see, highly critical. It has also, though, taken the form of the rigorous analysis of the underlying assumptions of Western culture and philosophy, and has begun to play a role in recent attempts to place the peculiarly Western brands of philosophy within a wider horizon. This point is emphasised by Coward (1990: 148) in his study of the relationship between Derrida and Indian philosophy where he concludes that the importance of the East–West dialogue lay

> not just in the building of a bridgehead between the two traditions, important as that is in itself, but the benefit is also one of a deeper self-understanding achieved by examining one's own thinking in relation to the thought of the other. More simply put it is sometimes through others that we come to know ourselves.

Finally, this whole 'sub-tradition' represents the historical and intellectual background to the discussion of Jung which follows, the context within which we can better make sense of his own dialogue with the East. This dialogue of Jung's has often – when not simply ignored – been read as an adjunct to his central psychological theories, in particular to his theory of the archetypes and the collective unconscious. This view is not entirely mistaken, but it represents only part of the truth, for Jung's attempts to grapple with Eastern thought has a significance which transcends the bounds of his analytical psychology, and is part of what we have called the conversation of mankind, that peculiar form of self-reflexive discourse that has gripped the imagination of so many European thinkers over the past few centuries.

3

JUNG AND HERMENEUTICS

The brief summary that has just been given of the dialogue 'between the ends of the earth' is useful as a counterweight to the generally held view that there is something intrinsic to the cultures of Asia and Europe which prevents them from communicating with each other. However, in our attempts to span supposed cultural chasms, we would be wrong to underestimate the difficulties, philosophical, historical, and technical, that stand in the way of this enterprise. Erich Fromm, who sought to establish a bridge between psychoanalysis and Zen Buddhism, began his study by wondering if his discussion of the subject could result in 'anything but the statement that there exists no relationship except that of radical and unbridgeable difference' (1986: 14). Jung himself found cultural bridge-building no easy task. He was often worried by the alien nature of the texts he was studying, and in his Commentary on *The Secret of the Golden Flower* he confessed himself to be 'profoundly impressed by the strangeness of this Chinese text' (CW13.1). The purpose of this chapter is to offer a model of inter-cultural communication, while at the same time accounting for the enormous difficulties that stand in its way. This model will enable us to understand Jung's hesitations as he embarked on his examination of Oriental texts, and to assess his achievement in this undertaking.

COMMUNICATING ACROSS BOUNDARIES

Admitting the possibility of inter-cultural communication does not give us a passport to cross borders with total impunity. Historicism at least cautions us to be wary of leaping across divides without taking appropriate account of cultural and linguistic differences. It is understandable that we should seek to discover someone with similar views to ourselves on the other side of the border, and so to achieve a bond of sympathy, perhaps even of unanimity, but this natural desire carries with it evident risks. No doubt many spurious parallels can be drawn between Eastern and Western systems of thought, inspired by the desire to make certain Asian philosophies interesting and acceptable by Western standards. We need to be reminded every so often that, in one sense, everything is similar to everything else, or can be made to appear so, and hence that comparisons can easily lapse into a state of empty truisms. Just as Orientalism, in Said's sense, carries with it the dangers of projecting Western prejudices and pretensions onto other cultures, so also, in a different sense, it can become nothing more than the sentimental desire to achieve empathy at any cost.

Take the example of the field of psychotherapy. Jung was by no means alone in drawing attention to interesting parallels between yoga practices on the one hand and the methods and approaches of psychotherapy on the other. It is not uncommon nowadays to read that 'Buddhism is a form of psychotherapy' or that 'Zen Enlightenment is similar to the kind of insight gained in the course of successful psychoanalysis'. Nevertheless, however illuminating such insights may be, it is necessary to bear in mind that these practices derive from very different cultural roots and arise out of different traditions. Thus, psychotherapy is a product of the scientific and philosophical tradition of the West, with its emphasis on analysis and objectivity, as well as from Christian, liberal humanist and existentialist traditions, whereas the ways of yoga and Buddhism derive from what can better be described as spiritual traditions whose goal is wisdom and whose methods are seen as transcending the intellect. Even innocent-sounding statements like 'Buddhism is essentially about human development', or 'the intrinsic purpose of [Buddhist teaching] is personal growth' (Claxton, 1986: 165) carry a burden of controversial assumptions. There are important questions here about whether Western therapeutic concepts can adequately convey the meaning of Oriental terms, and whether the whole enterprise of psychotherapy can be seen as having anything more than a superficial likeness to its supposed counterparts in the East.

There are also well-known technical problems with translation. As the American logician Quine has reminded us, there lies at the heart of any attempt to translate from one language to another a radical and inescapable indeterminacy, for we have no standpoint outside of language from which to judge the adequacy of the procedure, and no access to 'meaning' other than through specific languages. This question is especially urgent in the translation of Eastern philosophical texts, and we shall see later that this presents significant problems for Jung's reading of Eastern texts. The Buddhist scholar Herbert Guenther points out that terms such as 'mind' are difficult enough to make sense of in our own native language, let alone when we use them as translations for Sanskrit or Tibetan words, and goes on to comment that language 'is a treacherous instrument' and that the 'question, whether the authors of the original texts actually meant the same as we do by those words about whose meaning we ourselves are not quite clear, should always be present, not only when translating texts but still more when dealing with a systematic presentation of Eastern philosophies' (1989: 37–8). Tibetan terms are embedded in a long philosophical and religious tradition and cannot simply be lifted out by means of 'sky hooks' and re-implanted in a different linguistic environment. In a similar vein Raimundo

Panikkar, a key participant in the East–West dialogue, points to the difficulties that have been experienced, ever since the Jesuits first went to China, of translating such terms as 'God', 'person' and 'love' (1979: 278), and Jung himself warned of the 'dubious applicability' of the term 'psychology' to Eastern ideas and practices (CW11.759).

Nevertheless, the simple fact is that people do communicate across borders and boundaries. This is clearly the case at the everyday level where individuals manage, albeit often with difficulty, to communicate with other individuals, ranging from spouses and neighbours to bosses and foreign hotel proprietors. It could be said that people cross conceptual and cultural boundaries whenever they read a book, travel abroad, or even engage in the most trivial of conversations; indeed it is arguable that *every* act of communication is an act of decipherment and of translation. There are indeed different levels of communication which give rise to different levels of difficulty; 'You are a cad' might present fewer difficulties in practice than 'Thou art that', but the underlying philosophical issue remains the same. Problems of interpretation and basic comprehension are therefore not problems that are confined to inter-cultural communication, and it is easy to see that the force of Quine's translation argument could apply equally within, as much as between, cultures and traditions. As Halbfass points out:

Understanding, as well as misunderstanding, takes place in the European encounter with Indian and Oriental thought, just as it takes place in Europe's relationship with its own Greek sources, and just as it has taken place in the encounter between other traditions.

(Halbfass, 1988: 166)

In the light of this we might well ask whether the understanding of our own philosophical tradition is any less fraught with difficulties than understanding, say, a Buddhist tradition. Erich Fromm comments that 'Zen is not more difficult for the European than Heraclitus [or] Meister Eckhart' (1986: 70). Indeed, twentieth-century philosophers such as Heidegger or Wittgenstein appear to many contemporaries to be considerably less accessible than supposedly obscure and alien texts such as the *I Ching* or the *Tao Te Ching*. Part of the appeal of Eastern philosophy in recent times lies in the fact that to many people it appears to make more sense than their own home-grown varieties.

Again, of course, there is room here for self-deception and wishful thinking, but the history of Western philosophy is itself a battleground of conflicting interpretation and factionalism which does not always convey the sense of a shared tradition in which we comfortably dwell. Similarly the Western religious tradition is far from being monolithic but is fractured by doctrinal schisms and competing sub-cultures. As Radhakrishnan has argued, the European mystical tradition which stems from Plato and Plotinus, Clement and Origen, has more in common with, and makes more sense in the context of, Eastern mystical traditions such as that of Sankara than the more orthodox Christian tradition (1939: 296; see also Otto, 1957). Some have even suggested that aspects of one's own culture can be illuminated by mediating its ideas through foreign philosophical ideas and theories. This has certainly been the case with philosophers from China, Japan, India, and Sri Lanka who in recent years have increasingly made use of the concepts and methodologies of Western philosophy in order to illuminate their own philosophical inheritance. The Indian philosopher J.L. Mehta has pointed out that the use of the English language and European philosophical and religious concepts played an important role in the revival of traditional Vedānta philosophy in the nineteenth century (1985: 163). Furthermore, many modern Asian philosophers have entered into and contributed to debates within Western philosophy without any apparent intrinsic difficulties.[1]

Considerations such as these must inevitably lead one to question the usefulness of phrases like 'our culture', or 'our tradition', and open up the possibility of speaking of a world culture and a single tradition in which there are many relatively distinct though interconnected elements which overlap and criss-cross. If practical illustration were needed of the capacity of ideas to travel, as it were, across cultural and linguistic boundaries, then Buddhism itself offers an instructive example, for since its very inception it has been engaged in a creative interaction with other cultures. Throughout human history, indeed, cultures have interacted with each other in all kinds of ways, flowing into each other, learning, consciously or unconsciously, from each other. As B.K. Matilal has put it:

> Cultures and societies . . . are not like watertight compartments, which may seldom confront one another in reality and interact. They do interact with each other, sometimes generating violence, sometimes peacefully and almost unconsciously accepting value trade-offs and value rejections.
>
> (Quoted in Deutsch, 1991: 151)

These interactions have increased exponentially in the twentieth century with the increasing movement of peoples and the accelerating flow of information and of international communication. Two world wars and the end of colonialism have provoked increasing self-questioning on the part of European peoples and an unprecedented willingness to engage in dialogue rather than confrontation. In the case of East–West interaction the pioneering efforts of Ricci, Leibniz, Schlegel, and others mentioned in the previous chapter, have witnessed an extraordinary apotheosis in the twentieth century, growth in academic research having given the West access to the intellectual and culture treasure houses of the East, and helping to open up communication with Eastern ideas and culture at all levels.

With the development of contacts between East and West, and of academic interest in comparative studies, not to mention the popular enthusiasm for all things Eastern that has burgeoned in the past few decades, attention has increasingly been paid to the philosophical issues that I have mentioned above. A volume with the title *Interpreting Across Boundaries: New Essays in Comparative Philosophy* (quoted in Larson and Deutsch, 1991: 151), containing a wide range of essays by various scholars, is typical of the growing recognition of the importance of methodological questions in this sphere, as well as on the need for a widening of dialogue between the two cultures.

Such a volume is an acknowledgement of the fact that dialogue between the intellectual traditions of East and West is no longer a rare curiosity, if it ever was, but has become part of cultural and academic life. Many of the stereotypes to which we drew attention in the previous chapter, underpinned by theories about the difference between Eastern and Western mentalities, have been the product of ignorance, and the growth of Oriental scholarship in recent decades has allowed us to demystify some of the traditional assumptions about the supposed inaccessibility of the Oriental mind.[2] Since the turn of the century comparative studies in the fields of philosophy, theology, and psychology have grown from the scholarly efforts of relatively isolated individuals such as Friedrich Max Müller and Paul Masson-Oursel, and have in recent years achieved the proportions of a veritable industry. This fact in itself is hardly sufficient to dispel all philosophical doubts, but it is important to recognise the depth and extent of the East–West dialogue and to counteract the assumption that it is a marginal activity carried on by a few adepts with little or no impact on the culture in general.

Our task in this chapter, then, is not to demonstrate *that* the activity of inter-cultural communication is possible, but rather to show *how* it is possible, and in doing so to provide a model with which to understand Jung's own attempts at cross-cultural communication.[3]

In recent years *dialogue* has become a key word. In 1964 the historian of religions W. Cantwell Smith remarked that 'dialogue between members of differing traditions is nowadays replacing polemics, debate, and the monologue preaching of traditional missionary policy' (Smith, 1964: 177). In the intervening years this claim has been amply borne out by the ever-increasing commitment to this form of communication in a whole variety of contexts and disciplines. The term has achieved its widest currency amongst theologians. The Protestant-inspired ecumenical movement and the new spirit of openness inspired by the Second Vatican Council have both marked the emergence within the Christian Churches of a climate favouring dialogue, first and foremost between the traditionally embattled sects, but now increasingly with non-Christian religions. This development has moved Cantwell Smith to suggest that we in the twentieth century can no longer consider ouselves to be denizens of distinct cultural enclaves, but 'are heirs to the whole religious history of mankind' (Smith, 1981: 18).[4]

Amongst philosophers the concept has achieved at least an airing, if not a wide usage, due in large measure to the writings of Rorty and Bernstein, who are convinced that the traditional task of seaching for foundations and for a rational consensus in knowledge must now be replaced by the more modest aim of engaging in 'the conversation of mankind'. In their view the quest for immovable foundations, and the constructing of totalising systems and grand metaphysical narratives, which has characterised the Western philosophical endeavour, have lost all credibility. This is a situation which leads, they claim, not to scepticism and nihilism, but rather to a new and more robust pluralism, and a reconstruction of philosophy based on open-ended dialogue, conversation, and communication across hitherto well-established boundaries. They do not explicitly advocate an East–West dialogue, and indeed

Rorty speaks in an untypically limiting way of 'the continuing conversation of the *West*' (1979: 394, my italics), but the role for philosophy which they propose is one which has important implications for those engaged in the relationship between Eastern and Western thought.

Dialogue is the sort of activity to which no one can take exception; it is presumed to be a 'good thing'. But what exactly is it? How can we define it? Within the huge literature that has appropriated its benign aura there are surprisingly few attempts to subject it to close analytical scrutiny. Amongst these attempts phrases such as the following tend to recur: 'A reaching out of one person to another', 'Openness towards another's point of view', 'Capacity to listen and to change one's views'. And furthermore it is usually contrasted with 'debate' in which one side is expected to win, or with 'dialectic' in which there is some inevitable resolution of differences. In general it seems to imply a lack of dogmatism, a capacity for self-criticism, a willingness to take into account a plurality of ideas, and a quasi-dialectical procedure in which ideas evolve by means of comparison and contrast.

HERMENEUTICS

It is within the field of philosophical *hermeneutics* that a clearly worked-out concept of dialogue has emerged. As indicated in Chapter 1, I intend to make systematic use of hermeneutics, in particular that of H.-G. Gadamer, in making sense of Jung's dialogue with the East, and so we must now sketch its outlines and draw out its relevance to our present enquiries.[5]

The term 'hermeneutics' was first used in the seventeenth century to signify the principles and methods needed to interpret the meaning of the Bible, and in the hands of the German theologian Schleiermacher (1768–1834) the term was extended to embrace not only sacred texts, but any written text, and beyond that the whole sphere of human symbolic expression. He saw hermeneutics as 'the art of understanding' that humans employ whenever they try to understand a text, a human artefact, or another human being. In the hands of the philosopher Wilhelm Dilthey (1833–1911) hermeneutics became the key to understanding the distinctive nature of the human, as opposed to the natural, sciences. One of the most important contemporary exponents of hermeneutics is the German philosopher, Hans-Georg Gadamer, a pupil of Heidegger. In 1960 he published *Warheit und Methode* (translated in 1975 as *Truth and Method*) in which he restated the traditional principles of hermeneutics, not as an art or technique of textual interpretation, nor even as an account of the methodological basis of the human sciences, but as a philosophical account of the conditions that underlie human understanding as such. For him, hermeneutics 'denotes the basic being-in-motion of [man's being] which constitutes its finiteness and historicity, and hence includes the whole of its experience of the world' (1975: xviii; see also p. 433). Interpretation is not, according to Gadamer, 'an occasional additional act subsequent to understanding', but is precisely the specific form of understanding itself (p. 274).[6]

The main features of Gadamer's philosophy which concern us here can be summed up in the following points. (1) All thinking is historically embedded, and human reason 'exists for us only in concrete, historical terms, i.e. it is not its own master, but remains constantly dependent on given circumstances in which it operates' (1975: 245). (2) Hence all human thinking presupposes a tradition in which the thinker participates, and on which the very sense of his thinking is contingent. (3) From this it follows that we can never cast off prejudices in the way that Enlightenment thinkers advocated, for our thinking always carries with it pre-judgements as necessary conditions for making judgements at all. This does not mean that we are trapped blindly in our prejudices, for an essential part of historical understanding involves a critical reflection of our own historical situation and on the 'fore-structures' of our thinking, as well as on that of the 'text' being investigated. (4) In our attempts to understand the past we cannot leap out of history, out of the prejudices that our historical condition imposes on us, and grasp an idea *sub specie aeternitatis*. Historical understanding involves what Gadamer has called a 'fusion' or 'overlapping' of horizons, an horizon being 'the range of vision that includes everything that can be seen from a particular vantage point' (p. 171). (5) Finally there is the central idea of the 'hermeneutical circle' which in many ways sums up this whole approach. This means that all historical understanding involves 'the movement . . . constantly from the whole to the part and back to the whole', an 'interplay of the movement of tradition and the movement of the interpreter' (pp. 259 and 261), a continuing dialectical exchange in which we pursue the sense of a text by reiterative interplay of meaning between part and whole, between text and context, between interpreter and interpreted.

From these pointers we can reconstruct in general terms the way in which Gadamer evisages the process of making sense of an historical text. Such a text will present itself to us initially as strange and remote, rather in the way that a person newly introduced to us may seem alien and forbidding. 'Everything that is set down in writing is to some extent foreign and strange' (p. 487), so there is a 'barrier of alienness, that our understanding has to overcome' (p. 306). Meaning is not easily recoverable, and historical texts, even whole traditions, can sometimes appear to have lost their sense irretrievably. This alienness is not, it must be emphasised, a feature confined to historical texts, but is according to Gadamer an essential feature of human understanding as such, for all knowing involves a gap between what is familiar and what is unfamiliar. Temporal distance, furthermore, is no intrinsic barrier, no 'yawning abyss', but rather 'a positive and productive possibility' (p. 264), for it forces us to recognise differences and to forgo the easy assumption that we are in tune with the spirit of a past age. The activity of understanding demands the attempt to overcome this strangeness, to bridge the gulf, and hence the interpreter of a text 'like the interpreter of a divine or human utterance, has the task of overcoming and removing the strangeness and making its assimilation possible' (p. 487).

How is this possible? How can we overcome, even to a limited extent, the strangeness of a text, a tradition, a human being? We have seen that for Gadamer there can be no direct line to the meaning of the text, no unmediated insight or intuition which, by an examination of the text in isolation, will reveal its secrets to us – 'that false romanticism of immediacy' as he calls it (1975: 361). 'Meaning' is not some kind of entity hidden within the text, waiting to be uncovered, but rather arises from the encounter between reader and text. The model that Gadamer employs is essentially that of human communication: 'Our starting point is the proposition that to understand means primarily for two people to understand one another. Understanding is primarily agreement or harmony with another person' (p. 158). Clearly we are here moving closer once more to our idea of dialogue. But as with human dialogue we need first to understand where the other person is located – 'where they are at', to use an apposite colloquialism. Hence, as far as our text is concerned, we must endeavour to see it in its historical context, and to locate it within its own historical tradition, for 'the text is part of the whole of the tradition in which the age . . . seeks to understand itself' (p. 263). This means, amongst other things, that we must allow the text to address us, that we must open ourselves up to what it has to say to us. But, conversely, this also implies that we must recognise the historical identity of our own position and perspective, for 'True historical thinking must take into account its own historicality' (p. 267). There must therefore be in any historical inquiry a measure of self-criticism whereby we maintain a more or less constant awareness of prejudices and assumptions that we bring along with us. Furthermore, it is the very difference, and distance, that separates us from our text that helps to provide this self-criticism, for it is only when confronted with the other that we can honestly mirror our critical attention back on ourselves; the encounter with a text from the past can provide us with the stimulus whereby it becomes possible to identify the burden of historical prejudice and assumption that we carry (see p. 266).

It is true, of course, that we cannot literally have a conversation with a text: 'a text does not speak to us in the same way as does another person'. It is we who make it speak, says Gadamer, not in some arbitrary way, but by posing questions to which the text provides answers, and by opening ourselves up to whatever it is that the text presents to us. Thus, '[just] as one person seeks to reach agreement with his partner concerning an object, so the interpreter understands the object of which the text speaks' (pp. 340–1). Unlike the physical *processes* which are the object of the natural sciences, the object of hermeneutical inquiry is *meaning*, and hence the reading of a text can be seen as involving a relationship analogous to that of two persons in dialogue. We shall need to examine later the question of whether this honorific sense of dialogue is adequate to sustain the weight that Jung and others engaged in the so-called dialogue with the East place upon it.

Furthermore, such a dialogue, Gadamer surmises, involves a transformation of its participants: 'we do not remain what we were' (p. 341). Unlike in a debate, where the aim is to defeat one's opponent, and hence to remain as one was, dialogue implies the willingness to move forward and to allow one's initial position to develop in unforeseen ways. For Gadamer this is not just an epistemic change, a reassembling of our stock of knowledge, but a metamorphosis in our very being through the opening up of new horizons and possibilities. According to Richard Rorty this implies that for Gadamer the traditional aim of Western philosophy – the quest for epistemic certainty – is replaced by the wider goal of self-transformation (Rorty, 1979: 357).

Just as with a participant in an everyday dialogue, historical inquirers must necessarily operate from within their own unique point of view. The historian is not a pure spirit, but enters the inquiry from a specific and historically shaped perspective, with a set of assumptions and prejudices lying beneath, and a set of questions lying on, the surface of consciousness. Human understanding in general, Gadamer held, always carries with it what, following Heidegger, he called a 'fore-structure', a set of pre-shaping expectations and assumptions, and historical understanding in particular 'always involves something like the application of the text to be understood to the present situation of the interpreter' (1975: 274). 'Application', a key term for Gadamer, is not necessarily a conscious or deliberate activity, but rather an essential factor in the process of understanding, and hence 'all reading involves application, so that a person reading a text is himself part of the meaning he apprehends' (p. 304). From this it follows that 'It is senseless to speak of a perfect knowledge of history', for its activity is always 'motivated in a special way by the present and its interests' (p. 253). To think historically (p. 358)

> always involves establishing a connection between those ideas and one's own thinking. To try to eliminate one's own concepts in interpretation is not only impossible, but manifestly absurd. To interpret means precisely to use one's own preconceptions so that the meaning of the text can really be made to speak to us.

An important consequence of this view is that there can be no single correct interpretation of a text. The quest for an interpretation that is correct in itself would be 'a foolish ideal that failed to take account of the nature of tradition [for] the historical life of a tradition depends on constantly new assimilation and interpretation' (p. 358). There can be no Archimedean point outside of all historical traditions, outside of all languages, from which to get an absolutely secure purchase on the meaning of a text. This could be described as a form of relativism – namely, the view that all claims to truth can only be judged in the light of rules and principles which are integral to specific historical conditions and which therefore have no absolute or culture-free validity. The hermeneutical circle can, therefore, never be closed; indeed it has been suggested that it is really more like a spiral which turns on itself endlessly.[7]

The relativity of languages might seem to present an especial difficulty when it comes to communication between different traditions. According to Gadamer all understanding is grounded in *tradition*, and the fusion of horizons which is at the core of historical understanding can only arise through the mediation of a shared tradition. 'Understanding', he writes, 'is not to be thought of so much as an action of one's subjectivity, but as the placing of oneself within a process of tradition' (p. 258). It might seem to follow from this that any attempt to fuse one's conceptual horizons with one from a tradition as different as the East is from the West must inevitably be frustrated. However, it is important to realise that Western interpreters of the East are not *in principle* in any different position from those who are indigenous to Oriental traditions and who interpret them from within. The gap is greater, the horizons to be fused more remote from each other, technical difficulties of translation more acute, but in the end confronting the otherness of the East is in principle no different from confronting the otherness of one's next-door neighbour. Moreover, Gadamer's notion of a 'tradition', and his sense of 'belonging' to a tradition, are questionable, a point made by Jurgen Habermas in his debate with Gadamer where the latter is accused of adopting an uncritical notion of tradition, one which fosters dogmatism and authoritarianism (see Bleicher, 1982: 245–72). As I suggested earlier, even a cursory examination of history, as well as of our own present condition, reveals a picture infinitely more complex than that of a series of distinct cultural entities which can be individuated as distinct traditions. We are presented rather with a picture of more or less continuous interaction between, and acute divisions within, so-called traditions, which overlap, interact, and fragment in ways that elude our overly simple conceptual schemes. Furthermore, cultural traditions are capable of generating self-criticism, a fact which I have emphasised in the case of the modern West which, since the time of Descartes, has been engaged in more or less continuous bouts of self-reassessment. This point is acknowledged by Gadamer when he writes that 'However much it is in the nature of tradition to exist only through being appropriated, it still is part of the nature of man to be able to break with tradition, to criticise and dissolve it' (1975: xxv).

As far as the interaction between the traditions of East and West are concerned, we saw in the last chapter the extent to which, contrary to received orthodoxy, a 'fusion of horizons' has been taking place for a long time between East and West. And with regard to the inner coherence of these two traditions, it hardly needs to be pointed out that there are as many cultural divisions within them as there are differences between them. In short, the phenomenon of human communication, and hence of the hermeneutical endeavour to understand and interpret across boundaries, cannot be confined within artificially prescribed cultural enclaves or traditions. Halbfass, in his discussion of the use of Gadamerian hermeneutics in the context of the East–West dialogue, admirably sums up this point when he comments that there is

> no compelling reason why [Gadamer's] hermeneutical concepts and perspectives should not be applicable in a wider, trans-cultural context. Indeed we belong to the European tradition which has its origins in Greece. But this tradition has its own modes of openness and self-transcendence. Within the European tradition itself there has been a 'fusion' of different cultural horizons – Greek, Roman, Hebrew, etc. That we relate to other

traditions does not imply that we are estranged from 'our own' tradition. The phenomena of understanding and misunderstanding, which occur within a particular tradition, need not be fundamentally different from those which we encounter when we try to approach other traditions.

(1988: 165)

This, then, is our model of dialogue, and we must now make use of it to help illuminate Jung's own dialogue with the East.

JUNG AS HERMENEUT

Jung was in many ways a natural hermeneut. Whether dealing with patients, with Western philosophies, with mediaeval alchemy, or with the traditions and texts of the East, his method was one of dialogue in which he sought to construct a bridge of understanding, while yet retaining the principle of otherness. His method of understanding in all these, and other, spheres was characterised by holism, contextualism, open-endedness, tolerance, self-reflectiveness, and historical relativism – all features typical of the hermeneutical approach. However strange and alien the behaviour of a patient or the belief system of a remote culture might appear, it was never for him irremediably closed off, but presented the possibility for a form of understanding that is essentially that of one human being for another.

This approach is evident early in Jung's career. On the evidence arising in the course of his treatment of schizophrenics while an intern at the Burgholzli Hospital from 1900 to 1909, he argued, contrary to prevailing opinion, that it was possible to make sense of the strange behaviour and utterances of schizophrenic patients in their own terms (see MDR: Ch. 4, and CW3, *passim*). By dint of carefully listening and relating to these patients he came to the conclusion that symptoms, which had hitherto been regarded as senseless and crazy, perhaps explicable only in terms of physiological causes, could be 'read' and 'interpreted' in meaningful ways. This essentially hermeneutical approach became a model for him in his later dealings, not only with patients, but with a whole range of psychological, cultural, and intellectual phenomena.

Therapy became for him, therefore, not an adaptation of the methods of the natural sciences, but purely and simply an extension of human dialogue, a personal relationship in which 'I confront the patient as one human being to another', and in which analysis is 'a dialogue demanding two partners' (MDR: 153). The essence of the mental distress which he observed in his consulting room appeared to him to be, not that of functional disorder by analogy with physical disease, but rather the loss of a sense of meaning and purpose. He saw the analyst's work as more like that of a philologist seeking to interpret a difficult text than a natural scientist making observations and postulating general theories. He was a good hermeneut, as Robert Steele notes, 'because he clearly conceptualized what was involved in the activity of interpretation. He recognized that

47

the interpreter and the interpreted – the unconscious, a patient, or a text – must enter into a genuine dialogue' (Steele, 1982: 352). Furthermore, in such a dialogue the therapist cannot conceive of himself or herself as an objective observer since the analyst is just as involved in the process as the patient. 'Never forget', he warned, 'that the analysis of a patient analyses yourself, as you are just as much in it as he is' (CW18.1072).[8]

He extended this model in two opposite though complementary directions. The first was towards the inner microcosm of the psyche where he came to see the dynamic relationship between conscious and unconscious processes as having the characteristics of a human dialogue, a process he called the 'transcendent function':

> It is exactly as if a dialogue were taking place between two human beings with equal rights, each of whom gives the other credit for a valid argument and considers it worthwhile to modify the conflicting standpoints by means of thorough comparison and discussion or else to distinguish them clearly from one another. Since the way to agreement seldom stands open, in most cases a long conflict will have to be borne, demanding sacrifices from both sides.
>
> (CW8.186)

Self-knowledge means engaging in the often painful process of relating to and coming to terms with aspects of oneself which are partially hidden. The unconscious is not an absolute unknown, and in analysis, which could be seen as the formalisation of the path of self-knowledge, 'a dialectical discussion [takes place] between the conscious mind and the unconscious' (CW12.3).

The second direction in which he extended this model was to the macrocosmic world of symbolic products and belief systems, a world which for him included Gnosticism, mediaeval alchemy, Christian theology, aspects of the occult, and the philosophical texts the East. In the process of formulating his theory of the archetypes and the collective unconscious he sought to relate his own insights to a whole range of philosophical, historical and mythological precedents, and to show thereby that mankind in all its strange and diverse manifestations was capable of being comprehended within a single discourse. Unlike Freud who displayed what Philip Rieff has described as a 'bias against the past', Jung showed great sensitivity towards the influences that helped to shape his own intellectual development, and was constantly engaged in a to-and-fro dialogue with a whole range of thinkers from Lao-tzu and Plato to Kant and Nietzsche.

His interest in the world of symbolic expression was also, in a way, therapeutic. The urgent spiritual needs of our time, he surmised, could only be met if we were prepared to transform and revivify our modern consciousness through dialogue with the myths and traditions of past ages. Christianity itself, he pointed out, had demonstrated its vitality in its early days by its capacity to assimilate earlier myths, and the importance of hermeneutics (he actually uses the term in this context) lay in the 'beneficial effect on the psyche by consciously linking the distant past . . . with the present'. He went on to say that a religion that can no longer assimilate myths, and translate them into its own language, 'is forgetting its proper function' which is to act as 'a bridge to the ever-living past' which it makes 'alive and present for us' (CW14.474n).

In both of these directions – the micro and the macro – a noticeable feature is Jung's readiness to engage with and to confront the 'uncanny', the 'strange', the '*other*', or what he called the '*shadow*'. Many examples could be cited from various aspects of his life and his work, for example: his decision to pursue a career in the then unfashionable specialism of psychiatry; his study of occult phenomena for his doctoral dissertation; his fascination for the strange symptoms of schizophrenics; his espousal of the Freudian cause; his interest in the new physics; and, of course, his abiding fascination with the esoteric traditions of both East and West. At a more personal level there are the poignant examples, documented in his autobiographical essay, *Memories, Dreams, Reflections*, of his confrontation with the strange and frequently disturbing manifestations of his own unconscious, especially during the years following the rupture of his relationship with Freud. There is clearly a pattern here. It was not that of rebelliousness against the status quo, for he was by and large very respectable, conventional, and conservative in his outlook and behaviour. It was more to do with a need to find accommodation with and to integrate the strange and often hidden, unconscious depths of the human psyche, whether in his own case, or in that of a patient, or as manifested in the broader fields of human culture. He appears to have recognised from a very early age that to know oneself means to grapple with a stranger in one's innermost midst. So it was, too, on the wider plane of history and culture, the domain of the collective unconscious and the shared archetypes of mankind; here too we can only make sense of what we as human beings are if we are prepared to enter the labyrinth of the unknown.[9]

On entering the labyrinth of Oriental thought his first reaction was, as we have seen, one of alienation. When confronted with an ancient Chinese text such as the *I Ching* his initial reaction was to be aware of its strangeness and to feel a certain sympathy for those Western scholars who found in it little more than a collection of magic spells 'too abstruse to be intelligible' (CW11.965). Eastern cultures display an attitude of mind and a vision which, it seems, is 'quite foreign to the European' (CW11.908), and we would do well to confess that 'fundamentally, we do not understand the utter unworldliness' of a text such as *The Secret of the Golden Flower* (CW13.6).

At the very minimum this is a matter of linguistic difference. Although he knew no Oriental languages, Jung was well attuned through his wide knowledge of European tongues to the vagueries of translation, especially of crucial philosophical terms. He noted that 'Oriental religious conceptions are usually so very different from our Western ones that even the bare translation of the words often presents the greatest difficulties'. Original Buddhist and Taoist writings contain views and ideas 'which are more or less unassimilable for ordinary Europeans', and hence it is often best to leave certain crucial terms untranslated (CW11.877).

But it goes deeper than this, for in studying Eastern thought and culture he became acutely aware not just of linguistic differences, but that the ways of thinking of Eastern peoples may depart radically from those of Europe. His whole hermeneutical approach was premised on the belief that, in order to understand the other, one must start by recognising the chasm which needs to be crossed. Dialogue with the strange other – schizoid patient or Taoist text – was never for him a cosy chat with a familiar acquaintance, but a struggle to come to terms with the rifts that criss-cross and break up the terrain of the psychic life of mankind.

This helps us to understand Jung's consistent refusal to succumb to the allures of the East and to adopt its beliefs and practices, a temptation not always resisted by some of his more recent admirers. He made it abundantly clear that he was not interested in the revival of past belief systems, and was very critical of the Theosophists and Anthroposophists who, in his opinion, were simply putting on 'outworn clothes' rather than using old ideas in order to develop new ideas of their own. In a true dialogue the individuality of the participants is retained, even though in the end they are transformed by the interaction. So, too, in engaging with the myths and symbols of the past we need to be aware that we are speaking from our inescapably present historical situation to a past which is also inescapably situated in its own historical context. What is required in this sort of dialogue is not blind reverence or emulation, but an empathy with what is other and different, a willingness to communicate with what is strange and alien in order to enhance our present understanding. Through a process of question and answer, of give and take, we come to see the other point of view, thereby enhancing our own. In such a hermeneutical exchange we are not merely preserving or reconstituting the past, therefore, but saving the present from ossification and providing for the possibility of renewal. Historical comparison 'is not a mere learned hobby but very practical and useful [for it] opens the door to life and humanity again, which had seemed inexorably closed' (CW18.1269).[10]

Jung made a number of references to hermeneutics as the art of textual interpretation, and in 1916 he appropriated the term to characterise his method of unlocking the symbolic meaning of patients' fantasies. Such a method involved the elucidation, by making use of appropriate analogies, of 'something that is still entirely unknown or still in the process of formation' (CW7.492). He elaborated this in the following passage:

> The essence of hermeneutics, an art widely practised in former times, consists in adding further analogies to the one already supplied by the symbol: in the first place subjective analogies produced at random by the patient, then objective analogies provided by the analyst out of his general knowledge. This procedure widens and enriches the initial symbol, and the final outome is an infinitely complex and variegated picture the elements of which can be reduced to their respective *tertia comparationis*. Certain lines of psychological development then stand out that are at once individual and collective. There is no science on earth by which these lines could be proved 'right'.

> (CW7.493)

It is evident from this passage that he envisaged the practice of hermeneutics as leading beyond the psyche of the individual patient, and embracing collective or cultural meanings, that, in his own words, 'By means of the hermeneutic treatment of fantasies we arrive, in theory, at a synthesis of the individual with the *collective* psyche' (CW7.479; emphasis added). This is in effect the 'hermeneutical circle' that we discussed earlier, namely the process whereby, through a spiralling series of comparisons between the narrow and the wider context, an individual text or symbol is progressively illuminated. It also represents the core of the methodology through which he sought to establish the universal characteristics of the collective unconscious.

In later years he used the word 'hermeneutics' sparingly, and the term he coined which best expresses this feature of his method was *amplification*. I am not aware that he used it explicitly in relation to Oriental texts, but a moment's reflection will show its relevance. It is essentially a therapeutic method which seeks to clarify – to make ample – mental contents by linking them within an ever-widening network of meanings, expressed in symbols and images, through using all kinds of metaphors and analogies derived from mythological and cultural parallels. The techique rests on the belief that 'images [are] embedded in a comprehensive system of thought that ascribes an order to the world' (CW9i.11), so allowing patients to widen their purely personal attitude by placing it in the context of universal, archetypal, meanings. Thus, Jung spoke of the need in analysis to recognise that 'Even the most individual systems are not absolutely unique, but offer striking and unmistakable analogies with other systems' (CW3.413). The employment of this method, furthermore, again helps to differentiate Jung's method from that of the physical sciences, for, whereas in the case of the latter what is sought is law-like regularities of observed phenomena, Jung's method was concerned with relationships of meaning, with the comparison of symbols and images.

His whole approach to the East could be characterised as one of amplification. Just as his main task in analysis was the clarification of his patients' problems, so, similarly, in his wider cultural explorations, was his central concern with his own indigenous culture and its discontents. And just as patients need to see their symptoms in relation to the archetypes that are the collective possession of human beings as such, so also must an individual culture understand itself within the framework of the global culture. The method, as in the case of an individual patient, is one which attempts to make comparisons and to draw analogies across cultural boundaries, thereby seeking to enrich the fabric of meaningful discourse both of oneself and of the other. On this view, a global understanding is a necessary condition for *self*-understanding, for just as it is the mark of a mature person to be open to, and able to integrate, new and strange exeriences, so too is a mature community one that is able to assimilate a variety of perspectives.

The question of self-understanding points to a further comparison with Gadamer for, like the latter, Jung's primary concern was not that of pure disinterested scholarship, but rather one of *education* whereby the narrow intolerance of individual nations is tempered by a sincere and reflexive attempt to understand the other. For Gadamer the key term here is *Bildung*, a German word which refers to the process of human self-cultivation whereby individuals and groups expand their cultural horizons and extend the range of their sympathies. In his own words: 'It consists in learning to allow what is different from oneself and to find universal viewpoints', and its basic idea is 'To seek one's own in the alien, to become at home in it . . . [and] whose being is only to return to itself from what is other' (1975: 14–15). Without this hermeneutical amplification we are easy victims to narrow-mindedness, and from thence to self-righteousness, resentment of the unfamiliar, and blinkered dogmatism. In making use of this method Jung was clearly linked, as well, to that tradition, outlined in the last chapter, whose encounter with the East has aimed at the relativising of its own world-view through critical self-understanding. While recognising the element of truth in Said's critique, and noting the fantasy elements which have often characterised East–West studies, and are present too in Jung's own approach, it is at the same time important to acknowledge that the East–West dialogue, in seeking to place the West's world-view in a more ample perspective, is a prime example of mankind's efforts at self-education.

This particular dialogue is an educational task that is of benefit not only to the West. For the most part, Jung's ideas have been well received by many in the East precisely because they have been seen as a means, not just towards the West's self-understanding, but also towards that of the East. The Japanese philosopher Mokusen Miyuki, for example, has argued that Buddhist concepts can benefit greatly from being looked at from within the context of modern psychology (see Katz, 1983: 97), and another Japanese professor has commented that 'It is clear to me that Jung can contribute to our spiritual tradition and religion a reality basis that we have partly lost' (quoted in von Franz, 1975: 116). In this sense Jung has been a factor, along with other Europeans engaged in the East–West dialogue, in contributing towards the self-awareness and self-understanding of Eastern peoples themselves. On a wider stage it is worth recalling that the West's intrusions into the East, whether in the shape of Christian missions or of the Theosophical Society, have played an important role in the revival of self-awareness on the part of Eastern religious traditions.

The method of amplification, then, became for Jung a hermeneutical key with which to unlock the ideas of the East, as indeed also those of the Gnostics and the alchemists. It implies a developing awareness of the place from which one begins one's task of understanding, a sensitivity to one's own needs and projects, a capacity to become critically aware of one's own prejudices and assumptions, and an openness to the possibility of transcending one's present limitations. Further, as with the analytical 'talking cure', it involves the give-and-take, the to-and-fro, of a conversation in which awareness of one's own standpoint is balanced by awareness of the other's.

It must be emphasised that this whole approach is concerned with the *possibility* of understanding between cultures, and by no means guarantees success or relative ease of exchange. The adoption of the hermeneutical approach contains no promise of final or complete understanding of another culture and its symbolic products. Getting to know another culture or the texts from a distant tradition, like getting to know another human person, takes time, and the process of overcoming difference is for Jung, as for Gadamer, a task that encounters serious difficulties and requires considerable resources of patience and courage. Dialogue, whether with one's own unconscious, with a schizophrenic patient, or with the *I Ching*, is, as we noted above, no fireside chat, no comfortable meeting of mutually compatible minds, but an encounter from which there is not necessarily a fully satisfying outcome. There is about the whole hermeneutical approach an acceptance on the one hand of the radical finitude of the human mind and the human condition, historically grounded and limited, and on the other of the infinite possibilities that language, dialogue and interpretation open up for us. As Gadamer has expressed it, there is within human speaking 'an infinity of meaning to be elaborated and interpreted' (1975: 416).

This means that there is no possibility of a final definitive interpretation of a text. Where the natural sciences have in past times been seen as offering a steady and inexorable path towards a true and perhaps even a complete understanding of the world, and where modern philosophy since Descartes has pursued the goal of epistemic certainty, hermeneutics is self-consciously anchored in the relative and partial perspectives of historically located human beings. Accordingly, Gadamer emphasises that there cannot be

> any one interpretation that is correct 'in itself', precisely because every interpretation is concerned with the text itself. The historical life of a tradition depends on constantly new assimilation and interpretation. An interpretation that was correct 'in itself' would be a foolish ideal that failed to take account of the nature of tradition. Every interpretation has to adapt itself to the hermeneutical situation to which it belongs.
>
> Gadamer, 1975: 358)

Whether or not this leads to out and out relativism is a matter of dispute; if there is no correct interpretation 'in itself', then it might seem to imply that any one interpretation is as good as any other.[11] Jung himself sometimes appeared to lean towards a relativistic viewpoint with such remarks as 'I hold the truth of my own views to be equally relative [to those of Freud and Adler], and regard myself also as the exponent of a certain predisposition. . . . We should be modest and grant validity to a number of apparently contradictory opinions' (MM: 65). This attitude is especially apparent in his discussion of Eastern thought and culture in relation to the West. In marked contrast with the attitude of many Western thinkers from Hegel onwards, he declined to give the one any privileged or superior status over the other but sought to emphasise the purely relative validity of cultural values and beliefs. Alongside his belief that 'To the Oriental . . . the world must appear very different from what it does to the Occidental' (CW6.494), we find in Jung's writings the persistent claim that Western civilisation in general, and Western scientific rationalism in particular, can make no claim to inherent superiority. His physical and intellectual travels to the East enabled him to put European culture, with all its evident achievements, into a wider perspective, and to conclude that 'Western consciousness is by no means the only kind of consciousness there is; it is historically conditioned and geographically limited' (CW13.84). Furthermore, he rejected what he described as 'that megalomania of ours which leads us to suppose . . . that Christianity is the only truth, and the white Christ the only Redeemer' (MM: 246). Whatever the philosophical problems that lie beneath this attitude, it is clearly an attitude that has close parallels with the hermeneutical approach of Gadamer and his intellectual predecessors, and one which fitted him well for the task of constructing a dialogical bridge to the strange texts and ideas of the East. We turn to the details of this task in Part II.

Part II

DIALOGUE

4

JUNG'S DIALOGUE WITH THE EAST

Jung's interest in the East and his enthusiasm for the philosophical traditions of China and India were life-long. It is true that he lamented the wholesale plundering of the treasures of the East to sate Western appetites for spiritual sustenance, and warned repeatedly against the unthinking adoption of Eastern ways. But at the same time he believed that the West had much to learn from the study of Eastern thought, and that the Orient offered a way of subjecting the presuppositions and prejudices of the West to productive criticism. Though steeped in Western culture and not without admiration for its achievements, including those of science and technology, he was critical of its one-sidedness and of its tendency to self-inflation and self-aggrandisement. As we noted at the end of the previous chapter, he did not regard Western consciousness as the highest or most developed form of human consciousness. He pointed out that geographically Europe is just a peninsular of Asia, and that Christianity is of Asian origins. Many of our modern achievements, he noted, have been anticipated in the East by many centuries: for example, philosophical relativism and the recent concept of indeterminism in physics are both, he claimed, to be found in centuries-old Buddhist teachings, and psychoanalysis itself is 'only a beginner's attempt compared to what is an immemorial art in the East' (MM: 249–50; see also CW10.188). Moreover, the very health and even survival of our culture may depend on our ability to learn from the East, for Western civilisation is, he believed, in a state of crisis, it 'sickens with a thousand ills' and, without abandoning its own roots and its own traditions, can learn much from the East which 'teaches us another, broader, more profound, and higher understanding' (CW13.2). In this chapter we shall elaborate these themes in general terms, leaving to the following chapters the task of examining them in closer detail.

THE HISTORY OF JUNG'S INTEREST IN THE EAST

It has has often been suggested that Jung's interest in the East began with his reading of Richard Wilhelm's translation of *The Secret of the Golden Flower* in

1928 and ended ten years later with his trip to India and Ceylon, but in fact his interest began in childhood and extended right to the end of his life. Even before he could read, Jung pestered his mother to read to him from a book containing stories of Brahmā, Vishnu, and Shiva which he found 'an inexhaustible source of interest' (MDR: 32). And he was still grappling with Buddhist ideas shortly before his death.

During his early formative years a man of such wide-ranging intellectual sympathies as Jung could hardly fail to have been affected by the great surge of interest in Oriental ideas which swept over Europe in the final decades of the nineteenth century. Not only were there great advances in scholarship which bore fruit in such enterprises as Rhys Davids' Pali Text Society and Max Müller's *Sacred Books of the East* series, as well as in the writings of indologists such as Oldenberg and Deussen, but Eastern thought in general, and Buddhism most especially, had begun to enter deeply into the consciousness of educated Europeans and Americans. Jung was clearly familiar with Edwin Arnold's popular Buddhist poem, *The Light of Asia* (first published in 1879), and though he was critical of the Theosophical Society, he was certainly aware of its great influence and its significance for European culture at the turn of the century. This was a time which has often been seen as one of spiritual revival, a period of spiritual renaissance reacting against scientific rationalism, positivism, and materialism, a revival which manifested itself in a growing interest in the world of the spirit, in the occult, and in Eastern mysticism. H. Stuart-Hughes in his study of European consciousness at the turn of the century has written of the reaction against the 'self-satisfied cult of material progress found at that time', and the powerful surge in favour of the irrational, the non-logical, the uncivilised, and the inexplicable both at the academic and at the popular level (1979: 35; see also Hardy, 1987: Ch. 15). It is in this context that we must try to understand Jung's developing interest and involvement in the East. Though, as I shall argue, his work in this field has many unique and original features, it was not something idiosyncratic and bizarre, as some critics have tried to suggest, but rather was part of an identifiable phase in European culture. Though he undoubtedly played a seminal role in the propagation of Oriental enthusiasms in the twentieth century, his work must also be seen in the context of a much wider historical development, one that has not always been fully recognised and documented.

Brief references to Oriental ideas appear in the so-called *Zofingia* lectures of his student days, and here we can discern clear anticipations of many of the themes of his mature thought. But by the time he came to write his two early major works, *Symbols of Transformation* (CW5; 1912) and *Psychological Types* (CW6; 1921), he had acquired an extensive knowledge of Vedic, Buddhist, and Taoist ideas and mythology which he treated on a par, and closely interwove, with symbolic material from Western sources. The bibliography to *Symbols of Transformation* indicates extensive reading in primary as well as secondary texts: he showed familiarity with the *I Ching*, the *Rig Veda*, the *Rāmāyana, and the Bhagavad Gitā*, as well as with the writings of leading indologists such as F. Max

Müller, H. Oldenberg, and Paul Deussen. Here the hermeneutical approach, with its engagement with a variety of cultural forms in dialogue, is deployed to great effect, and we see for the first time Jung's willingness to draw systematic parallels between Eastern and Western symbols. *Psychological Types* includes a lengthy discussion of Brahmanic and Taoist notions of opposites, and makes much use of Eastern mythical and philosophical concepts in elaborating his newly emerging concept of the psyche. It is in this work that Jung came to recognise the importance of psychic processes, especially those involving the interplay of opposites, in shaping religious attitudes and world-views, and where he first elaborated his notion of the relativity of the God-concept to the human psyche, a crucial insight which owed much to Eastern philosophy.

One of the most important influences in the shaping of Jung's interest in Eastern philosophy was undoubtedly the great nineteenth-century German philosopher Schopenhauer. His *World as Will and Idea*, which Jung discovered while still at school, had a great influence on the development of his thinking in general, but the close affinity which Schopenhauer drew between his own philosophy and that of both the Vedānta and Buddhist philosophies must have made a powerful impact on him, for it gave, as Jung expressed it, 'reality to [the] dawning rays of Oriental wisdom' (CW6.223). As we saw in Chapter 2, Schopenhauer's influence on the emerging climate of Orientalism in the nineteenth century was crucial, and though he may have been responsible for conveying a distorted image of some aspects of Eastern philosophy, giving to Buddhism a pessimistic image which mirrored that of his own philosophy, he undoubtedly helped to facilitate the East–West dialogue. In view of his frequently acknowledged debt to Schopenhauer it is hardly surprising, therefore, that Jung too sought to associate his own thinking with that of the philosophies of the East.[1]

During the 1920s Jung's interest in Oriental ideas received a further stimulus from the acquaintance with two men, Herman Keyserling and Richard Wilhelm. Keyserling was a widely travelled amateur social philosopher whose book, *The Travel Diary of a Philosopher*, first published in 1919, attempted to grasp the 'soul' of the East, and sought to propagate an internationalist outlook in an epoch increasingly dominated by narrow nationalisms. He was deeply concerned with the theme of spiritual regeneration, and in a pamphlet written in 1912 entitled *The East and the West and their Search for the Common Truth* he spoke of the 'extraordinary interest in all things Eastern – Eastern thought, art, religion and culture in general' that had blossomed in the West in recent decades, and urged the need for some kind of synthesis between Eastern and Western thought. He believed that the West had lost its spiritual bearings and needed to tap the wisdom of the East. In pursuit of this goal he founded the School of Wisdom at Darmstadt, whose aim was to foster mutual respect and understanding by setting up a dialogue between East and West. Jung's friendship with Keyserling lasted from the early 1920s up to the time of the latter's death in 1946, and though their relationship was often inharmonious, they undoubtedly gave each other inspiration and support in their respective enterprises.[2]

It was while attending a meeting at Darmstadt in 1923 that Jung first met Richard Wilhelm, a Christian missionary and sinologist, who was to have a great impact on his intellectual development. They met, as Jung put it, 'in a field of humanity which begins beyond the academic boundary posts', where a 'spark leapt across and kindled a light that was to become for me one of the most significant events of my life' (CW15.74). He wrote, in his memorial tribute to his friend, that Wilhelm's life-work was 'of immense importance to me because it clarified and confirmed so much that I had been seeking, striving for, thinking', and he felt himself 'so very much enriched by him that it seems to me as if I had received more from him than from any other man' (CW15.96). This remark is especially interesting, not only in view of the fact that Freud is usually perceived as the chief influence on Jung, but also because of the general perception that the East was little more than just a marginal interest and influence in the development of Jung's thought.

What struck Jung most of all was the fact that Wilhelm, although a missionary who had worked in China for the conversion of non-believers to the Christian faith, had been able to develop a refined appreciation for Chinese thought, seemingly so alien to the European mind, and had even gone so far as to express great satisfaction that he had never actually baptised a single Chinese! It would seem that Wilhelm, like Jung, was a natural hermeneut. He had, Jung noted, 'the gift of being able to listen without bias to the revelations of a foreign mentality, and to accomplish that miracle of empathy which enabled him to make the intellectual treasures of China accessible to Europe' (MDR: 407). He approached the East 'freely, without prejudice, without the assumption of knowing better; he opened his heart and mind to it [and] let himself be gripped and shaped by it' (CW15.93). By attempting to sacrifice his European prejudices he had been able 'to open himself without reserve to a profoundly alien spirit', and to 'feel his way into the spirit of the East' (CW15.75-6), a sacrifice which took its toll on his health.[3] He had 'created a bridge between East and West and gave to the Occident the precious heritage of a culture thousands of years old, a culture perhaps destined to disappear for ever' (CW15.74). Especially impressive, Jung thought, was his translation of the *I Ching* which 'succeeded in bringing to life again, in new form, this ancient work in which not only many sinologists but most modern Chinese see nothing more than a collection of absurd magical spells' (CW15.77).

Wilhelm's importance for Jung goes beyond this, however, for his meeting with the sinologist not only stimulated further his interest in the Orient (he had actually been experimenting with the *I Ching* in Legge's translation for several years before they met), but pointed the way out of the intellectual isolation in which he had found himself after his break with Freud in 1912. Wilhelm's translation of the Taoist text, *The Secret of the Golden Flower*, provided Jung with two important kinds of support. In the first place it encouraged him to have confidence in the validity of his own therapeutic technique, for he discovered that he 'had been unconsciously following that secret way which for centuries had been the preoccupation of the best minds of the East' (CW13.10). Even more significantly, in the second place, he believed that it offered crucial evidence in support of his investigations into the archetypes of the collective unconscious, helping to confirm him in his view that 'the human psyche possesses a common substratum transcending all differences in culture and consciousness' (CW13.11). In addition to this, Wilhelm's translation and interpretation of the *I Ching* was to have an important influence on the formulation much later of Jung's concept of 'synchronicity' and on his attempts to build a bridge between ancient wisdom and modern science. We shall look at these points in more detail in the next chapter.

Any account of the history of Jung's relationship with the East would be incomplete without reference to the *Eranos* seminars which were held annually from 1933 at a villa overlooking Lake Maggiore. Initially the conferences had no title, but later Rudolf Otto suggested the name *Eranos*, a banquet to which participants bring their own contributions. They were international gatherings attended by a wide range of scholars including the indologist Heinrich Zimmer, the physicist Erwin Schrödinger, the anthropologist Paul Radin, the theologians Martin Buber and Paul Tillich, and the historians of comparative religion Rudolf Otto and Micea Eliade, and while the initial impetus for the gatherings lay in the task of finding common ground between Eastern and Western thought, the seminars broadened out to embrace a wide range of subjects relating to the history and psychology of religious experience. Jung, who attended most years from 1933 to 1951, was a key figure in setting the tone and the agenda of the proceedings, and it was there that he first presented ground-breaking ideas on alchemy, archetypal theory, and synchronicity. The seminars were organised by an enterprising Dutchwoman, Olga Fröbe-Kapteyn, who came from the Anglo-Indian theosophical tradition, and who described her original intention thus:

> The Eranos conferences have set themselves the goal of mediating between East and West. The task of this mediation, and the need to create a place for the promotion of such an understanding of the spiritual realm, have become ever clearer. . . . The question of a fruitful confrontation of East and West is above all a psychological one. The clear-cut questions posed by Western people in matters of religion and psychology can undoubtedly find added, meaningful fructification in the wisdom of the Orient. It is not the emulation of Eastern methods and teachings that is important, nor the neglecting or replacing of Western knowledge about these things, but the fact that Eastern wisdom, symbolism, and methods can help us to rediscover the spiritual values that are most distinctively our own.
>
> (Quoted in Wehr, 1987: 263)

I have quoted this passage at length since it sums up, not only the spirit in which these seminars were conceived, but also, as will soon be evident, Jung's own approach.[4]

The story of Jung's relationship with the East reached its high point with his visit to India in 1938. The opportunity to undertake this journey came, not from his own initiative, but by way of an invitation from the British Government in India to take part in the celebrations to mark the twenty-fifth anniversary of the founding of the University of Calcutta. He took the opportunity to make an extended visit to various parts of India and Ceylon (now Sri Lanka), and to make the acquaintance of a number of Indian scholars and gurus, giving lectures at various universities, and visiting some important historical and religious sites. The temple at Konarak (Orissa), with its 'obscene sculptures', and the stupas of Sanchi, where the Buddha delivered his 'fire sermon', each in its own way affected him deeply. He was moved, too, by the timelessness and the deep historical roots that underpinned every aspect of Indian culture, and was impressed with what he saw as their sense of wholeness and their ability to live at ease with themselves and with nature.

Nevertheless, one senses that Jung was ill-at-ease in the Indian sub-continent and that many aspects of his experience there irritated him, even though on the whole his visit, as he later put it, 'did not pass me by without a trace [but] left tracks which lead from one infinity to another infinity' (MDR: 314). A distinct feeling of ambivalence towards the East becomes noticeable, and his normal hermeneutical openness to the 'other' gives way at times to bafflement and to a tendency to retreat into his European enclave. This ambivalence was partly due no doubt to the fact that in 1938 the main focus of his interest had shifted away from the East and towards European alchemy. He described the journey as 'an intermezzo in the intensive study of alchemical philosophy on which I was engaged at the time' (MDR: 304), and spent much of his spare time in India and on the long sea voyage studying a Latin alchemical text. It is significant that prior to his return he had a powerful dream which he interpreted as calling him back 'to the too-long neglected concerns of the Occident', the dream reminding him that 'India was not my task, but only part of the way' (MDR: 313). In recalling his visit many years later he pictured himself as remaining within himself 'like a homunculus in a retort', of pursuing his own truth, in spite of the exotic and thought-provoking distractions that surrounded him. It is also significant that he avoided meeting 'so-called "holy men"', lest he should be tempted, as he put it, to 'accept from others what I could not attain on my own' (MDR: 305).

Pervading his whole Indian experience was a feeling of distance, even of alienation, with regard to the indigenous culture, a profound ambivalence to what he referred to as 'the dreamlike world of India' with its 'foreign mentality and culture'. To be sure, there was no sense in all of this of cultural or racial superiority. In his article 'What India Can Teach Us', written shortly after his return to Zürich, he compared Indian civilisation very favourably with that of Europe, seeing it as more balanced psychologically than the West and hence less prone to the outbreaks of barbarism which at that time were only too evident in the supposedly advanced civilisation of Europe (see CW10.1011–12). But at various points in the accounts he gave of his journey, such as when confronting the 'exquisitely obscene' sculptures that adorned the temple at Konarak, or when walking through a bustling bazaar in Bombay, Jung was strongly aware that his own assumptions, his very European notion of what is real and what is not, were being called into question; it was as if 'My own world of European consciousness had become peculiarly thin, like a network of telegraph wires high above the ground' (CW10.987). And elsewhere he suggested that 'It is quite possible that India is the real world, and that the white man lives in a madhouse of abstractions' (CW10.988). A similar challenge to what was central to his own world-view seems to have played a part in his failing to visit Shri Ramana Maharshi, one of India's great spiritual leaders, preferring instead to converse with one of the Maharshi's disciples, a humble, unassuming man who remained in touch with the 'real' world in order to feed his children. The very holiness of the Maharshi, like 'the whitest spot on a white surface', roused the sceptic in Jung, and seems to have symbolised for him 'the unfathomableness of India' (CW11.952–3). Such disturbing reactions, and the whole equivocal mood that pervaded his visit to India, raise important questions about Jung's whole attitude towards the East–West dialogue, and will resurface in our later discussion of criticisms of Jung's attempt to build a bridge between East and West.[5]

This is not the end of the story. Though Jung expressed the need to devote himself to 'the long-neglected concerns of the Occident', his self-education in the ways of the Eastern mind by no means ceased after his return to Europe. It is true that in his writings over the last three decades of his life we see a preoccupation not only with alchemy but with matters relating to Christian theology, but he continued to study and find inspiration from Eastern texts. Thus in 1950 he remarked to a correspondent that he 'was again immersed in the study of [Ch'uang-tzu's] writings' (*Letters I*: 560), and in the year before he died he was again busy studying the Buddha's sermons, 'trying to get near to the remarkable psychology of the Buddha himself' (*Letters II*: 548). There is plenty of evidence that Eastern ideas continued to play a role in this last productive period of his life. In 1956, for example, he contributed a statement, along with Thomas Mann and Albert Schweitzer, to a publication of the discourses of the Buddha, in which he acknowledged 'the immense help and stimulation I have received from the Buddhist teachings', expressing his conviction that these teachings 'offer Western man ways and means of disciplining his inner psychic life' (CW18.1580 and 1577).

Two further and more substantial examples of his continuing interest in the East must be mentioned. The first was the Foreword he contributed to Wilhelm's translation of the *I Ching*, published in 1950, which gave him the opportunity not only to engage in a remarkable hermeneutical dialogue with the text, but also to indulge in speculations which challenged the accepted Western concept of causation. These speculations were amplified a short time later in one of his most original late works, *Synchronicity: An Acausal Connecting Principle*, where he sketched some intriguing parallels between Taoist cosmology and the world-view that was emerging from the revolution in twentieth-century physics. Both of these writings will be examined in more detail in later chapters.

The dialogue with the East, therefore, is a theme which runs throughout his life's work. He wrote no major or systematic treatise on the subject, and his writings in this area consist mainly of short essays and of introductions to translations of Oriental texts by Wilhelm and others. They are not the works of a sinologist or an indologist, for he had no facility in the languages of China or India, nor do they constitute a systematically worked-out position on the subject. Furthermore, as we have seen, he expressed the need to maintain a certain distance from Oriental thought, speaking of the 'strangeness', even the 'incomprehensibility' of the Eastern psyche, and warning against the adoption by Europeans of its spiritual practices. Why, then, did he embark on a dialogue with the East, and what did he hope to achieve by it?

THE REALITY OF THE PSYCHE

One possible answer to this question lies in Jung's belief in the fundamental reality of the human psyche, a reality which is not derivative but is in some sense the 'world's pivot', 'a precondition of being'. To see the point of this we need first to return to Jung's relationship with Richard Wilhelm. What both men discovered was that each in his own apparently distinct discipline had been moving imperceptibly towards the other. The isolation in which, as I mentioned above, Jung found himself after his break with Freud, came to an end with this new relationship, and he once more found his way 'back into the world', for it enabled him to find corroboration for his newly emerging theory of the human psyche. The text of *The Secret of the Golden Flower*, though hardly less opaque than the Gnostic ones that he had felt obliged to put on one side, opened up for Jung 'a bridge of psychological understanding between East and West', and convinced him that there existed an 'agreement between the psychic states and symbolisms of East and West' (CW13.83).

Most importantly this agreement gave him renewed confidence in the plausibility of his new theory of archetypes, for the text offered clear evidence of psychic processes and images that bore unmistakable resemblance to processes and images that hitherto he had observed only within a purely European environment. In this way it enabled him to place his theory of the human psyche in a much wider context, and so to give it potentially universal application. Freud has sometimes been accused of basing his psychoanalytical theories on the rather narrow empirical foundation provided by his Viennese patients. The same accusation cannot be levelled against Jung who deliberately set out to underpin his own theory with evidence from as wide an historical and cultural spectrum as possible. His travels in Africa, where he came in close contact with a pre-modern mentality, and in America where he studied the dreams of people of non-European origin, and conversed with the chief of the Pueblo Indians, his investigation of the ancient Gnostics, and more especially of the long tradition of European alchemy, his interest in the occultist traditions, in mediaeval Christian theology – all of these constituted a rich variety of evidence in support of his new theory of the human psyche. They gave him confidence to believe that in his archetypal theory he was dealing with a universal characteristic of human nature, and not with a purely European variant. It is true that it was from European alchemy that he harvested his richest crop of evidence; 'The possibility of a comparison with alchemy, and the uninterrupted intellectual chain back to Gnosticism, gave substance to my psychology', he wrote (MDR: 231), but light on European alchemy came to him 'only after I had read the text of the *Golden Flower*' (MDR: 230). At this stage of his development it was most especially his studies of the religious ideas of the East which gave him, as he expressed it, 'no end of support in my psychological endeavours' (*Letters I*: 128), for therein he discovered 'very many parallels with the psychic processes we observe in Western man' (*Letters II*: 195). It is in this framework that we must try to understand his intellectual voyages to the East.

All of these excursions enabled him to adopt a comparative approach, to view the European psyche and culture, and his own theories, from an external perspective. He often spoke of the search for an 'archimedean point', a firm place or fulcrum outside his own framework of thought from which he could gain an objective viewpoint to examine his own presuppositions. He fully recognised that philosophically no such intellectual fulcrum was available to him; his Kantian background prevented him from supposing that he could in any way escape from the limits of his own mode of understanding, and he frequently observed that our philosophical outlooks are shaped by cultural and psychological dispositions. Nevertheless from a pragmatic standpoint the East offered him a serviceable substitute for the unattainable Archimedean fulcrum which, though not having any absolute status, at least enabled him to examine the presuppositions of his own culture from an entirely different viewpoint. Like Voltaire and the other *philosophes* who turned Eastwards in their attempts to re-examine the assumptions of their own civilisation, Jung too found in his studies of texts from India and China a mirror with which to practice a kind of critical self-analysis. Such a mirror would provide 'a deeper understanding of our Occidental prejudices . . . the indispensable basis for a critique of Western psychology' (CW18.1483), and even wider than that would offer the means towards a re-examination of modern Western culture.

One important consequence for Jung of this re-examination was, as we have seen, the confirmation that there existed a universal component in the human psyche, and hence a rejection of any idea that Europe represented any fundamentally superior phase in the evolution of mankind. The theme of the underlying unity of mankind pervades Jung's thought in general, and was at the core of his theory of the collective unconscious which sees consciousness as underpinned by archetypal structures which transcend both individual and cultural boundaries. Thus, in his commentary on *The Secret of the Golden Flower*, he wrote that the 'human psyche possesses a common substratum transcending all differences in culture and consciousness', and a few years later in his Tavistock Lectures he insisted that 'somewhere you are the same as the Negro or the Chinese. . . . In the collective unconscious you are the same as a man of another race' (CW18.93). 'Our world has shrunk', he noted elsewhere, 'and it is dawning on us that

65

humanity is *one*, with *one* psyche' (CW10.779, Jung's emphasis). Indeed, despite the wide gulf that in many respects separates Jung's thinking from that of the eighteenth-century Enlightenment, his whole approach has this much in common with the thinkers of that period in that it amounts to nothing less than a theory of a universal human nature, a universal essence that unites mankind beneath the variegated surfaces of different cultures and epochs. The fascination with the East which he shared with the *philosophes* is not surprising, therefore, since it manifests an assumption which they held in common.

Looking at ourselves from the standpoint of Asia enables us, then, to take a sober and more objective look at ourselves, and to cut down to size our hitherto inflated conception of our own superiority. Going beyond this, Jung believed that from this perspective we can see that the differences between East and West are not to be understood in terms of some inevitable historical progress, as Hegel had imagined, let alone of some inherent racial superiority, but in terms of *complementary opposites*. The central spiritual message of *The Secret of the Golden Flower* lay, in Jung's view, in the concept of psychic integration, the ideal of the reconciliation of the conscious and unconscious elements in the life of the psyche into a balanced and harmonious whole. The idea of complementary opposites, of course, pervades Eastern thought, both in its Indian and in its Chinese forms, and for Jung this represented a significant point of contact with his own thinking. The concept of a dynamic interplay between opposing elements was at the root of many of his own hypotheses, and as far as the life of the psyche is concerned he taught that 'opposites are the ineradicable and indispensable preconditions' (CW14.206). This ancient notion, which in the West can be traced back to Heraclitus, is called *enantiodromia*, which Jung defined as 'the play of opposites in the course of events – the view that everything that exists turns into its opposite' (CW6.708).

This idea of a dynamic conjunction between opposites played a crucial role in Jung's dialogue with Oriental thought, and was first discussed in depth, along with the idea of *tao*, in 1921 in *Psychological Types* (see CW6.358–70). His general attitude is summed up in his comment that 'the mind of the Far East is related to our Western consciousness as the unconscious is, that is, as the left hand to the right' (CW18.1484). The strange otherness of the East, which many have interpreted as a sign of relative backwardness, evidence that the peoples of Asia are stuck in the childhood stage of mankind, Jung construed in terms of his belief that the psyche itself is polarised between opposing tendencies, and that psychic health is to be sought in the balancing of these opposites. The discovery of what he saw as a distinct Eastern mentality was not, therefore, the discovery of some earlier stage in the development of the human race, a view which had many supporters in Jung's day, but rather the discovery of a complementary aspect of the human personality. While the West had developed and refined the extraverted aspects of the psyche, associated with rational understanding and control of the external world, the cultures of the East had by contrast developed those psychological qualities of introversion associated with the understanding

66

and control of the inner world; in Jung's words, 'Western man seems predominantly extraverted, Eastern man predominantly introverted. The former projects the meaning and considers that it exists in objects; the latter feels the meaning in himself' (MDR: 348–9). Just as the individual psyche has the opposing dispositions of introversion and extraversion, and needs to achieve some kind of balance between these two, so too whole cultures can be seen to manifest these dispositions, and can become unbalanced by the over-development of one function or the other.

The question of opposites in relation to the East also concerned Jung at a more metaphysical level. The question of evil and its relation to good within the context of Christian theological assumptions had preoccupied him since his youth, and was the subject of one of his last books, *Answer to Job*. The crux of the issue for him lay in his doubts concerning the orthodox Christian view, first, that good and evil represent polar opposites, seemingly irreconcilable with each other, and, secondly, that evil does not exist in the same sense as good, but is rather the negation of the latter – the doctrine of *privatio boni*, as it is called. He felt that the image of Christ in particular was too one-sidedly good and spiritual, and that by comparison with this the Eastern idea of opposites, such as the Chinese *yang/yin* duality, was 'closer to the truth' since it more adequately expressed the fullness and the wholeness of the human personality. On his Indian journey he was impressed with the fact that with the Indian culture – as also with the Chinese – 'good and evil are meaningfully contained in nature, and are merely varying degrees of the same thing' (MDR: 305). Some twenty years earlier in *Psychological Types* he had argued that it was 'necessary to draw a parallel between Schiller's ideas and those of the East because in this way Schiller's might be freed from the all too constricting mantle of aestheticism', a notion which typically underestimated the significance of the darker factors in human nature (CW6.194). The Indian idea of the liberation from opposites, though not fully in line with Jung's own thinking, was at least premised on a recognition of the full range of human psychic potentiality. Similarly in the case of Chinese thought, '*Tao* is the right way . . . the middle road between opposites, freed from them and yet uniting them in itself' (CW6.192). In discussions such as these we can see clear examples of the way in which Jung's hermeneutical approach to the East enabled him to throw light on his own psychology as well as the underlying assumptions of Western culture.

The problem with the West, Jung believed, is that it has cultivated the extraverted function at the expense of the introverted. The extraordinary developments in science and technology in the West are more or less admirable in themselves; contrary to some hostile opinions, Jung was not opposed to science and technology as such. But these latter have tended to focus our attention on the outer world at the expense of the inner, furnishing us with unprecedented levels of knowledge of the material world, but distracting us from the path of *self*-knowledge. 'From the Eastern point of view', Jung comments, 'this complete objectivity is appalling [for] the outer man has gained ascendancy to such an extent that he was alienated from his innermost being' (CW11.785). 'No one', he declared, 'has any time for self-knowledge or believes that it could serve any sensible purpose. . . . We believe exclusively in doing and do not ask about the doer' (CW14.709). This one-sided emphasis in the West, associated with the refinement of the conscious rational mind, has led to the 'breathless drive for power and aggrandisement', and needs to be balanced in favour of those functions of feeling and intuition about which the East has so much to teach us. The East, by contrast, represented for Jung a different point of view which would compensate for what he called the 'barbarous one-sidedness' of Western civilisation. It represented in his eyes the capacity for self-awareness, and hence for uncovering and releasing the self-liberating powers of the mind, thereby opening up the possibility of the sort of psychic integration and contentment which so painfully eluded the Western grasp.

It would appear then that for Jung the East, in recognising the need to achieve some sort of balance between opposites, has gained a superior insight from which the West can learn. However, in practice, he thought, the East is as one-sided as the West, for it has overstressed the inner intuitive side of the psyche or mind just as the modern West has overstressed the rational and the scientific. Jung observed that

> the two standpoints, however contradictory, each have their psychological justification. Both are one-sided in that they fail to see and take account of those factors which do not fit in with their typical attitude. The one underrates the world of consciousness, the other the world of the One Mind. The result is that, in their extremism, both lose half of the universe; their life is shut off from total reality.
>
> (CW11.786)

But for Jung the West's situation is inherently more dangerous, not just because he saw Europe as his special vocation, but because in his opinion the West is going through an unprecedented spiritual crisis. This crisis is a recurrent theme in Jung's writings and was clearly a matter of deep concern to him. His preoccupation with the broader moral and social questions surrounding psychotherapy is evident as early as 1912 when he wrote that 'in the patient a conflict . . . is connected with the great problems of society', and that neurosis 'is intimately bound up with the problem of our time' (CW7.438 and 430), namely the fact that in modern societies the traditional props of our personal and social lives were being progressively pulled away. In 1931 he wrote that 'We are living undeniably in a period of the greatest restlessness, nervous tension, confusion and disorientation of outlook', and that 'everywhere the mental state of European man shows an alarming lack of balance', a comment appearing in a collection of essays entitled *Modern Man in Search of a Soul* (MM: 266). Both in his consulting room and in his observations of the world at large he noted that traditional religious symbols and beliefs had grown empty, and that 'Christian tenets have lost their authority and their psychological justification' (MM: 268). Traditional metaphysical certainties and inherited truths have ceased to convince, for 'natural science has long ago torn this lovely veil to shreds' (MM: 235). Moreover, the assiduous cultivation of rational consciousness in Western civilisation has tended to detach us from our instinctive roots in the collective unconscious, thereby engendering a feeling of rootlessness and unbelonging.

Though in Jung's view this crisis had reached a high degree of intensity in recent times, he believed that it can be traced back to the periods of the Reformation, the Scientific Revolution, and the Enlightenment. During these periods European culture turned its back on its ancient traditions with their rich store of archetypal myths, images and rituals, and as a result was set adrift, having lost touch with its sources of individual and cultural meaning, and become thereby a prey to all sorts of impersonal social and political forces. Some twenty-six years after *Modern Man*, following the long night of Nazism and world war, he wrote with equal urgency in *The Undiscovered Self* of the 'collective possession', amounting to a 'psychic epidemic', that had been unleashed by a civilisation that has lost touch with its unconscious roots, and spoke of the dangers inherent in a culture which has reduced the human individual to a statistic. We have, he lamented, come to adopt a 'statistical world picture [which] displaces the individual in favour of anonymous units that pile up into mass formations', and which accepts 'the abstract idea of the State as the principle of political reality' (US: 13). Peter Homans, in his analysis of Jung's reponse to the problem of modernity, characterises his psychology as 'an extreme response to the pluralization of modern society, in which the individual [is] oppressed by the conformity-inducing forces of collective life', and sees his therapeutic strategy as addressed, not just to the problems of the individual patient, but 'to the problem of modernity, understood as mass man in a mass society' (1979: 143 and 179).

This diagnosis of the condition of the modern Western world was by no means unique, of course. There have been plenty of commentators from Kierkegaard, Marx, and Nietzsche, through Weber and Durkheim to Marcuse, Habermas and beyond who have offered critiques, from various perspectives, of the supposedly perilous condition of modern culture. The distinctive contribution that Jung made to this debate was to see it in terms of psychological categories, and to recognise the contribution that the East may make to its possible resolution. He had, as we noted earlier, realised that the growing interest, amounting almost to an obsession, with Oriental philosophies, was more than just an historical curiosity but amounted to a symptom of the West's spiritual malaise. The educated classes in the late nineteenth century, in their search for a substitute for Christianity, had in many instances turned Eastwards via such organisations as the Theosophical Society which offered them fresh spiritual insights unencumbered by the intellectual and historical burdens of indigenous belief systems.

Jung's Eastward turn must necessarily be understood in this context, and his struggle with Eastern ideas seen as closely linked to his preoccupation with the predicament of modern man. While wary of what he deprecatingly called 'the allurements of the odorous East', he sought an understanding with the East that would help in the formulation of a spiritual cure for the West. In alchemical terms, the East represented not the gold but the philosopher's stone, the catalyst through which spiritual transformation might take place; the East was, he believed, 'at the bottom of the spiritual change we are passing through today', out of whose depths 'new spiritual forms will arise' (MM: 250).

Jung recognised that there is certainly a danger in all of this that we might simply seek to escape Eastwards from our Western troubles, 'try to cover our nakedness with the the gorgeous trappings of the East', as he put it (CW9i.28), that we would simply plunder 'the symbolic treasure rooms of the East' which, though the Christian view of the world has paled for many people, 'are still full of marvels' (CW9i.11). As we shall see later, he was very critical of those who, like the Theosophists, vested themselves in the ways of the East like a new fashion in clothing. But underneath he perceived a deeper purpose, and in the East he saw a more profound quality that was the true object of his own searchings and those of his spiritually hungry epoch. This could be described as a sense of inwardness, an inclination to turn away from external reality, to explore and understand the world within the individual psyche or mind, and a readiness to find wisdom – one's 'Buddha nature' – within oneself. By contrast with the predominant Western outlook, 'Oriental philosophy has been concerned with these interior psychic processes for many hundreds of years' (CW7. 124–5), a fact which was not only of great importance for Jung's own comparative psychololgical research, but pointed the way towards a rediscovery in the West of its own spiritual values.

The general cultural setting in which these ideas were embedded interested him little; even their doctrines and metaphysical beliefs were, as we shall see later, placed in agnostic parentheses, for what he sought in his dialogue with the East was not its specific practices or beliefs but its commitment to the exploration of the inner world of the psyche, a world of equal extent and importance, in his view, to that of the outer physical world. Western man, he surmised, has demonstrated a superb capacity for understanding and controlling this physical world, conveniently splitting off the mental from the material and concentrating its talents on the latter. The East points towards the possibility of a more balanced outlook by bringing what Jung called the 'subjective factor' into play.

What was of importance to Jung, therefore, was that the East gave central ontological status to mind. There the psyche is treated, not just as a secondary, even derivative, phenomenon, as has been the tendency in Western thought since the Age of Enlightenment, but is seen as the essence and ground of all things. This is especially true in the central philosophical traditions of India where primacy is given to mind and consciousness, with the material world taking a secondary place. In the Vedānta philosophy and in certain Buddhist schools, such as the Yogacara, the world as it appears to our senses is seen as a kind of illusion, as a product of our modes of perception and understanding rather than as a reality in its own right, and hence, whereas 'for us the essence of that which works is the world of appearance; for the Indian it is the soul. The world for him is a mere show or façade, and his reality comes close to what we would call a dream'

(CW11.910). The East is wiser than the West, according to Jung, 'for it finds the essence of all things grounded in the psyche'; it recognises that 'The psyche alone has immediate reality' (CW8.384).

This was a central tenet of Jung's own thinking. For him the human mind is not just a dim reflection of the material world, but is a kind of cosmos in its own right, a reality 'of unimaginable complexity and diversity, an internal, non-spatial universe [which is] the only equivalent of the universe without' (CW4.764). It is, moreover, a world with which we have immediate acquaintance, for while, in his view, the material world is known indirectly, and strictly speaking has the status of a hypothesis, we are directly aware of the contents of consciousness, of mind. Indeed we are 'so enclosed by psychic images that we cannot penetrate to the essence of things external to ourselves. All our knowledge is conditioned by the psyche which, because it alone is immediate, is superlatively real' (MM: 220). This implies for Jung that without consciousness 'there would, practically speaking, be no world, for the world exists as such only in so far as it is consciously reflected and consciously expressed by a psyche'. For this reason 'the psyche is endowed with the dignity of a cosmic principle, which philosophically and in fact gives it a position coequal with the principle of physical being' (US: 46–7).

This approach enabled Jung to build his bridge to the East, where he found ideas of an essentially similar nature. There he discovered not only a deep and long-held concern with the mental world but the belief, in various forms, that reality *is* mind-like. In both Hinduism and *Mahāyāna* Buddhism the world as we know it through our senses is not the ultimate reality but, to those with insight to understand, a manifestation of eternal Mind.

Jung's whole approach here is undoubtedly philosophically contentious. It owed much to the idealism of Kant and Schopenhauer, but often showed little awareness of the epistemological complexity of the issues involved; for example, the idea that we are somehow 'enclosed' within a world of mental images suggests a solipsistic conclusion which Jung would presumably have wanted to avoid. Furthermore, from an historical point of view it represented a drastically over-simplified picture of the contrast between Eastern and Western philosophical outlooks, and was limited by a somewhat un-hermeneutical indifference to the broader cultural and social context of ideas. We shall need to address these matters, and other related difficulties, in more detail later (see Chapter 9).

INDIVIDUATION AND WHOLENESS

His interest was, of course, not primarily theoretical but practical. The wisdom that he claimed to perceive there was not of an abstract metaphysical kind but one which helped him to address the problem of the West's spiritual crisis. He had no desire to import Eastern metaphysical systems to the West, but rather to enable the West to find its own path to spiritual enlightenment. Like Gnosticism, and later alchemy, the East provided a model of inner exploration and mind-training, a pointer to the way in which the inner recesses of the psyche can be investigated and cultivated. It pointed to a way of experience rather than a way of faith. To some extent Christianity has also performed this role, for example in the *Spiritual Exercises* of St Ignatius and in such works as *The Imitation of Christ*, but in Jung's view the Churches, with their emphasis on doctrine, on faith, and on ritual observance, have never really encouraged the faithful to explore this inner world, and indeed have often been suspicious of their own saints who, like the Eastern mystics, have explored the inner world of the spirit. Furthermore, the Christian view of the world has now paled for many people, its archetypally rich symbolism no longer holds people's imaginations, and its doctrines have 'stiffened into mere objects of belief', lacking therefore the vitality of direct personal experience.

The East's emphasis on inwardness, self-awareness, self-analysis, was perhaps as one-sided as the West's predominantly extraverted attitude, but it did, according to Jung, offer the opportunity to reassess the relative importance of the world of mind and consciousness, and to discover a more adequate balance between the spiritual and the material. He regretted the fact that in our culture the pursuit of self-knowledge is not highly valued, and that such activities as meditation and contemplation have a bad reputation, often regarded as 'a particularly reprehensible form of idleness or pathological narcissism' (CW14.709). He believed that Oriental cultures, both Chinese and Indian, but most especially Buddhism, had developed ways of tapping into and assimilating material from the deeper levels of the psyche, the unconscious, which in the West we have tended to block off through our excessive refinement of rational consciousness. This does not amount to a denial of the value of rationality, of course, for Jung fully understood its importance in the economy of individual and social life, but involves a recognition of our need for psychic *wholeness* whereby we come to terms with the non-rational aspects of our nature. This concept is indeed central to Jung's relationship with Eastern thought, and needs to be explored further.

Wholeness is a key notion in Jung's thinking, and in general terms his way of looking at the human psyche could be described as 'holistic'. This now somewhat overworked term was first coined in 1926 by Jan Smuts, and was used by Jung in 1936 to characterise his approach to 'the systematic observation of the psyche as a whole' (CW6.966), and as early as 1913 he was using such terms as 'unity', 'totality', and 'wholeness' in relation to the psyche (CW4.556). He frequently spoke of the need to address the patient as a whole person rather than as a collection of acts or dreams, to 'turn our attention from the visible disease and direct it upon the man as a whole' (MM: 222). In terms of human *praxis*, wholeness is to be equated with mental health, and represents the goal of human activity, the fullest realisation of the human personality which alone, he believed, can give the individual a sense of true value and purpose in life.

The holistic attitudes of certain Eastern philosophies matched well with Jung's own outlook, and though he held back from endorsing the monistic, 'all-is-one' metaphysics of Indian Vedānta, he drew support in a variety of ways from these philosophical traditions. One well-known example is the Tantric Mandala which he interpreted as a symbol of psychic wholeness, and in which he found corroboration for his view that the psyche has a natural inclination to integrate and harmonise its various aspects. Another concerns his elaboration of the concept of synchronicity in relation to the cosmological presuppositions of the *I Ching*, a text which, he argued, 'does not aim at grasping details for their own sake, but at a view which sees the detail as part of a whole' (SY: 49). Here he found support for his view that the causalistic world-view of modern science needs to be supplemented by an approach which takes account of the overall pattern, as opposed to the one-by-one sequence, of events. Both of these examples will be examined in detail in later chapters. Many other individual parallels could be cited, but in broad terms the Eastern outlook offered him a way of looking at the world, not reductively as in much modern Western thought, but in terms of its interconnections and its indivisible wholeness.

The holistic attitude of Eastern philosophies was, then, highly congenial to Jung, especially in their refusal to draw any absolute distinction between the world of mind and spirit on the one hand and the body and material world on the other.[6] He was convinced that at the heart of what he called 'the psychic insufficiency of Western culture as compared with that of the East' (MM: 62) lay in its bifurcation between the spiritual and the physical. This has taken a well-publicised form in Descartes' distinction between two different types of substance, the mental and the material, which has provided philosophers ever since with endlessly bemusing puzzles. But this is not just a problem for philosophers, for its roots go deep into our culture. Jung pointed out that Christianity itself has tended to foster a dualistic outlook by creating a fundamental chasm between mankind on the one hand and the divinity on the other. God in the Christian tradition is seen as 'wholly other', as infinitely higher and more perfect than man who can thereby only sense his own worthlessness and his own alienation from the ground of his being. Modern man has, according to Jung, widened this chasm through the development of science and technology. The benefits of these developments can hardly be denied, but at the same time they have helped to tear mankind loose from his traditions, from his sense of oneness with the earth and with his fellow human beings, from what the anthropologist Lévy-Bruhl called the *participation mystique*, and has resulted in what Jung described as 'a new disease: the conflict between science and religion' (CW11.762). Certainly he has achieved thereby a higher level of consciousness, a refinement of our sense of individual autonomy and of our rational intelligence, but it has also meant the loss of contact with the unconscious sources of our psychic life and a consequential loss of meaning, a consequence that was only too obvious to Jung in his consulting room. The East by contrast, at least in its philosophical and religious traditions, offered a model of psychic wholeness which, Jung believed, could help the spiritually suffering peoples of the West to rediscover their own selfhood, not through imitation, but 'on our own ground with our own methods' (CW11.773).

Wholeness constituted for Jung the goal and purpose of psychic growth, and was central to his conception of the *self*. The process of self-transformation whereby this goal is pursued he called *individuation*, the bringing together of the disparate parts of the self, both conscious and unconscious, into a state of balance or equilibrium, a state of more complete self-realisation. He believed that all living things, through the interaction of opposing elements within themselves, have a natural tendency towards a state of harmonious balance, but with human beings this tendency becomes a deliberate process through which a conscious sense of meaning and purpose can be achieved.

'Self' is the key term here and needs some further elucidation. In the West, according to Jung, we commonly identify the self with the conscious ego which in turn is seen as playing a lead role in the human personality. In certain Western philosophical traditions going back to Descartes, the ego is seen as the central rational core of the person with the other aspects of the personality, such as the passions, revolving round it like satellites. Freud was an heir to this tradition in that he viewed the ego, in his later writings at any rate, as the central agency of the personality. Jung proposed a very different model, one which involved a veritable 'Copernican revolution' in psychology in that the total psyche – the self – becomes the centre, with the ego relegated to a subordinate status. The self, according to Jung, is 'an unconscious prefiguration of the ego. It is not I who create myself, but rather I happen to myself.' Thus the 'ego stands to the self as the moved to the mover, or as object to subject, because the determining factors which radiate out from the self surround the ego on all sides and are therefore supraordinate to it' (CW11.391). The self, then, is the totality of psychic function, 'the sum total of [man's] conscious and unconscious contents' (CW11.140). Furthermore, this self is not a static entity but 'a dynamic process', 'an active force' whose essence is one of continual transformation and rejuvenation' (CW9ii.411). Jung rejected the idea of the simple unity of consciousness as a 'naive assumption', and argued instead that the psyche contains within itself a plurality of centres and functions, both conscious and unconscious, and that in the natural course of development the psyche seeks to bring these diverse elements into some kind of unity. This unity, he insisted, is not that of undifferentiated oneness, but rather a harmony, a balance sought through the interplay of opposing but complementary forces. It is in effect a self-regulating system which seeks a balance between various opposing tendencies, and which has, in the words of one commentator, 'not only a tendency to polarization but also an inclination to strike a balance, even to establish continuous states of equilibrium' (Frey-Rohn, 1974: 170).

Jung's exploration of Eastern thought helped to confirm him in the essential correctness of this view. The idea of the psyche as a teleological system which seeks integration had been on his mind since his Freudian days, and was a major factor in distancing him from his colleague's more reductive view of the psyche. The term 'individuation' had also long been known to him from his reading of Schopenhauer. But it was not until 1929 that his concept of individuation was first explicitly formulated, and there can be no doubt that his reading of *The Secret of the Golden Flower* played a part in its evolution. Furthermore, in his

Commentary on this text he began to speculate on its practical implications, and to draw attention to the close parallels between his own therapeutic method and certain ancient Chinese alchemical practices. He noted with satisfaction that in his own technique of psychic healing he 'had been unconsciously following that secret way which for centuries had been the preoccupation of the best minds of the East', and that the content of the text demonstrated 'a living parallel to what takes place in the psychic development of my patients' (CW13.10).

Jung's study of *The Secret of the Golden Flower* was only one of the many places where he sought to delineate a close parallel between his own therapeutic methods and the ancient spiritual practices of the East. Elsewhere he drew attention to the fact that 'Taoist philosophy as well as Yoga have very many parallels with the psychic process we can observe in Western man' (*Letters I*: 195). In recent decades we have become familiar with the practice of yoga, not only as a method of physical and mental relaxation, but as a spiritual path. Jung was one of the first Westerners to recognise this and to harness it to indigenous concerns. As we shall see later, he used the term 'yoga' to refer to the whole range of spiritual practices, Taoist as well as Buddhist and Hindu, and in his discussion of Jung's ideas on yoga, H. Coward points out that 'the spiritual development of the personality [is] the goal of all yoga', and that as a general term yoga 'is the foundation of everything spiritual not only for India, but also for Tibet, China and Japan' (1985: 3). As far as Jung was concerned what bound all these traditions together was the pursuit of liberation through the transcendence of opposites (ranging from hot/cold, through love/hate and honour/disgrace to good/evil and spirit/matter). In this he saw a close parallel with his own therapeutic practice. Thus, the Indian concept of *moksa*, or liberation, though not, as we shall see later, entirely consonant with Jung's own views, was in many ways close to his own idea of psychic liberation and enabled him to clarify his concept of the 'self' as the goal of the individuation process. Similarly in Tantric yoga, which envisages a form of vital energy circulating through the *chakras*, Jung discovered certain symbolic parallels with his own conception of psychic libido and with the general goal of psychic integration.

I must emphasise here that Jung did not advocate the practice of yoga, in any of its forms, by Westerners. He frequently used strong words to discourage those who unthinkingly adopted the methods of yoga; the following passage is typical:

> I wish particularly to warn against the oft attempted imitation of Indian practices and sentiments. As a rule nothing comes of it except an artificial stultification of our Western intelligence.

> (CW11.933)

This may seem strange in the light of his evident enthusiasm for the Orient, and also in view of the enormous influence he had on the pursuit of Oriental practices in the West. This point will be examined in greater depth later (see Chapter 8), but in the present context, where we are trying to understand the nature of, and motivation behind, Jung's Eastern explorations, we need to see that the aim of building a bridge of understanding was not the adoption of the ways of what he saw as an alien tradition, but the construction of our own way, making use of the materials of our own traditions. In adopting the methods of yoga we are in danger of trying to escape from our own problems; inspired by the East, we must in the final analysis 'build on our own ground with our own methods' (CW11.773).

Like many Westerners over the past one hundred and fifty years, Jung experienced a particularly strong affinity for Buddhism, and spoke late in life of 'the immense help and stimulation' he had personally received from it. In contradiction to his earlier reservation about adopting Eastern practices, he affirmed in 1956 that the teachings of the Buddha offered 'Western man ways and means of disciplining his inner psychic life . . . [that] can give him a helpful training when either Christian ritual has lost its meaning or the authority of religious ideas has collapsed' (CW18.1577). The theme of personal transformation and the attainment of wholeness was especially evident in his discussion of Zen Buddhism. He was fully aware of the great cultural and linguistic chasm that divided the West from Zen, admitting that concepts such as *satori* are 'practically impossible for the European to appreciate' (CW11.877), and that 'the correspondence between *satori* and Western experience is limited to those few Christian mystics whose paradoxical statements skirt the edge of heterodoxy or actually overstep it' (CW11.894). Nevertheless he believed that some kind of bridge, however fragile, could be thrown across the gap, and went on to suggest that the concept of *satori* might be understood in the context of the relatively new practice of psychotherapy. Thus, while doubting the desirability or even the possibility of transplanting Zen into Western conditions, he conjectured that psychotherapists might find it useful to study Zen practices and to compare their own methods of psychic transformation with 'this Eastern method of psychic "healing" – i.e., "making whole"' (CW11.905).

The Eastern idea of liberation helped Jung to clarify his ideas about the self in another way. Up to this point we have emphasised the parallels and affinities that he observed between his own theories and Oriental traditions, thereby deriving some measure of support and confirmation from them. But he was also aware of differences, and the realisation of these differences helped him to place his views of the human psyche into clearer focus. The Hindu and the Buddhist traditions are often painted in sharply contrasting colours, but they both share the view that ultimate, final, absolute liberation is possible. The Hindu concept of *moksa* means the final liberation from all worldly bonds, from death and the cycle of rebirth through union with *Brahman*. The Buddhist concept of *nirvāna* similarly implies the release from the wheel of rebirth and freedom from attachment to illusions and desires. In contrast with this, Jung distanced himself from any concept of ultimate perfection or release, for, as he put it, 'complete liberation means death'. The path of individuation, though parallel in some respects to the path that leads to moksa or *nirvāna*, differs in at least one fundamental respect: no ultimate perfection is possible for man. Despite the common concern with the relief of suffering, Jung took the view that the dynamic interplay of opposites that is the very driving force of life, and which in the Hindu tradition is also the source of suffering, cannot be halted, and that the balance or harmony at which the human psyche aims is not the balance of stasis but of dynamic equilibrium. Suffering is therefore not something that can be finally overcome through the individuation process, and it is here that the contrast with Eastern ideas is most sharp: 'The Oriental wants to get rid of suffering by casting it off. Western man tries to suppress suffering with drugs. But suffering has to be overcome, and the only way to overcome it is to endure it' (*Letters I*: 236). 'Complete redemption from the sufferings of this world is and must remain an illusion' (CW16.400). Thus individuation is not a final cure for life's ills, an ultimate state of perfection that we might aim to achieve, but is itself a way, a path: life always has to be tackled anew.

Jung was also adamant that the goal of individuation, though similar to that of yoga, cannot be understood in terms of the absorption of the self into some higher form of universal consciousness. In the Vedānta philosophy, *moksa* is understood not just as a higher state of consciousness, and the attainment of a state of ecstasy, but as a condition known as *samādhi*, in which the individual conscious ego is to all intents and purposes dissolved. This represented for Jung a philosophical and psychological impossibility, 'a contradiction in terms since exclusion, selection, and discrimination are the root and essence of everything that lays claim to the name "consciousness"' (CW9i.520). Yoga can lead to 'a remarkable extension of consciousness', to profound feats of introspection, but strictly speaking it cannot lead to an ego-less state, for in such a case there would be no one left to experience it. 'There must always be something or somebody left over to experience the realization, to say "I know at-one-ment, I know there is no distinction"' (CW11.817). Now it may be the case that this view represented a failure of imagination on Jung's part, an inability to extricate himself from the confines of European thought and language, with its fundamental distinction between self and other, but from Jung's point of view it helped to clarify his own conception of the ego and its relation to the self. For where he concurred with Indian thought was in his belief that individuation implies, as Coward puts it, 'the shifting of the center of the personality away from the ego and towards the self' (1985: 86). It involves a sort of 'Copernican revolution' in which the ego, from being seen as the centre of the psychic universe, revolves round the self in the way that the earth revolves round the sun, and in which the self is, as he put it, 'an unconscious prefiguration of the ego', and thus the 'ego stands to the self as the moved to the mover, or as object to subject, because the determining factors which radiate out from the self surround the ego on all sides and are therefore supraordinate to it' (CW11.391). He drew the line, however, at the point where the ego is seen to be obliterated finally and entirely through identification with some higher trascendent reality.

In drawing attention to these differences we also become aware again of the fact that Jung's relation to the East was profoundly ambivalent. There were, as we have seen, many affinities that Jung himself was not only aware of but made use of in the elaboration of his own ideas. His whole conception of the human psyche as a primary dynamic reality engaged in a process of radical self-transformation has deep resonances with the ideas of Vedāntists, Buddhists and Taoists. The same goes for his holistic approach to the human person, and his preference for a world-view that seeks to integrate matter and spirit as complementary opposites rather than as separate realities. His dialogue with the East, then, was certainly not a polemical confrontation. But neither was it an amiable and uncontentious conversation, let alone an exercise in unbounded admiration. As with any full-blooded dialogue there were differences, misunderstandings, and contradictions, as well as progressions and illuminations.

JUNG'S OWN INDIVIDUATION

In this chapter I have sought to explain both differences and affinities in purely theoretical terms, terms relating to the evolution and formulation of Jung's own theories and practices. But what of Jung himself? How does this fit into his own personal story?

It is beyond the scope and competence of this book, which is essentially concerned with the history of ideas, to offer any sort of analysis of Jung's theoretical development in psychological terms, whether Jungian or otherwise. Nevertheless, in concluding this chapter we need at least to touch on the question of the psychological significance for Jung himself of his dialogue with the East, and the role it played in his own individuation process. While the symbol of Christ is frequently discussed in his writings as an archetype of wholeness, it is doubtful whether he personally derived much spiritual satisfaction from this image. Though he persisted throughout his life in identifying himself with the Christian tradition, there is no doubt that from his schooldays onwards he felt a deep and painful ambivalence with regard to the Christian religion, exacerbated by the suppressed doubts of his father, a Lutheran pastor. The profoundly transformative experiences of his life, such as the early fantasy of God destroying Basel Cathedral, and his later encounter with Philemon and other fantasy images, had a significance, both in terms of their symbolic meaning and their unconscious origin, which appeared to fall outside the bounds of Christian doctrine. The example of Philemon is an especially telling one. In his autobiography Jung recalled that, in the years of inner struggle following the break with Freud, a wise prophet-like figure emerged repeatedly from his unconscious and became for him a kind of spiritual guide, an embodiment of a 'superior insight'. This figure, which he called Philemon, was very real to him, and according to Jung brought home to him the objective reality of the psyche. Fifteen years later when he was in India he met a cultivated elderly Indian who told him, much to Jung's amazement, that his guru was a dead person, and who went on to observe that '"Most people have living gurus. But there are always some who have a spirit for teacher"' (MDR: 209). This enabled Jung to reassure himself that his relationship with Philemon, without necessarily being anything to do with the spirit world, was a form of experience that was not as fanciful and absurd as he had feared but bore a close analogy with relatively common experiences within the Hindu tradition. 'Evidently', he remarked with relief, 'I had not plummeted out of the human world, but had only experienced the sort of thing that could happen to others who made similar efforts' (*ibid.*).

The relationship with his inner guide represented the side of Jung which we have identified in terms of his fascination with the 'other', with the shadow, with the world of the strange and the fantastic, and of his fascination with his inner world of powerfully visualised personalities and forces, an aspect of himself which he described as his '"Other", personality No.2' (MDR: 62) – this side of him evidently responded readily to the symbolic world he discovered in the Oriental texts such as *The Secret of the Golden Flower* and the *I Ching*, and in the teachings of yoga, as it had done to the remarks of his Indian friend. It is clear that he found therein not only inspiration and confirmation of an intellectual kind but also something which addressed his own urgent psychological need for wholeness, that had the potential to satisfy a yearning within his own psyche which traditional Christian and Western modes of experience (with the possible exception of alchemy) seemed unable to satisfy.

5

TAOISM

Jung neither visited China nor learned its language, but references to its thought and culture abound in his published works, and he clearly felt a great affinity for what he saw as its philosophical and psychological outlook. Confucianism, with its emphasis on the external political and moral order, interested him little, and mention is made of it only in passing.[1] Taoism, however, which he tended to look upon as typical of Chinese thinking as a whole, preoccupied him in a variety of different ways, and played an important role in the formation of his psychological theories. Thus, he found its holistic outlook and its affinity for the natural world especially congenial. Its romantic impatience with rational and conventional structures and its eagerness to make contact with the primordial sources of life was immediately attractive to him. He was drawn, too, to its dynamic cosmology based on the idea of ever-changing and ever-interacting forces, characterised in terms of energy (*ch'i*) which flows through the whole of nature, human and non-human. In the central concept of *tao* (the way) he saw a close affinity with his idea of synchronicity, and in the idea of *wu-wei* (action through non-action) he recognised a psychological attitude which ran closely parallel to his own approach to the unconscious mind. And finally the concepts of *yang* and *yin*, opposing yet complementary principles that underpin all of reality and human experience, matched with remarkable exactness his conception of the psyche as a self-balancing system governed by the tension of opposing principles. His earliest extended references to Taoist ideas occurred in *Psychological Types* (1921) where, in the context of a discussion concerning pairs of psychological opposites, he defined the aim of Taoism as the 'deliverance from the cosmic tension of opposites by a return to *tao*' (CW6.370), a conception which clearly anticipated his own key idea of 'individuation'. But his main discussions of Taoist ideas were contained in the psychological analysis of two Chinese texts, *The Secret of the Golden Flower* and the *I Ching*, and these, along with his idea of 'synchronicity', will occupy us in the following sections.

THE SECRET OF THE GOLDEN FLOWER

We saw in the previous chapter that the discovery of the Taoist alchemical text, *The Secret of the Golden Flower*, marked a turning point in Jung's life. It constituted, as he put it, 'the first event which broke through my isolation', and provided him with 'undreamed-of confirmation' of ideas concerning the human psyche that he was developing at that time (MDR: 222–3). It is remarkable indeed that it was this strange text – which seemed to him on first reading so obscure, so alien, leading him to puzzle 'as to how and where the Chinese world of thought might be joined to ours' (CW13.3) – that helped to lead him out of his intellectual isolation, and enabled him to map out his future life-path with clarity and assurance.

The text itself had been translated by Richard Wilhelm from a Chinese treatise dating from about the eighth century CE, and was the product of an esoteric Taoist movement known as The Order of the Golden Elixir of Life which was devoted to the enhancement of life and longevity through the practice of yoga and meditation. It also showed evidence of Buddhist influence in its references to the illusoriness of life and the quest for *nirvāna*. It is a relatively short treatise which essentially comprises a set of spiritual/psychological exercises aimed at self-transformation through detachment from outer material goals, and at the attainment of an inner freedom symbolised by the Golden Flower.

Describing it as a work of 'alchemy' can be misleading for the Western reader. It contains nothing of the chemical contrivances – the furnaces, retorts, sublimations, putrefactions – that fill the pages of European alchemical works, but rather is concerned throughout with the process of inner transformation. In contrast with the more popular Taoist schools, which used the techniques of magic, mediumship, and physical potions, it advocated methods which Wilhelm describes as 'purely psychological'. The search for an elixir of life, making use of alchemical methods in the bid to find the 'golden pill' (the 'philosopher's stone', in European terms), had for centuries been a central aim of popular Taoism. *The Golden Flower*, however, represented an alternative, mystical tradition which dated back nearly a millennium to the founder of philosophical Taoism, Lao-tzu. Any alchemical allusions which remained in texts such as *The Golden Flower* had become, in Wilhelm's words, 'symbols of psychological processes', an interpretation which clearly appealed to Jung and became a key to the whole understanding of the language of alchemy, European as well as Chinese.[2]

In 1928 Wilhelm invited Jung to write a commentary on *The Golden Flower*. He accepted with enthusiasm since it provided him with welcome support for his ideas and the opportunity to publish, at least in provisional form, the results of investigations in which he had been engaged for some years. It is a remarkable piece of writing which, while acknowledging the cultural and historical distance involved, manages to draw from it psychological insights which put it in contact with Western consciousness. There is no question here of modern Westerners being urged to become honorary members of The Order of the Golden Elixir of

Life, or of engaging in the arduous sprirtual path prescribed by the text, but rather we are invited by means of the text to re-examine the nature of the psychic life, and in so doing to recognise the one-sidedness of our Western modes of understanding. In Jung's view, the most important thing for the West to learn today is that the psyche 'has the same validity as the empirical world, and . . . that the former has just as much "reality" as the latter' (CW13.75).

Jung's immediate stated aim in his Commentary was 'to build a bridge of psychological understanding between East and West' (CW13.83). Bearing in mind that the text derived from an esoteric tradition and hence was not intended for the eyes of the uninitiated, it would be easy, he confessed, either to dismiss the work as the product of the 'overwrought mystical intuitions of pathological cranks and recluses', or like Faust to allow oneself to be overwhelmed by its magical charms and to forsake the sure foundations of Western rationalism for its mysterious Oriental allures. The Commentary sought a middle way, one which acknowledged the profound importance of the text, while at the same time seeking to mediate its heady contents by means of the sober hermeneutical discipline of dialogue. In his Foreword to the second German edition of 1938 Jung was careful to warn his readers against certain misunderstandings: the bridge that he sought to construct in his Commentary was not intended as 'a recipe for achieving happiness', a technique for self-development to be imitated by Westerners, nor was it a method which he instilled into his patients for therapeutic purposes (CW13: 4). In approaching this text, he insisted, we need to remain true to ourselves, to build on our own foundations, to resist the temptation to depreciate the Western intellect, while at the same time avoiding the trap of undervaluing a text which does not immediately fit into our Western categories.

To appreciate the 'middle way' which Jung adopted in his interpretation of the text we need to see it in the context of certain intellectual strategies which he was pursuing at that period.

The first, relatively narrow, strategy arose from his theory of archetypes and the collective unconscious. Over the past decade he had been forging what he believed to be a revolutionary new conception of the human psyche, one which took its rise from Freud but which departed from the psychoanalytic theories of his former colleague in certain crucial respects. While accepting the idea of a personal unconscious, formed by the repression of conscious contents, he postu-lated in addition a *collective* unconscious comprising what he at first termed 'primordial images' but later came to refer to as 'archetypes'. The psychic structures of individual persons must be understood, not just in terms of their own individual histories, but in terms of the history of the human race, that in some sense we actually inherit patterns of psychic behaviour, just as we inherit, so he believed, patterns of physical behaviour. According to this hypothesis, each individual inherits not just a kit of biological instincts but dispositions to think, experience, and symbolise in ways which, though shaped on the surface by culture and history, are at a deep level the common denominators of the human psyche. He had earlier thought of this psychic inheritance in terms of images like those to be found in the fantasies of individuals and in the myths and symbols of human cultures, but by the time he wrote his Commentary on *The Golden Flower* he had arrived at the conclusion that it was not actual but *virtual* or *potential* images that were inherited. As members of the human race we inherit the capacity to develop distinctive psychic contents related to certain basic aspects of the human condition, which in turn are shaped by the peculiarities of the individual culture in which we are reared.

Not only did this idea fly in the face of current psychological orthodoxy, which rejected any form of innateness in the human psyche, but it was a theory for which he could supply only a narrow range of confirmatory evidence. Since the theory made claims about the universal condition of mankind, it was not at all satisfactory to offer in its support evidence culled merely from the study of a few European psychiatric patients, or even from a study of the mythologies of Western Europe. His results, 'based on fifteen years of effort', he admitted, 'seemed inconclusive, because no possibility of comparison offered itself'. He 'knew of no realm of human experience with which I might have backed up my findings with some degree of assurance', except for scattered and fragmentary reports from the early Christian Gnostics (CW13: 3). *The Secret of the Golden Flower* happily confronted him with new evidence from an entirely different culture for it contained, as he put it, 'exactly those items I had long sought for in vain among the Gnostics' (CW13: 4).

The second, somewhat broader, strategy involved the question which, as we saw in the last chapter, was increasingly occupying his mind at that time, namely the loss of meaning in Western culture. In 1931 he wrote that 'modern man has suffered an almost fatal shock, psychologically speaking, and as a result has fallen into profound uncertainty' (MM: 231), an uncertainty which had resulted from the loss of traditional religious ideals, indeed of the whole metaphysical foundations of our spiritual and moral life. This spiritual shock has forced us to turn our attention towards new sources of meaning, for 'no psychic value can disappear without being replaced by another of equivalent intensity' (MM: 242). It is hardly surprising, therefore, that the European has been drawn towards the cultures of the East which appear to offer the possibility of some sort of spiritual renewal. Science has proved an invaluable tool, Jung insisted, but 'it obscures our insight only when it claims that the understanding it conveys is the only kind there is' (CW13.2). What the West needs most urgently is an alternative to our scientific culture, a 'broader, more profound, and higher understanding', and in pursuit of this we need to take seriously the philosophical approach of the East, though without simply becoming its 'pitiable imitator'.

These two points of departure – the broad and the narrow – are not unconnected, for the theory of the collective unconscious was more than just a theory about the structure of the unconscious mind; it also represented an attempt to understand the symbolic nature of the human psyche, and thereby to address the question of man as a meaning-creating being. The archetypal inheritance represented for him a structure of meaning, a framework of images which guided mankind, a set of signposts, as it were, which could be used to make sense of the essential parameters of human existence. The imaginal life of humans, therefore, is not just a set of features alongside bodily functions, or an amusing by-product of evolution, but is the means through which the psyche creates a meaningful world. In the West we have for too long sought to downplay and to dismiss mythical images, and along with them the fantasy world of the mind, as irrelevant, superstitious, even pathological, we have 'often denigrated the imaginative quality of human life, at best relegating it to the province of art and poetry, at worst placing it within the range of abnormal phenomena' (Avens, 1980: 11). Certainly one of Jung's most important contributions to modern thought was his attempt to re-evaluate the role of the imaginal and symbolic in psychic life, and his interpretation of this Taoist text played a significant role in this.

The Secret of the Golden Flower, therefore, provided Jung with the opportunity not only to articulate and reinforce his new theory of the collective unconscious but to engage with what he saw as the most important question facing modern European civilisation. By building a bridge of understanding with the Orient, he was not only opening up a dialogue with a strange and long-forgotten alchemical text, but was opening up a new means of discourse with the human psyche itself. A deep and sympathetic reading of this text led him to conclude that it was describing processes that were recognisably similar to those postulated by analytical psychology, and indeed confirmed him in his belief that these processes transcend racial differences and point to 'a common substratum transcending all differences in culture and consciousness' (CW13.11), a common substratum that he identified with the archetypes of the unconscious.

The crisis facing us in the West, he believed, lay in our inability adequately to make contact with and to express these archetypal images. The extraordinarily high development of rational consciousness in our modern culture has led to a one-sided development in which 'the unconscious is thrust into the background', seemingly emancipating itself from irrational forces, a 'Promethean freedom' which soars above the earth, but is in danger of sudden collapse. By contrast with this one-sided development, *The Golden Flower* offered a model of balanced psychic development in which the externalising forces of *yang* are balanced by the rooted inwardness of *yin*. The concept of *tao*, which is central to Chinese thinking and to this text in particular, signifies a union of opposites, 'a reunion with the unconscious laws of our being', and hence represents an image of wholeness. The key to this psychic balance and wholeness lies in the release of the power of fantasy and imagination. The development of full personality, and thereby the ability to achieve a sense of rootedness in life, lies, he believed, in our ability to accept all aspects of our personality, in 'saying yea to oneself' (CW13.24).

The Secret of the Golden Flower is not a philosophical treatise but rather a veritable repository of symbols and images that can be used to facilitate the alchemical transformation of the self. Jung focused first on the mandala image, which, as we shall see in a later chapter, represented for him a symbol of psychic wholeness. Mandalas do not appear as actual images in the text, but rather through the image of circulation. The text suggests the idea of transformation, not as a linear, but as a circular process, in effect like the hermeneutical circle we noted earlier, in which a rotation from one pole to another, from light to darkness, brings about a progressive sense of integration and completeness. This circular movement 'has the moral significance of activating the light and dark forces of human nature' (CW13.39), a procedure in which all sides of the personality come into play, and which leads to self-knowledge. The 'circumambulation of the self' was a favourite image of Jung's that he used to express the dynamic process of self-discovery whereby the ego is seen to be contained in the wider dimensions of the self, the self being both the centre and the circumference of the psychic life. The circular motion implies a sense of both a marking off and of a process of integration which are essential to the process of individuation, the coming-to-be of the self. In the alchemical language of the text this process was expressed in terms of the 'creative point' out of which the life-giving interplay of opposites proceeds. In this way the text can be read as a symbol of psychic integration, as being concerned at a deep level with the very same issues that Jung dealt with in his consulting room.

The emergence of a fuller and more balanced self through this activity is by no means smooth and easy, but requires the breaking down of the psyche, and the revelation of multiplicity within its apparent unity. The emphasis on wholeness and unity as the goal of psychic transformation – the individuation process – can lead the unwary to suppose that for Jung the human psyche is ideally some kind of homogeneous substance, and that the splitting of the self is always pathological. Quite the contrary, Jung saw the self as a multiplicity of related elements, a dynamic system of psychic processes that seeks, not the elimination of multiplicity, but the bringing of this multiplicity into awareness and into balance. His view on this matter is close to that of modern systems theory which views wholes in terms of the homeostatic balance between competing forces, such as, for example, in an ecosystem or an organism.

In *The Secret of the Golden Flower* the quest for spiritual enlightenment has, as Jung read it, a similar structure. Though the goal of the quest is unity – the perfection of the 'diamond body' as the text calls it – the means to that end takes the adept through the dangerous labyrinth of the unconscious in which all kinds of strange shapes and spirit-beings emerge. It has a kind of disintegrating effect brought about by the emergence into consciousness of 'thought-figures' that take on the shape of a variety of numinous forms. These figures should not be avoided or repressed, but rather contemplated and taken possession of, for it is only through such figures and their integration that the full power of the human spirit unfolds itself. To illustrate this Jung reproduced a series of images from the text which depict a sage in meditation. In the first picture he is in a state of undisturbed bliss, gathering light into himself, and out of this undivided state emerges progressively a series of fantasy images that represent the bearers of spiritual powers. The singularity of his consciousness is thus split into multiplicity, yet finally he remains still and undisturbed at the centre, having retained in himself the multitude of images which finally he must see as, in the words of the author, 'only empty colours and forms' (CW13.46).

For Jung these bizarre spirit-beings are nothing other than 'fragmentary psychic systems'. No doubt the adept will tend to see them as gods, *Bodhisattvas*, or as spirit-beings of some kind, but here as elsewhere Jung, reading the text as a psychologist, interpreted them as semi-autonomous psychic contents. Putting aside, as matters of faith, metaphysical questions about the actual existence of such beings, he saw in such phenomena a clear manifestation of psychic complexes, of quasi-personalities. At one extreme these 'personalities' may have a disintegrating effect that tends towards a psychotic condition, they may tend to split off and take on an independence which threatens the coherence of the psyche as a whole; such a condition would be recognised in former times as a state of divine or diabolical possession. At the other end of the spectrum they have the potentiality to be integrated within the whole self, to be explored and exploited on the road towards individuation.

Jung called the technique for dealing with such fantasy images in a constructive way 'active imagination' – a method which in fact received its first public airing in his Commentary. He had originally stumbled upon this method when struggling with the upwelling of powerful images that occurred in his period of 'confrontation with the unconscious' following his break with Freud, thereafter fashioning it into a therapeutic tool that he used as a supplement to dream analysis. He described it later as 'a method . . . of introspection for observing the stream of interior images' (CW9i.319), for 'raising unconscious contents to consciousness' (CW11.137n), and for 'switching off consciousness, at least to a relative extent, thus giving the unconscious contents a chance to develop' (CW11.875). In practical terms patients are asked to place themselves in a relaxed state of mind and to suspend rational judgement as far as possible, allowing images and fantasies to emerge and unfold, which are then to be observed and followed through 'with absolute objectivity'. It is in effect a form of 'visionary meditation', whose aim is to bring unconscious material into conscious awareness and to integrate it into the whole personality, a process which in general terms Jung called the 'transcendent function'.

The extraordinary inner world of images and the methods for dealing with them which Jung came across in *The Golden Flower* seemed to offer a process which was almost exactly isomorphic with his own therapeutic system, and one which confirmed for him the importance of creative fantasy in the economy of the psyche. What the text offered, it seemed to him, was nothing less than a discipline for the attainment of psychic health, a discipline which consisted precisely in doing nothing (*wu-wei*), or rather in letting things happen, for, as the text explains, 'the light circulates according to its own law' (CW13.20). The contents of the unconscious can be ignored or repressed, or they can be allowed to errupt and to swamp consciousness in a potentially dangerous way. The Taoist treatise described for him a way in which these very real inner forces can be acknowledged, controlled, and directed for the benefit of the psyche by inducing a greater sense of wholeness.[3]

Jung's interpretation of *The Secret of the Golden Flower* offers a model, therefore, of psychic integration and health. In earlier times these psychic contents were projected onto the external cosmos as divine beings or forces, and have been dealt with by means of ritual and prayer. In our own more sceptical day, however, we have concluded that these beings and forces are the result of primitive superstition and simply do not exist. Herein, according to Jung, lies a great psychic danger. We imagine that by denying the existence of these forces we have got rid of them, but as elements that arise from the unconscious they continue to have a powerful effect on us:

> They become an inexplicable source of disturbance which we finally assume must exist somewhere outside ourselves. The resultant projection creates a dangerous situation in that the disturbing effects are now attributed to a wicked will outside ourselves, which is naturally not to be found anywhere but with our neighbour *de l'autre côté de la rivière*. This leads to collective delusions, 'incidents', revolutions, war – in a word, to destructive mass psychoses.
>
> (CW13.52)

Self-knowledge, the recognition of the power of the unconscious, must in modern times be our way of dealing with these hidden forces.

> The person who has understood what is meant by psychic reality need have no fear that he has fallen back into primitive demonology. If the unconscious figures are not acknowledged as spontaneous agents, we become victims of a one-sided belief in the power of consciousness, leading finally to acute tension. A catastrophe is then bound to happen because, for all our consciousness, the dark powers of the psyche have been overlooked.
>
> (CW13.62)

In other words, our inability to recognise the unconscious forces at work within us, and our delusions about the supremacy of rational consciousness, lead to a new form of possession in which we are taken over, not by demons, but by 'phobias, obsessions, and so forth; in a word, neurotic symptoms'. The gods have become diseases, even psychic epidemics (CW13.54).

To sum up, then, the importance to us of *The Golden Flower* lies in its power to persuade us of the reality of the psychic forces that lie within, 'to accord to the psyche', as Jung put it, 'the same validity as the empirical world, and to admit that the former has just as much "reality" as the latter' (CW13.75). It can teach us, first, that these unconscious forces cannot be dismissed as mere illusions, and, secondly, that unless they are acknowledged and integrated they will wreak personal and communal havoc. He believed that we in the West have tended to depreciate everything psychic, and our emphasis on rational consciousness and the ego has prevented us from recognising the importance of factors which lie beneath the level of consciousness. An understanding of this ancient text can therefore lead us to an enhanced understanding of the unconscious and thereby enable us to free ourselves from its domination. We need to recognise that the unconscious is 'a codetermining factor along with consciousness', thereby shifting the centre of gravity of our whole personality, a new centre which 'might be called the self' (CW13.67). This is in effect the process he described as 'individuation', a process which requires us to treat the unconscious with the same respect as the conscious mind.

The text teaches us, too, of the power and importance of fantasy and imagination, for it is through releasing these powers that we are able to tap into those repressed and despised layers of our personalities, and to embark on the path of individuation. These faculties have been systematically rejected and neglected in the West: 'In the East there is an abundance of conceptions and teachings that give full expression to the creative fantasy. . . . We, on the other hand, regard fantasy as worthless subjective day-dreaming' (CW13.63).

The dialogical bridge that Jung sought to erect between East and West was one which, in the end, appears to affirm, as much as to transcend, cultural differences. In reading the Commentary one is struck by the passionate desire, indeed the urgent need, to understand and to learn from the methods of Chinese yoga. Yet there is also repeated affirmation of its otherness. East and West remain for Jung radically different in their outlooks and values; each is, as he put it, 'historically conditioned and geographically limited', each representing only one aspect of mankind. 'What a contrast, what an unfathomable difference, what an abyss of history', he is moved to exclaim when juxtaposing the Christian symbol of the crucifixion with the image of the Golden Flower (CW13.79). In the Western Christian tradition stress has been laid on the incarnation of Christ and on the need for the seekers after salvation to subordinate themselves to divine providence, and to acquire through the imitation of Christ the merits that Christ alone has earned. The East, on the other hand, teaches the path not of imitation but of autonomy, of *self*-realisation. The training of the mind, the exploration of the unconscious, the eliciting of images in meditation exercises, though conducted under the guidance of a teacher, are in the last analysis impelled from within by the individual and finally rely on his or her own efforts.

However, it is precisely at this point, Jung suggests, that contact is made between the two ends of the bridge, for it is here that Westerners can begin to learn about the psychological demands of self-realisation and to articulate their own unique way of pursuing it, 'so that, after all, it might be possible for each to realize himself in his own way' (CW13.81). In this manner it is possible, despite the evident differences, to find some kind of agreement between the psychic states and symbolisms of East and West, and to combine together in the pursuit of self-realisation 'which unites the most diverse cultures in a common task' (CW13.83). Yet this common task, and the assimilation of the ideas of the East, we can undertake only 'by standing firmly on our own soil' (CW13.72).

This final sentiment sums up the hermeneutical spirit of the Commentary. We cannot reconstruct the mentality of ancient Taoists; we cannot leap into the minds or the texts of the past, even of our own past, let alone those of a distant culture, for a deep gulf divides us. Yet this gulf, the very otherness that we face, can serve to illuminate and to place into fresh and critical perspective our own position, and indeed can enable us to come to some understanding of the 'other' too. After the dialogue (though of course there is, strictly speaking, no end to this process) we come to understand our position better, and to modify and correct it through comparison and contrast with that of the other, and in doing so we come to recognise the human solidarity, the common core of humanity that unites us in our differences. The distance that at first seemed so inexorably to divide us becomes the very means whereby that distance can be overcome. In one sense the tradition out of which *The Secret of the Golden Flower* has sprung appears to be definitively different from our own, indeed closed for ever to the modern mind, including that of the modern Chinese. And yet through engaging in a seemingly impossible intercourse we come to recognise and to participate in a wider tradition that reaches down into our archetypal roots, leading us thereby to recognise the limits and inadequacies of our own beliefs and practices. This is a pattern we shall recognise in the other examples of dialogue that follow.

THE *I CHING*

This hermeneutical pattern is especially evident in Jung's reading of the *I Ching*, where once again Richard Wilhelm acted as intermediary. In his memorial address delivered in 1930, Jung spoke of his 'rare good fortune' in experiencing through Wilhelm's translation of this ancient Chinese text

> such a comprehensive and richly coloured picture of a foreign culture. What is even more important is that he has inoculated us with the living germ of the Chinese spirit, capable of working a fundamental change in our view of the world. We are no longer reduced to being admiring or critical observers, but find ourselves partaking of the spirit of the East to the extent that we succeed in experiencing the living power of the *I Ching*.
>
> (CW15.78)

Whereas *The Golden Flower* was was an esoteric work with a very restricted readership, the *I Ching* was a central text of Chinese culture, possibly the oldest of the so-called *Five Classics*, and could justifiably be described as one of the most important books in the world's literature. Wilhelm (1968: xlvii) wrote of it that

> Its origin goes back to mythical antiquity, and it has occupied the attention of the most eminent scholars in China down to the present day. Nearly all that is greatest and most significant in the three thousand years of Chinese cultural history has either taken its inspiration from this book, or has exerted an influence on the interpretation of its text. Therefore it may safely be said that the seasoned wisdom of thousands of years has gone into the making of the *I Ching*. Small wonder then that both of the two branches of Chinese philosophy, Confucianism and Taoism, have their common roots here.

The title, *I Ching*, is usually translated as *The Book of Changes* which, according to Wilhelm, expresses the idea of the typical changes and transformations that take place in individual and public life, and which at a deeper level point to the Chinese idea of the constantly changing and transitory nature of all phenomena, arising out of the interplay of the opposing forces of *yang* and *yin*. The text itself is built around a sequence of six-line figures called 'hexagrams', whose six horizontal lines are either unbroken (*yang*) or divided into two (*yin*). There are sixty-four of these symbols, a number which represents the sum of all possible combinations of the six broken and unbroken lines. Corresponding to each hexagram is a text comprising a 'Judgement', an 'Image', and six brief 'Lines' (or verses) which correspond to the six lines of the hexagram. The work has also accumulated a set of Commentaries, mostly by Confucius and his followers, which expand, elaborate on, and explain the original text. Each of the hexagrams is thought of as corresponding to a configuration of transitional states in the cosmos, symbolising between them all that happens in heaven and on earth. The corresponding sections of the text relate these symbols to generalised human situations, offering both a summary of these situations and general advice or pointers on how to approach and cope with them.

Although the *I Ching* was, in time, associated with occult doctrines and was used as source of oracles and divination, the text does not offer precise prophesies or predictions, but by giving the user a suggestive image of the possibilities and potentialities inherent in a state of affairs, the text can be applied to the user's own situation. It will be evident from this that the book lends itself to a dialogical approach: the user asks the *I Ching* a question; the text 'replies'; the user interprets the reply in terms of the context that gave rise to the question. It was certainly the case that, as traditionally employed in China by Taoist priests and their followers, the book was treated as the mouthpiece of unseen spirits; as Jung noted: 'according to the old tradition, it is "spiritual agencies", acting in a mysterious way, that make the yarrow-stalks give a meaningful answer' (CW11.975). But the very nature of the text allowed Jung to place these beliefs in parentheses, as it were, and to treat the work as a 'book of wisdom', and in his investigation of the text no assumptions are made about the metaphysical beliefs that may in the past have underpinned the work, but rather the exercise is treated purely as a 'psychological procedure'.

In 1949, some years after Wilhelm's death, Jung was asked to write a foreword to the English edition of the *I Ching*, an invitation which he readily accepted. His approach was similar to the previous text. As with *The Secret of the Golden Flower*, Jung recognised the formidable divide that separated the modern reader from this book which, at first glance, is so obscure and seemingly unintelligible – a book which is the product of 'a remote and mysterious mentality' (CW11.1001), which 'departs so completely from our way of thinking' (CW11.967) and which displays a strangeness, Jung noted, not unlike that of the delusions of the insane or primitive superstitions. It would be easy, then, to dismiss it – as have many Westerners, and indeed many modern Chinese scholars – as nothing but 'a collection of magic spells'. Not surprisingly, Jung himself felt considerable unease at the prospect of writing an introduction to such an archaic-sounding book while at the same time claiming for himself scientific status.

In approaching this work, then, Jung clearly felt himself confronted with a chasm separating him, with his European culture and presuppositions, from this strange text from a seemingly quite different world. How, then, was he to carry out the commission? He devised two ways of bridging the divide, each, though different from the other, a method of dialogue, the first thoroughly practical, the second more theoretical. Neither way involved a full-frontal intellectual attack on the work with detailed analyses and definitive interpretations, for as he pointed out, unlike a typical Western philosophical or scientific text, 'the *I Ching* does not offer itself with proofs and results', but, like a part of nature, 'waits until it is discovered'. This meant, he admitted, that not all would be persuaded by his approach, for the *I Ching*

> offers neither facts nor power, but for lovers of self-knowledge, of wisdom – if there be such – it seems to be the right book. To one person its spirit appears as clear as day; to another, shadowy as twilight; to a third, dark as night. He who is not pleased by it does not have to use it, and he who is against it is not obliged to find it true.

(CW11.1018)

The book is, of course, not a theoretical treatise but a practical manual for use in a variety of everyday situations, and it was for this reason that Jung chose to devote most of his Foreword to a practical experiment in which he put the text to work. He had in fact been making use of the *I Ching* as a method of exploring the unconscious, his own and that of his patients, for some years prior to receiving Wilhelm's translation. In his autobiography he recalled that during one summer in the early 1920s he made, as he put it, 'an all-out attack on the riddle of the book', and would sit for hours practising the technique, testing the oracle's answers against the question posed to it, and producing some remarkable results which he could not explain to himself (see MDR: 405). He now sought to confront the text again, and in effect to hold a dialogue with it as if it were a living person. 'Why not venture a dialogue', he asked, 'with an ancient book that purports to be animated?', and treat the answers which the text gave 'as though the *I Ching* itself were the speaking person' (CW11.976–7). The question he chose to put concerned directly his actual current task: what did the text think of his 'intention to introduce [the *I Ching*] to the English-speaking public'? (CW11.975).

He elicited its reply by making use of the traditional method of chance selection of a passage from the text. This method normally involved the employment of a bundle of marked yarrow stalks from which a series of six individual stalks were removed at random. This could be done either by removing the requisite number 'blind' by hand, or by the operation of shaking the bundle vertically in a container until one emerged above the level of the others. For convenience sake, Jung chose to make use of coins, three in all, which he tossed six times, the outcome of which was the chance selection of one of the hexagrams. Using this technique, he simply asked the text his question concerning his intention to write a foreword to the text. The answer he obtained was hexagram 50, *ting*, THE CAULDRON. The text is as follows:

THE JUDGEMENT:

Supreme good fortune. Success.

THE IMAGE:

Fire over wood:
The image of the CAULDRON.
Thus the superior man consolidates his fate
By making his position correct.

THE LINES:

1. a *ting* with legs upturned.
   Furthers removal of stagnating stuff.
   One takes a concubine for the sake of her son.
   No blame.

2. There is food in the *ting*.
   My comrades are envious,
   But they cannot harm me.
   Good fortune.

3. The handle of the *ting* is altered.
   One is impeded in his way of life.
   The fat of the pheasant is not eaten.
   Once rain falls, remorse is spent.
   Good fortune comes in the end.

4. The legs of the *ting* are broken.
   The prince's meal is spilled
   And his person is spoiled.
   Misfortune.

5. The *ting* has yellow handles, golden carrying rings.
   Perseverence furthers.

6. The *ting* has rings of jade.
   Great good fortune.
   Nothing that would not act to further.

(See Wilhelm, 1968: 193–7, and CW11. 194–9)

Jung began with the second and third lines since, according to a rule concerning the relative value of the various lines, these are to be especially emphasised. His construal is based on the assumption that *ting* – a sacrificial vessel – may be taken to refer to the *I Ching*, and that the ritual food cooked therein symbolises the spiritual nourishment contained in the text. His interpretation is given in the following passage:

> The answer given in these two salient lines to the question I put to the *I Ching* requires no particular subtlety for its interpretation, no artifices, and no unusual knowledge. Anyone with a little common sense can understand the meaning of the answer; it is the answer of one who has a good opinion of himself, but whose value is neither generally recognized nor even widely known. The answering subject has an interesting notion of itself: it looks upon itself as a vessel in which sacrificial offerings are brought to the gods, ritual food for their nourishment. It conceives of itself as a cult utensil serving to provide spiritual nourishment for the unconscious elements or forces ('spiritual agencies') that have been projected as gods – in other words, to give these forces the attention they need in order to play their part in the life of the individual.

(CW11.982)

Jung's interpretation of the other lines of the hexagram can be summarised as follows: The first suggests that the *I Ching* is like an unused vessel that needs to be shaken out to remove stagnating matter, and that, like a man who turns to a concubine in order to have a son, the text must turn to a foreigner to have its due effect. The text of the fourth line sees the *I Ching* being put to use, but in a very clumsy and inappropriate manner; the text, Jung surmises, 'is evidently insisting here on its dignity as a ritual vessel and protesting against being profanely used' (CW11.989). The golden handles in the fifth line suggest that the *I Ching* has a new way of grasping it, and that understanding is furthered through perseverence. Finally, in the sixth line, 'the *I Ching* expresses itself . . . as being not only well satisfied but indeed very optimistic' (CW11.993). With regard to the 'Judgement', Jung was modest enough not to comment on this, but with hindsight, taking into consideration the subsequent fate in the West of the work for which he is writing the Foreword, the judgement seems peculiarly apt.

The process does not end here, however. According to ancient usage, lines designated by a six or a nine have an inner tension that causes them to change into their opposite, thereby producing hexagram 35, *chin*, PROGRESS. Wilhelm comments on this hexagram that it 'represents the sun rising over the earth [and] is therefore the symbol of rapid, easy progress, which at the same time means ever widening expansion and clarity' (1968: 136). Jung himself commented that 'The subject of this hexagram is someone who meets with all sorts of vicissitudes of fortune in his climb upward' (CW11.997). Unlike the previous hexagram, he did not deal with this one in detail; its general drift seemed clear to him, and as with the previous one suggested good fortune in the West for this controversial work. Nevertheless, one line held his attention: 'Perseverence brings good fortune / Then one obtains great happiness from one's ancestress'. In the case of the interpretations already discussed, Jung employed a hermeneutical method that can best be described as 'commonsense', since they require no special knowledge of myth or symbol. In this case, however, Jung drew on his psychological experience, on his knowledge of dreams and fairy tales, where

> the grandmother, or ancestress, often represents the unconscious, because the latter in a man contains the feminine component of the psyche. If the *I Ching* is not accepted by the conscious, at least the unconscious meets it halfway, for the *I Ching* is more closely connected with the unconscious than with the rational attitude of consciousness.

> (CW11.997)

Jung pursued the text with one more question, asking it to comment directly on his actions. The answer was hexagram 19, *k'an*, THE ABYSMAL. *K'an* is, as Jung noted, one of the less agreeable hexagrams, with its repetition of the trigram THE ABYSMAL, WATER. He was encouraged by the Judgement, which reads 'If you are sincere, you have success in your heart / And whatever you do succeeds'. But the general weight of the text leans towards danger, and urges caution and circumspection in the face of difficulties. But this precisely reflected his mood and the tentative manner of his approach to the text, he recalled, for even before he had embarked on this experiment he was aware that the *I Ching* represented 'a deep and dangerous waterhole in which one might easily be bogged down' (CW11.1015). The imagery of the hexagram, with its dangerous abyss and overflowing water, spoke to him of the unconscious, expressing feelings of uncertainty and risk in the face of the unknown, and warning him of the danger of inadvertently coming under the influence of powerful unconscious forces. Hence the text was in effect confirming him in the appropriateness of his cautious approach. He could, as he notes, have embarked on a full-blown psychological commentary on the whole book, but chose instead a more modest path. This is the way, in the words of the text, in which the 'superior man . . . carries on the business of teaching'.

What is the reader to make of this? Is it anything more than an imaginative, but in the final analysis bogus, exercise in special pleading? Or, perhaps worse, was Jung being duped into accepting, despite his reservations, an ancient superstition, of supposing that a ghostly presence resided in the text, addressing him like a disembodied voice at a seance? He did in fact agree that 'any number of answers to my question were possible. . .' (CW11.985), but he went on to point out that only one was actually given. Furthermore, a repetition of the experiment would be logically impossible 'for the simple reason that the original situation cannot be reconstructed' (CW11.985). This is an interesting observation which goes to the heart of the hermeneutical approach. If he were making use of the method of the natural sciences then, as he noted, it would be necessary for the experiment to be repeatable in all relevant respects an indefinite number of times by any competent observer. But clearly these conditions could not be met, for the situation in which he, C.G. Jung, found himself at that moment were unique and could not be re-enacted by another experimenter. It could not be repeated by another since the questions concerned precisely his own relationship with the *I Ching* at that particular moment, in those particular circumstances. Nor could it even be repeated by Jung himself since the results of the first experiment would provide a new context for, and inevitably affect the results of, the second. From the standpoint of hermeneutics the significance of this lies in the fact that understanding a human situation, such as in the study of history, is in principle quite different from understanding a physical phenomenon, for whereas in the case of the latter we are concerned with the development of general laws which are applicable universally, in the case of the former our concern is with the individual and the unique, with a meaning that is situated in a particular context. Hermeneutical understanding, as we have seen, involves a circular movement that oscillates from the part to the whole, each in a sense illuminating the other; as Gadamer put it, 'we must understand the whole in terms of the detail and the detail in terms of the whole' (1975: 258). Thus the significance of Jung's dialogue arises not from the application of general principles but rather from a to-and-fro interaction between the text and Jung's question.[4]

How do we know – indeed how was Jung to know – that he was being 'objective' in all of this? Could his reading of the text be nothing more than an arbitrary projection on his part? Since the situation cannot be repeated, by what criteria are we to judge the adequacy of his interpretation? Even if the hermeneutical approach is different from that of the natural sciences, it must still provide some means of distinguishing between well-grounded and unsound results.

The answer which Jung offered was that the results he obtained made the sort of sense he would expect if he were engaging in a dialogue with another intelligent and perceptive human being. The results were not just meaningful, but were relevant to the question asked and cast light on the immediate situation. 'Had a human being made such replies', he commented, 'I should, as a psychiatrist, have had to pronounce him of sound mind, at least on the basis of the material presented. Indeed I should not have been able to discover anything delirious, idiotic, or schizophrenic in the . . . answers' (CW11.1016).[5] And reflecting back on his earlier experiments he noted that he was struck in a similar way with the relevance of the answers obtained, and with the fact that 'a significant number of answers indeed hit the mark' (MDR: 406).[6]

Jung certainly recognised the possibility of projection, namely that his own unrealised thoughts and unconscious dispositions were simply being projected onto a text whose abstruse and ambiguous symbolism would be especially receptive to a wide range of possible construals (see CW11.1016). He did not appear especially bothered by such a possibility. The consistently meaningful and helpful character of the results he obtained, both in the experiment described in the Foreword and in his earlier experiments (which, he regretfully observed, he failed to record), suggested that the projection theory was inadequate and that some more complex theory was indicated. It is true that at times he seemed prepared to adopt a kind of agnostic fall-back position in which he left on one side theoretical questions, taking a purely pragmatic attitude to the text; as he put it rather wryly: 'The less one thinks about the theory of the *I Ching*, the more soundly one sleeps' (CW11.1017). Furthermore, as we noted above, he was adamant that no 'occult' explanation was to be inferred from the experiment (CW11.1000). But the consistently significant nature of the responses he obtained led him to speculate that some further explanation was required, and this in turn provided further evidence for a bold new theory which had been taking shape in his mind in the 1920s.

This leads us into the second, more theoretical, form of dialogue which he conducted with the *I Ching*, which revolves around his notion of *synchronicity*.

THE *I CHING* AND SYNCHRONICITY

The idea of synchronicity represents one of the most remarkable and contentious conjectures that emerged in the creative middle period of Jung's life. It is difficult to know exactly when he first conceived the idea, though the original stimulus seems to have come from a lecture he attended in about 1912 by Albert Einstein, which started him thinking about the relativity of time and space, and the possible implications of this for psychology (see *Letters II*: 109). The two men met socially on several occasions at this period, and their friendship led to Jung's later cooperation with Wolfgang Pauli, a major contributor to the emerging field of quantum physics, who enabled Jung to clarify and develop his ideas on synchronicity. He had certainly already begun to formulate the idea in his mind prior to his meeting with Richard Wilhelm in 1923, but it is clear that his association with Wilhelm and with his translation of the *I Ching* was of considerable importance in enabling him to develop and articulate it more fully. The term was in fact first used publicly by him in 1930 in his memorial address for Wilhelm.

He had since his early years been struck by coincidences occurring in his own life, and later as a therapist had been fascinated by cases of meaningful coincidence occurring with his patients, i.e. coincidences that appear to have a definite significance, and cannot easily be explained away in terms of pure chance.[7] This, along with his acquaintance with the profound new conceptions of reality emerging from quantum physics, led him to speculate that in addition to the principle of causality, it was necessary to postulate a parallel principle to account for the simultaneous occurrence of meaningfully connected events. He called this 'synchronicity', which he defined as 'the simultaneous occurrence of two meaningfully but not causally connected events' (SY: 36), and in 1951, after many years in which he felt reluctant to inflict such an eccentric notion on the public, he published his ideas in a little book called *Synchronicity: An Acausal Connecting Principle*.

Jung's initial reason for introducing this term was to account for meaningful coincidences. As an example of this, he quoted an incident where a patient was recounting a dream in which she was presented with a golden scarab, and at that very moment a scarab beetle began insistently to knock against the window. The scarab, he pointed out, was a classic example of a rebirth symbol, and the startling event just referred to was enough to move the patient forward after a period in which she seemed stuck and unable to make any progress. He also cited the work of J.B. Rhine, the American psychologist who, in a series of experiments into the phenomenon of extrasensory cognition, consistently produced results which went well beyond the probability of chance. Examples such as these, Jung believed, 'confront us with the fact that there are events which are related to one another ... *meaningfully*, without there being any possibility of proving that this relation is a causal one' (SY: 27). It would make sense, therefore, to postulate a new *acausal* principle of explanation to supplement the traditional causal explanation of events. Thus, in the case of the scarab, the linking of two events – the dream and the appearance of the beetle – could not be explained in causal terms alone, but required another principle which linked them within a framework of meaning concerned with the life-world of the patient. It is this principle which he named 'synchronicity'.

Now, while 'synchronicity' was coined to help account for a limited class of phenomena – namely, that of meaningful coincidences – it came to be seen by Jung as having a much wider application, and indeed suggested to him a quite revolutionary new conception of reality and of our relation to it as conscious beings.[8] Classical physics, created by Newton, canonised philosophically by Kant, and enshrined at the heart of the modern world-view, conceived the world as a domain of material entities governed by immutable causal laws. Accordingly, the occurrence of any event could be explained with reference to a set of antecedent causes which in turn were manifestations of universal, deterministic laws. If human actions and mental events are to be counted as part of this universe, then they too must be in principle explainable in similar terms. The principle of synchronicity appeared to run right in the face of this, for it postulated an alternative, albeit complementary, mode of explanation, one which employed concepts quite alien to those of classical physics. It suggested that 'besides the connection between cause and effect there is another factor in nature which expresses itself in the arrangement of events and appears to us as meaning' (SY: 95).

But how was Jung to make sense of this? He attempted to do so in the first place by drawing on ideas from the new physics of relativity and quantum mechanics, which in the inter-war years was beginning to challenge the conceptual framework of classical physics. With help from his friend the physicist Wolfgang Pauli, who was himself at the forefront of these developments, he suggested that the principle of causality that underlay classical physics was not an absolute principle at all, but was a matter only of statistical probability, relative only to a particular way of observing and investigating the world. Synchronistic events could therefore be viewed, not as conflicting with the causal principle, but as falling under a complementary principle. He also turned to the history of Western philosophy: to Kant, for whom the Newtonian concepts of space, time and causation were not intrinsic properties of things in themselves but of our ways of experiencing and understanding reality (SY: 28); to Schopenhauer, who had in many respects anticipated Jung's attempt to construct a principle of complementarity in our dealings with the world (SY: 16–17); and above all to Leibniz, whose monadology envisaged a world in which there is a non-causal parallelism between inner and outer events and a non-causal pre-established configuration, or harmony, between all elements of the natural world (SY: 112ff).[9] It was, however, the *I Ching* that provided him with the most useful mirror in which to scrutinise his strange new theory, and the most helpful participant in a dialogue aimed at elucidating it.

What seemed to him significant in such cases as the scarab beetle was not just that two events, seemingly connected, occurred simultaneously in such a way that a causal explanation seemed unlikely, but that these fitted into a larger nexus of interrelated meanings, a pattern of meaning which stretched out to embrace the whole psychic situation of the patient. He suggested that one of the limitations of the Rhine experiments was that they involved an isolation of the experimental subjects from their everyday circumstances, and that there was nothing in the experiments to illuminate the psychic background, except perhaps the fact that boredom with the experiments on the part of the subjects appeared to diminish their performance (SY: 26 and 48–50). The characteristic of *meaningful* coincidence which attracted his attention, then, was not just the remarkable concurrence of two otherwise unrelated events but rather that they fitted into a pattern of psychological meaning. In his analysis of the relevance of the new physics to the principle of synchronicity he had noted the importance of the idea of pattern and of interconnectedness, rather than of interaction between discrete particles as in classical physics. From this quarter there was emerging, he surmised, a new unitary conception of being, one which not only breaks down absolute barriers between entities and between space and time, but also between observer and observed, between subject and object, between mind and matter. It points, in other words, to what would nowadays be described as a *holistic* concept of being.

Now it was precisely this property of the *I Ching* that he seized on as providing a conceptual analogue for his own theory, in that it provided an intuitive technique, characteristic of Chinese thought, for grasping the total situation. 'Unlike the Greek-trained Western mind', he wrote, 'the Chinese mind does not aim at grasping details for their own sake, but at a view which sees the detail as part of the whole . . . and thus placing the details against a cosmic background – the interplay of Yin and Yang' (SY: 49). Seeing things as a whole in this way enabled the Chinese to look at certain patterns of events in an entirely different way from that of modern science, as he made clear in the following remarks in his Tavistock Lectures in 1935:

It is like this: you are standing on the sea-shore and the waves wash up an old hat, an old box, a shoe, a dead fish, and there they lie on the shore. You say: 'Chance, nonsense!' The Chinese mind asks: 'What does it mean that these things are together?' The Chinese mind experiments with that *being together* and *coming together at the right moment*, and it has an experimental method which is not known in the West, but which plays a large role in the philosophy of the East.

(CW18.144, Jung's italics)

What Jung was looking for was a method for developing his concept of synchronicity which both exemplified the element of acausal, chance coincidence, yet at the same time gave insight into the meaningful psychic background. The *I Ching* appeared to fulfil these two conditions: its technique depends on the random throw of coins or yarrow stalks, leading to a text which allows one to reflect on the current situation within a global context. What it does, in effect, is to 'explain the simultaneous occurrence of a psychic state with a physical process as *an equivalence of meaning* ... the same living reality was expressing itself in the psychic state as in the physical' (SY: 51, Jung's italics). In other words, the psychological significance of any given moment in time, embracing a whole range of hidden meanings and unconscious connections, is revealed through the hexagram, which in turn is arrived at through an apparently random procedure.

What intrigued Jung about the *I Ching*, therefore, was not just its potential as an aid to self-knowledge, nor even its apparent exemplification of the synchronistic process, but the fact that it pointed to a way of conceptualising reality in a wholly different way from that which had been established in the West from the time of the Scientific Revolution. In his view, the idea of synchronicity represented a break with the conceptual framework of classical physics, and the adumbration, in partnership with ideas emerging from the new physics, of a new and more ample conceptual framework. Lying behind the *I Ching*, and indeed behind the whole Chinese mentality, lay, he surmised, a way of comprehending reality which in many ways anticipated these new ideas, and which, through a process of dialogue, could be used to cast light on them.[10]

As we have seen, the essence of this ancient Chinese conception lay in its assumption of the fundamental unity of nature. To make sense of this, and of the use Jung made of it, let us examine this conception more closely.

Jung was once asked how it was that so highly cultivated a people as the Chinese had produced no science. He replied that 'this must be an optical illusion, since the Chinese did have a science whose standard text-book was the *I Ching*, but that the principle of this science, like so much else in China, was altogether different from the principle of our science' (CW15.80). He proceeded to amplify this by outlining the Taoist natural philosophy. Its central idea is, of course, that of *tao*. This crucial term has been given a variety of translations, such as 'God', 'providence', and 'the way', but for Jung the most appropriate was that adopted by Wilhelm, namely 'meaning'. This, he believed, conveyed the central idea of Chinese philosophy – namely that the world of nature, in which man is an integral part, is not a random or mindless collection of events but is linked together by some kind of hidden pattern of significance.[11] Such a pattern, according to one recent commentator, '[is] not based on mechanistic causation, but rather on an equivalency of meaning with respect to the phenomena contained therein' (Aziz, 1990: 136). Hence this pattern cannot be discerned by dissecting reality into its component parts, a method which typifies Western science, for meaning is essentially a function of interconnection; as the Taoist sage Chuang-tzu remarked, 'Tao is obscured when you fix your eye on the little segments of

99

existence only' (SY: 99). While in the dominant Western tradition the individual details of nature have been investigated for their own sake, the Taoist mind always seeks the total picture, and can only grasp the parts in terms of the whole. As Jung put it:

> While the Western mind carefully sifts, weighs, selects, classifies, isolates, the Chinese picture of the moment encompasses everything down to the minutest nonsensical detail, because all of the ingredients make up the observed moment.
>
> (CW11.969)

Any particular aspect of nature is linked with other aspects of nature in such a way that we can only grasp its significance in terms of these connections, and ultimately in terms of the whole. This means that there lies between the various aspects of nature a relationship that could be described as one of 'correspondence', or of 'correlation'. Many scholars have noted this as a central feature of Chinese cosmology. John B. Henderson (1984: 1), for example, writes:

> Correlative thought is the most basic ingredient of Chinese cosmology [which] in general draws systematic correspondences among aspects of various orders of reality or realms of the cosmos, such as the human body, the body politic, and the heavenly bodies. It assumes that these related orders as a whole are homologous, that they correspond with one another in some basic respect, even in some cases that their identities are contained one within the other.

Joseph Needham (1956: 281) has written about the Chinese world-view in similar terms:

> The key-word in Chinese thought is *Order* and above all *Pattern*. . . . The symbolic correlations or correspondences all formed part of one colossal pattern. Things behaved in particular ways not necessarily because of prior actions or impulsions of other things, but because their position in the ever-moving cyclical universe was such that they were endowed with intrinsic natures which made that behaviour inevitable for them. If they did not behave in those particular ways they would lose their relational positions in the whole. . . . They were thus parts in existential dependence upon the whole world-organism.

As Jung observed, this way of thinking is closely parallel to that of Mediaeval Europe, with its idea of the *unus mundus* (one world) involving a systematic correspondence between microcosm and macrocosm, and can be traced back to Greek conceptions of the bond of 'sympathy' that holds all things together in organic harmony (see SY: 100–1). It is also to be found, he noted, in astrology where the meaning of individual human lives and human acts is related to meanings symbolised in the cosmos, and manifested at certain crucial moments such as at birth. It must be emphasised that such correspondences are not physical but symbolical in kind, they depend on links of meaning that must be deciphered and read like a text, rather than observed and correlated within causal laws. Indeed one could describe this as an anthropomorphic model for in effect it suggests that the cosmos acts in ways analogous to a human psyche in which various aspects of a person correlate in such a way that they can be read like a text, or like 'a legible or understandable picture' (CW11.973), and where, moreover, a particular act or moment in an individual's life in some way encapsulates and reflects the whole of that person's existence.

It was not Jung's aim to recover and to dress up again for modern use these ancient world-views. Contrary to the opinion of certain hostile critics, who have seen Jung as a weary reactionary, turning away from the modern world and returning to pre-modern ideologies, he was highly critical of those 'spiritual beggars of our time who are too inclined to accept the alms of the East in bulk and to imitate its ways unthinkingly' (CW15.88). Rather than alms, it is hard work that can rid us of our beggary, and it is through the reconstruction of our own world-view with the materials of our own culture, not through borrowing another's, that we should find our way forward. The dialogue with the *I Ching*, therefore, is not like a preliminary negotiation by defeated generals in preparation for eventual capitulation, but more like a conversation with a stranger who, because of long familiarity with the terrain, can give us some guidance in our travels; but of course it is we ourselves, not the stranger, who must make the journey.

Jung's dialogue with the *I Ching*, therefore, is a means of carrying forward contemporary discussions about the reconceptualising of the physical world and of the relation between the physical world and the mind. It commences from our present standpoint, or more precisely from Jung's speculations within that standpoint, and works from there backwards, not directly but back and forth from the text to contemporary concerns, each consciously recognised as an expression of its own historical situation, but each progressively illuminating the other. It becomes thereby a way of putting these recent speculations, and especially those concerning synchronicity, in a wider context, helping us to see that there is an alternative to a purely causalistic account of nature. This is a pattern of argument with which we should be quite familiar by now, for once again Jung was making use of Eastern thought to cast light on and offer a critique of the basic assumptions and prejudices of Western thought. By placing ourselves sympathetically within another world-view, as it were, we are able to see the limitations of our own – to see that the Western outlook does not represent the final and absolute truth, but is only one 'truth' among many. 'We must remember', he wrote, 'that the rationalistic attitude of the West is not the only possible one and is not all-embracing, but is in many ways a prejudice and a bias that ought perhaps to be corrected' (SY: 95).

None of this demonstrates the validity of his theory of synchronicity, nor was it meant to. The theory was offered as 'work in progress', a bold conjecture designed to explain phenomena which the modern Western world-view left out of account, but which could once again be opened up for discussion in the context of the new physics. Jung warned that 'there can be no question of a complete description and explanation of these complicated phenomena, but only an attempt to broach the problem in such a way . . . as to open up a very obscure field which is philosophically of the greatest importance' (SY: 6). We need 'the courage to shock the prejudices of our age if we want to broaden the basis of our understanding of nature' (SY: 47). Taking this 'archaic book of "magic spells"' seriously was meant to deliver such a shock, and thereby to carry the discussion a stage further. In recent decades we have become accustomed to seeing our long-accepted theories and world-views challenged and overturned; the idea that the old Newtonian order is giving way to a 'new paradigm' which revives, while not simply recapitulating, traditional holistic and organic models, is widely debated, if not universally accepted. Jung's speculations concerning syn-chronicity, and his dialogue with the *I Ching*, can usefully be viewed as an early contribution to these debates.

6

YOGA

It is sometimes confusing for Jung's readers that he employed the term 'yoga' as a general term indicating the whole range of Eastern thought and meditational practice. Coward points out that, in his writings, the term 'is used to designate Eastern traditions as diverse as Hinduism, Indian Buddhism, Tibetan Buddhism, Japanese Buddhism, and Chinese Taoism' (1985: 3), going on to suggest that this is justifiable insofar as the way of release from suffering and self-realisation represent common themes of all Eastern thought and practice. But at the same time Jung also used the term in its more narrow and more usual sense to refer to the Indian practices of spiritual discipline which make use of mediation, breathing and postural techniques, and to the forms of spiritual knowledge which underly these practices. It is in this narrower sense that the term is being used in the present chapter. I shall begin by examining in general the relationship between Jung's thought on the one side, and yoga and Indian thought on the other, and then look more closely at the particular case of Tantric yoga.

YOGA AND INDIAN PHILOSOPHY

Indian philosophy played an important role in the development and formulation of Jung's thinking. As with Chinese thought, he held it in high regard, writing that 'Our Western superciliousness in the face of . . . Indian insights is a mark of our barbarian nature, which has not the remotest inkling of their extraordinary depth and astonishing psychological accuracy' (CW6.357). Especially dear to his heart, though, was that path within the Hindu tradition called yoga, which he described as 'the most eloquent expression of the Indian mind' (CW11.911), a spiritual achievement which represented 'one of the greatest things the human mind has created' (CW11.876).

Jung's interest in Indian thought in general dated from the intense period of study of religion and mythology in preparation for his book *Symbols of Transformation*, first published in 1912 – an interest which played an important role in the development of his theory of psychological types on which he was working

103

in the same period. In the 1920s this interest was given further impetus by Oscar Schmitz's book *Psychoanalyse und Yoga*, and by his friendship with the indologist Heinrich Zimmer, and he continued to draw close parallels between psychoanalysis and yoga and to develop the idea of a dialogue between the two. It was at this time that he recognised in yoga an approach which was in tune with his own developing concept of the 'self', and a technique which paralleled his exploration of the unconscious and his theory of individuation. He came to the conclusion that the experiencing and realisation of the self was 'the ultimate aim of Indian yoga', and hence that 'in considering the psychology of the self we should do well to have recourse to the treasures of Indian wisdom' (CW16.219). For this reason he recommended to his students the study of classical yoga, and maintained that 'psychologically we can learn a great deal from [it] and turn it to practical account' (CW16.219).

Like alchemy, yoga represented for Jung a rich symbolic system of personal transcendence which, unlike orthodox Christianity, addresses the needs of the whole psychosomatic system, and which, by slackening the control of the conscious ego, makes possible the exploration of the unconscious depths of the psyche. Furthermore, his 'discovery' of yoga came at a time when he was seeking to clarify his own theoretical position *vis-à-vis* that of Freud whose procedure was, he claimed, too analytical and reductive; by contrast, Jung was seeking to emphasise 'the purposiveness of unconscious tendencies with respect to personality development'. Again in contrast with Freud, he was developing his own idea of the libido as a general, non-specific psychic energy, and some of the main ideas of Hindu philosophy struck him as demonstrating a remarkable parallel with his own. It was in the context of this search for an alternative way of thinking about the psyche that 'important parallels with yoga have come to light, especially with Kundalini yoga and the symbolisim of Tantric yoga. These forms of yoga', he went on, 'with their rich symbolism afford me valuable comparative material for interpreting the collective unconscious' (CW11.875).

Let us look at some of these ideas more closely, especially at the way in which Jung interwove his own developing theory of analytical psychology with those of Indian yoga.[1]

We begin once again with *Psychological Types*, where much use was made of yoga in the forging of various new concepts which were to play central roles in the elaboration of Jung's mature thought. The idea of liberation from opposites was central here. When investigating Taoism in the previous chapter, we saw that Jung discovered in the Chinese concept of *tao*, and in the related concepts of *yang* and *yin*, a close analogy to his own idea that the self seeks redemption from unreconciled opposites. A similar dynamic is to be found, he believed, in yoga which he explained as '[the] method by which the libido is systematically "introverted" and liberated from the bondage of opposites . . . by which are to be understood every sort of affective state and emotional tie to the object' (CW6.189–90). The Sanskrit term for pairs of opposites is *dvandva*, which includes the pairs male/female, desire/anger, love/hate, honour/disgrace, as well

104

as fairly mundane pairs such as hot/cold. For the Indian, Jung maintained, the purpose of life is clear: 'It wants to free the individual altogether from the opposites inherent in human nature' (CW6.329).

He discovered that these ideas were closely linked to certain cosmogonic myths and philosophical ideas associated with the Hindu concepts of *Brahman* and *Ātman*. Essentially, *Brahman* is seen as the world-ground, the creator, the unitary cosmic principle out of which all life, all forms emerge as warring, pain-ridden opposites, which must then seek to overcome these divisions by being reunited with *Brahman*. This seemed to correspond closely with Jung's idea of libido: 'It is clear . . . that the *Brahman* concept, by virtue of all its attributes and symbols, coincides with that of a dynamic or creative principle which I have termed libido' (CW6.336). *Ātman* is the soul which, contrasted with most Western thinking, is seen as ultimately identical with *Brahman*; as Jung puts it: 'The fusion of the self with its relations to the object produces the identity of the self (*Ātman*) with the essence of the world [i.e. *Brahman*] so that the identity of the inner with the outer *Ātman* is cognized' (CW6.189). The apparent division between *Brahman* and *Ātman*, the outer and the inner, is achieved through the understanding that they are really in essence one and the same.

These teachings seemed to embody for Jung his own psychological insights in a projected form, namely the psychological process of introversion in which the conscious mind opens up to and seeks union with its opposite, the unconscious. The ultimate aim of yoga is the attainment of *Brahman*, the 'supreme light', or *ānanda* (bliss), a redemptory exercise involving, so he believed, a trance-like state, an immersion in the unconscious, in which all oppositions – subject and object, inner and outer – are transcended. In cosmogonic terms this involves the identity of *Ātman* (soul) with *Brahman* (ultimate reality), and is summed up in the famous Upanishadic phrase *tat tvam asi* (thou art that). *Brahman*, then, represents the idea of the total freedom of the individual 'from the opposites inherent in human nature . . . which is the state of redemption and at the same time God' (CW6.329).

On the face of it he thought that these notions must appear 'strange and inaccessible to the Greek-trained European mind' (CW11.908). Nevertheless, as a model of psychic integration it proved a suggestive prototype, one which was more fully developed later in the same work where the first outline of his central concept of *individuation* appears (CW6.757–62). Individuation refers to the natural process of differentiation whereby the individual personality is formed. As we saw earlier, Jung believed that all living things display this tendency, but that in the case of human beings this involved a unique process whereby we consciously bring into play antagonistic, and sometimes repressed, aspects of our personalities, and seek some kind of harmonious psychic integration or whole-ness. Treated psychologically the *Ātman–Brahman* concept offered Jung a close analogy to individuation, and suggested to him that his own 'strange and in-accessible' ideas had already been foreshadowed in metaphysical form several thousand years earlier.

We can also see in Jung's discussion of these Indian concepts the seeds of another important Jungian idea, closely related to individuation, namely that of the *self*. This concept, which was discussed in an earlier chapter, could be defined as the archetypal image of human wholeness and fulfilment in which conscious and unconscious are brought into harmony. In *Psychological Types* we can witness the birth of this Jungian notion through the conjunction, on the one hand, of Schiller's idea of spiritual sublimation through aesthetic experience, and on the other, of the Indian notion of the unity of $\overline{A}tman$ and *Brahman*. Schiller's 'aestheticism' proved inadequate and one-sided; according to Jung it 'is not fitted to solve the exceedingly serious and difficult task of educating man, for it always presupposes the very thing it should create – the capacity to love beauty . . . [and] always averts its face from anything evil, ugly, and difficult' (CW6.194). By contrast, the religious philosophy of India, with its capacity to confront and integrate the opposing tendencies within the human psyche, and the whole range of human potential, evil as well as good, 'grasped this problem in all its profundity and showed the kind of remedy needed to solve the conflict' (*ibid.*). What the Upanishadic teaching offers, then, is not just insight into one aspect of the human personality but into the true inner self. As Coward notes: 'At the moment of highest insight, the true inner self, that $\overline{A}tman$, is seen to be identical with the life essence of all the external universe (*Brahman*)'. Thus, he continues 'It is this uniting of the internal and external in the $\overline{A}tman$–*Brahman* symbol that becomes a model for Jung's concept of the self' (1985: 53).

Behind all of this lay Jung's belief, to which I drew attention above, in the non-derivative reality of the psyche; 'it seems to me far more reasonable', he claimed, 'to accord the psyche the same validity as the empirical world, and to admit that the former has just as much "reality" as the latter' (CW13.75); in short: 'The "reality of the psyche" is my working hypothesis' (CW18.1507). This psychic reality, furthermore, represented for Jung not some kind of inert substance but rather a form of energy (libido), which can be expressed in different kinds of desire and in a variety of symbolic forms. These insights fitted well with the Indian Sankhya-Yoga concept of *citta* which denotes the phenomenological reality of mind, and is viewed as the source of all perception and thinking. In a series of lectures on 'The Process of Individuation' given in Zürich in 1939, Jung discussed this concept at some length and linked his own idea of libido as a neutral (i.e. not exclusively sexual) source of psychic energy with the commonly held Indian notion that the world is a manifestation of a fundamental energic force. The yoga idea of *rajas*, for example, conveys the idea of human life as driven by striving, greed, lust, and restlessness, and is seen by Jung as directly analogous to his own idea of libido as psychic energy.

This receives further confirmation in the Hindu conception of *Brahman*. Coward points out that Jung, in elaborating his concept of libido, 'also appeals to the creative impulse inherent in the Hindu concept of the absolute or *Brahman* . . . as the creative principle within the cosmos . . . the uniting impulse which attempts to harmoniously tie all things together' (1985: 33). In support of his attempt to draw close analogies between his own conjectures and the ancient philosophy of India, Jung quotes a number of passages from the *Vedas*, and concludes that

> It is clear from these examples, which could be multiplied indefinitely, that the Brahman concept, by virtue of all its attributes and symbols, coincides with that dynamic or creative principle which I have termed libido.
>
> (CW6.336)

Support is further elicited from the Hindu concept of *rta*, a term which means something like the divine order which underlies all things, and refers to those processes of nature which remain constant. In other words, the overflowing, creative energy of *Brahman* is manifested not in chaos and disorder but in cosmic harmony, and human actions too must be carried out in obedience to *rta*, thereby linking the microcosm of the human world with the order of the macrocosm (the word 'rite' probably has its root on *rta*). For Jung, *rta* represents another symbol for libido; it is not only connected with the idea of an energic force underlying phenomena, but it also carries the sense of shaping this force and directing it along a path. Libido, too, as psychic energy, is not mere undirected force, but also 'necessarily includes the idea of a regulated process. . . . It is the path of our destiny and the law of our being' (CW6.355).

Libido, furthermore, like *rta*, carries with it the notion of aim or purposiveness. However, Jung insisted that this is not to be understood as an aim or purpose imposed from without, but rather one that arises spontaneously from within; *rta* is not to be confused with law imposed by a separately existing divinity, but arises naturally from within the creative process of *Brahman*. What the East teaches us, in Taoist as well as Hindu thought, is that the notion of order, whether in the cosmos at large or in human affairs, does not necessarily imply laws imposed from without, which is the Western prejudice; 'We are still so un-educated that we actually need laws from without, and a task-master or Father above, to show us what is good and the right thing to do' (CW6.357). We need, on the contrary, to find the law that arises out of our own sense of inner freedom, to trust in ourselves. The full realisation of human nature, Jung believed, must come from sources within the individual person, from its own tendency to find balance and harmony through the reconciliation of opposite tendencies.

The emphasis on *self*-realisation, and hence on the *individual* who pursues the path of salvation without the benefit of divine grace, should not obscure the role that the idea of the *collective* plays in Jung's theory of the psyche. The theory of the collective unconscious, and the related concept of commonly inherited archetypes, is perhaps one of the most characteristic of Jung's teachings, one which set him most clearly apart, not only from Freud but from the mainstream of twentieth-century psychological thinking. In constructing this theory during the period following his estrangement from Freud he was clearly encouraged and influenced by a similar idea in Indian philosophy, namely *karma*, and its related idea of rebirth. *Karma*, the belief that we each create our lives through our actions, and subsequently must accept and address the consequences of these actions, implies, according to Jung, 'the succession of birth and death . . . viewed as an endless continuity, as an eternal wheel rolling on for ever without a goal' (MDR: 348). Where the West has viewed each human life as essentially unique – a one-off occurrence – the East has typically viewed the individual life as only a transient phase in the eternal flow of life, and the individual soul as caught in the endless cycle of rebirth. There is no clear evidence of direct influence from *karma* to Jung's notion of archetypes and the collective unconscious, but from various remarks in his writings and lectures in the 1920s and 1930s it is evident that he found this Indian notion congenial and allowed it to inter-penetrate his own thinking; as Coward puts it: '[archetype] was an idea that evolved slowly in his mind, interacting constantly with the Indian notion of *karma*' (1985: 97). It certainly gave him confidence in his belief that the human mind must be under- stood in much wider terms than those commonly accepted in the West, and that individual consciousness is shaped by factors that are historically wider and deeper than those which occur during the lifetime of the individual.

At the same time it is important to draw attention to the differences between *karma* and archetypal theory. As Jung noted, the former 'implies a sort of psychic theory of heredity based on the hypothesis of reincarnation' (CW11.845), and this he found unacceptable. The archetypes, according to Jung, are not the product of individual inheritance, but are 'universal dispositions of the mind . . . [a] psychic structure which is inherited and which necessarily gives a certain form and direction to *all* experience' (CW11.845, my emphasis). In other words, where the Indian view implies that a person inherits the *karma* of an *individual* predecessor, Jung believed that the psychic attributes we inherit in the shape of archetypes are the *collective* property of mankind in general, and that, hence, 'there is no inheritance of individual prenatal, or pre-uterine, memories' (CW11.846). Furthermore, the idea of rebirth carried with it certain metaphysical assumptions implying 'an hypothesis of the supratemporality of the soul' (CW11.845), and as such he deemed it to fall outside his competence as a scientist. 'Neither our scientific knowledge nor our reason can keep in step with this idea', he claimed, and any proof concerning the pre- or post-natal existence of the soul 'would be just as impossible as the proof of God', from which he concluded that 'we may cautiously accept the idea of karma only if we under- stand it as psychic heredity in the very widest sense of the word', that is to say as psychic dispositions of the most general sort (CW11.845).

Jung's attitude in this matter typifies his whole approach to Indian thought, for he remained consistently sceptical concerning the metaphysical assumptions underlying these 'cosmogonic myths', treating them always as allegories for psychological processes. Nevertheless, it is clear that the ideas of yoga provided nutrients that had an important effect on the growth of his own concepts, and while it is impossible to determine the exact degree of influence that Indian thought played in the development of the theoretical basis of analytical psycho- logy, there can be no doubt that they were deeply implicated in the creative process in which Jung was engaged at that time.

Jung's interest in yoga can be placed in a broader context than that of analytical psychology, however. He frequently noted the extraordinary explosion of interest in yoga in recent times, and diagnosed this as a symptom of spiritual sickness, drawing a comparison between this phenomenon and the movement of religious syncretism that took place in the Hellenic world in the third and fourth centuries CE, when ideas from the East had also played a part in a Gnostic religious movement (see CW11.861). The decline of religion in the modern world and the widespread loss of traditional religious belief had led, as we described earlier, to a spiritual vacuum into which all kinds of exotic Eastern religions flooded. The enormous growth of technical and military power has given the modern European and American an unprecedented capacity to control and manipulate nature, yet we have little understanding of ourselves, of the persons who wield this power. It is not greater understanding of nature that we now need, but an improved understanding of ourselves.

In the light of this it is hardly surprising that the West has shown a great interest in the theory and practice of yoga. As Jung saw it, yoga represented first and foremost a discipline of self-discovery and self-development, a path of spiritual growth which involves the disciplining of the instinctual forces of the psyche and a penetration into the unconscious mind. As such it offers a necessary counter-balance to the extraverted tendencies of the West, a way of exploring and activating regions of the psyche which, in the West, have been ignored or even suppressed. Jung emphasised this point by drawing attention to what he saw as a sharp antithesis between the psychological attitudes of the East and the West. While in the West we tend to think of the spiritual world as involving an *upward* movement, as appropriately symbolised in the heaven-aspiring steeples of Gothic churches, the Indian, on the other hand, thinks in terms of a *downward* movement, of self-immersion or sinking in meditation, as symbolised by the location of altars beneath ground level (see CW11.911). The West, he insisted,

> is always seeking uplift, but the East seeks a sinking or deepening. Outer reality, with its bodiliness and weight, appears to make a much stronger and sharper impression on the European than it does on the Indian. Therefore the European seeks to raise himself above this world, while the Indian likes to turn back into the maternal depths of Nature.
>
> (CW11.936)

What the European needs most urgently is to achieve a greater balance between these two movements, not by negating the upward tendency, but by developing the capacity to move downwards, to explore the unconscious, and thereby to rediscover our lost psychological roots. For all the great Western achievements in controlling nature, we have by some peculiar irony lost contact with it – in particular, with that aspect of nature which lies within the collective unconscious. It is true that some methods comparable to those of yoga have been developed in Europe – for example, the Catholic cure of souls, and most especially the *Spiritual Exercises* of St Ignatius Loyola – but these represent only marginal aspects of Christian piety, and indeed, he argued, such methods are largely absent from the Protestant tradition.

We are tempted, therefore, in our spiritual hunger, to seek out and imitate the ways of the East. This, Jung believed, would be a grave mistake. We shall discuss later his reservations about adopting the ideas and methods of the East in general, but here we need to note that for him yoga, insofar as it represented an identification of the conscious mind with the unconscious, was especially dangerous for the European. 'I wish particularly to warn against the oft-attempted imitation of Indian practices and sentiments. As a rule nothing comes of it except an artificial stultification of our Western intelligence' (CW11.933). The negation of the conscious mind, which has been so carefully developed and refined in the Western tradition, can lead to a psychotic state in which individuals becomes trapped, trance-like, in their own unconscious.

What must be done, then, is to develop our own yoga, based on our own traditions, created with our own tools. But to do this we need to learn from the East. It is true that psychoanalysis constitutes the first glimmerings of a modern Western form of yoga, but compared with the ancient techniques of the Orient it was born only yesterday. Jung's dialogue with yoga was an attempt, therefore, to illuminate and amplify his own psychological insights by placing them within the context of this much older tradition. This dialogue was especially revealing in the case of Tantric (or Kundalini) yoga.

TANTRIC YOGA

In the autumn of 1932 the indologist J.W. Hauer gave a seminar on the Tantric *chakra* system to Jung and his pupils in Zürich. The ideas, which were already familiar to Jung through his reading of J.G. Woodroffe's *The Serpent Power*, were received with great interest by his pupils, but also with a considerable measure of confusion. Barbara Hannah, who was present, reports that 'we all got terribly out of ourselves and confused', and as a consequence Jung devoted his next three lectures to a psychological commentary on Hauer's exposition which, as she put it, 'got us back into ourselves' (Hannah, 1976: 206).

Tantric yoga is a system of esoteric practice for the attainment of spiritual perfection which has common strands in both Hindu and *Mahāyāna* Buddhist traditions. Its methods are unconventional, sometimes making use of ritualised sexual intercourse in the quest for enlightenment, though Jung does not enter into this aspect of Tantra. It lays little stress on religious or philosophical theories and is mostly concerned with meditation techniques whose aim is the purification of the body-mind through the control of physiological and psychological processes. These techniques focus on the female energy or force within the body, Shakti, also called *kundalinī* or serpent power. *Kundalinī* is encouraged to rise through a series of centres in the body, known as *chakras*, the aim being to activate its energy by various yoga techniques, and to raise it from the lowest to the highest *chakra*, there to be united with Shiva, the male principle, a union which brings about a state of supreme bliss beyond all dualities. In Jung's own words:

> a feminine creative force in the shape of a serpent, named *kundalinī*, rises up from the perineal centre, where she has been sleeping, and ascends through the *chakras*, thereby activating them and constellating their symbols. This 'Serpent Power' is personified as the *Mahādevishakti*, the goddess who brings everything into existence by means of *māyā*, the building material of reality.
>
> (CW 16.561)

The *chakras*, though localised in the body, are not strictly physical in nature, and are elements within a system known as the subtle body. Jung describes the system as follows:

> there are seven centres, called *chakras* or *padmas* (lotuses), which have fairly definite localizations in the body. They are, as it were, psychic localizations, and the higher ones correspond to the historical localizations of consciousness. The nethermost *chakra*, called *mūlādhāra*, is the perineal lotus and corrresponds to the cloacal zone in Freud's sexual theory. This centre, like all the others, is represented in the shape of a flower, with a circle in the middle, and has attributes which express in symbols the psychic qualities of that particular localization . . . . The next *chakra*, called *svādhisthāna*, is localized near the bladder and represents the sexual centre. Its main symbol is water or sea, and subsidiary symbols are the sickle moon as the feminine principle, and a devouring water monster called *makara*, which corresponds to the biblical and cabalistic Leviathan. . . . The third centre, called *manipūra*, corresponds to the solar plexus. . . . This third *chakra* is the emotional centre, and is the earliest known localization of consciousness. . . . The fourth *chakra*, called *anāhata*, is situated in the region of the heart and the diaphragm. In Homer the diaphragm . . . was the seat of feeling and thinking. The fifth and sixth, called *vishuddha* and *ājnā*, are situated respectively in the throat and between the eyebrows. The seventh, *sahasrāra*, is at the top of the skull.
>
> (CW 16.560)

The characteristics of Tantra which attracted Jung, and which drew him into a psychological dialogue with it, can be summed up in the following points. First, a dynamic, developmental view of the personality, with a strong teleological tendency towards self-fulfilment; thus, the *chakras* are not only centres of growth, but can be viewed as stages of development, symbolised by the ascent of the *kundalinī*. Secondly, a holistic outlook which draws no absolute distinction between psychic and somatic factors; thus the psyche is not a disembodied entity but is mapped onto the body's inner topography. Thirdly, a positive, life-affirming view of the body, the passions, and the shadowy regions of the psyche;

111

as Coward puts it: 'The Tantric approach was world-affirmative', and triumphs, not through the denial of the passions, but 'by way of the passions themselves' (1985: 110); similarly, the indologist Heinrich Zimmer referred to the 'essential principle of the Tantric idea that man, in general, must rise through and by means of nature, not by the rejection of nature' (quoted in Coward, 1985: 111). And fourthly, a symbolic system which employs complex images rather than words to express psychic processes, and which encourages us to view the psyche as a meaningful structure.

The holistic outlook was especially important for Jung. He viewed the self, as we indicated above, not as some kind of pontifical disembodied ego ruling over the personality like a monarch, but rather as the total personality in which the ego was an integral, but not a privileged, factor. He did not view the ego as a sovereign legislator to the personality, but rather as facilitating the emergence of the unconscious into consciousness. In 1916 he named this process the 'transcendent function'. He thought of it as a kind of dialogue, carried on in images rather than words, in which conscious and unconscious elements overcome their mutual indifference or even hostility and enter into partnership. It involved getting in touch with, respecting, and giving expression to impulses and images that arise from the unconscious, and a harmonising of the psyche by overcoming the oppositional effects of an over-evaluation of the conscious ego. This is essentially the process of individuation, and Kundalini appeared to Jung to 'offer a perfect analogy' for the process of psychological growth whereby 'what is unconscious becomes conscious in the form of a living process of growth' (CW13.35).

It was the elaboration of this analogy that was at the centre of Jung's hermeneutical dialogue with Tantra. As we saw in our discussion of Gadamer, the hermeneutical method involves more than the interpretation of a difficult text, but in addition demands an awareness of context surrounding and assumptions underlying the process. Jung makes this approach explicit at a number of points in his lectures, remarking, for example, that 'We can only understand [the Tantric] picture of the world in as much as we try to understand it in our own terms. Therefore I make the attempt to approach it from a psychological point of view' (Jung, 1975: 13). This meant that Jung had nothing to say about the metaphysical assumptions underlying the Tantric yoga system, he offered no discussion of the ontological status of the *chakras* or of the channels that supposedly connected them together, but as in all his writings about esoteric systems of thought he treated them in purely symbolic terms. What concerned him was not whether there 'really' is a system of energy centres within the body, but rather how we could understand and make sense, and perhaps make use, of these ideas in terms of our modern Western assumptions.

The *chakras* themselves, accordingly, are treated in purely symbolic terms. The word '*chakra*' literally means a circle, and can be envisaged as a centre of psychic energy, 'a living *Gestalt*', located in seven specific parts of the body. Each represents what Jung describes as 'a whole world', encompassing a constellation of related psychic qualities, amounting to what he elsewhere calls a fragmentary personality or personality complex (see CW3.77ff). They act as symbols of 'highly complex psychic facts . . . they represent a real effort to give us a symbolic theory of the psyche' (Jung, 1976: 21). Such symbols are necessary, Jung believed, because 'The psyche is something highly complicated, so vast in extent, so rich in elements unknown to us . . . that we always turn to [them] in order to try to represent what we know about' (*ibid.*). Jung maintained a specific view with regard to the nature and function of symbols in general. He saw them not as signs pointing to identifiable and circumscribable signifiers, but rather as 'an intuitive idea that cannot be formulated in any other or better way' (CW15.105), as something whose 'pregnant language cries out to us that they mean more than they say' (CW15.119). Furthermore, in Jung's thought they have more than a merely theoretical intent, for they have a role as an essential part of the functioning of the psyche, and it is this feature of the Tantric system that makes it so relevant to modern life where symbols are often treated in a purely scientific way. The following passage sums up Jung's viewpoint on this:

> The symbols of the *chakras*, then, afford us a standpoint that extends beyond the conscious. They are intuitions about the psyche as a whole, about its various conditions and possibilities. They symbolize the psyche from a cosmic standpoint.
>
> (Jung, 1976: 27)

The Kundalini *chakras*, then, by symbolising and linking together dynamically the various components and tendencies of the psyche can enable us to gain some understanding of the psyche as a whole.

Following these general considerations we can now examine how Jung engages with the individual *chakras* in turn. The lowest *chakra*, the *mūlādhāra*, located at the perineum, the lowest part of the trunk, symbolises the earth on which we rest and out of which we arise. It is the region associated with instincts and impulses, and is 'a dark and unconscious place' (Jung, 1975: 8–9), an area of life which we are inclined to forget, or even actively to repress. Here, Jung surmises, 'the self is asleep', for at the level of instinct the psyche acts in an unconscious and automatic way, as yet unguided by the active participation of consciousness. It represents, therefore, the ordinary everyday world, the world of unselfconscious routine, from which we need to be awakened if we are to become developed human beings.

The awakening occurs at, and is symbolised by, the next *chakra*, the *svādhisthāna chakra*, located at the sexual centre. While earth is the element associated with *mūlādhāra*, *svādhisthāna* is the place of water, and hence symbolises birth, and the ritualism of initiation and rebirth, as in baptism. In order to rise to the level of self-consciousness we need first to descend into the water of the unconscious. In the symbolism of this chakra we can observe in symbolic form the world-wide idea of baptism by water with its dangers of being drowned or devoured. . . . Today, instead of the sea or the leviathan, it is [psychological analysis] which is equally dangerous. One goes under the water, makes the acquaintance of the leviathan there, and that is either the source of regeneration or destruction.

(Jung, 1975: 11)

In *svādhisthāna*, then, is the arousing of the sleeping serpent, the first step towards individuation with all its expectations and dangers, and it is for this reason, as Coward points out, that 'Both Kundalini and Jung stress the dangers involved in this psychic awakening and thus the need for careful guidance' (1985: 117).

The *manipūra chakra*, situated in the belly, is symbolised by fire. Here, grumbling in the lower depths, and emerging into consciousness, we find the seat of the passions, an almost divine power, both creative and destructive. Following on from the baptism and rebirth of *svādhisthāna*, this centre concentrates within itself the emerging force of human feeling and emotion, full of dangers, yet also full of promise. This awesome power suggests the replacement of pleasure by power and domination, and perhaps for this reason *manipūra* is also 'the centre of the identification with God, where one becomes part of the divine substance' (Jung, 1975: 23). Although it is common to identify the emotions with the belly, the use of Tantric symbolism may be important for Westerners in helping them to avoid a too-easy identification of thinking with the head, and of the common separation of the head from the emotions. This *chakra* helps to remind us of the wholeness of the human person and that, with the emergence of consciousness and of a sense of one's own self, the body taken as a psychosomatic whole cannot be left on one side and ignored.

But it is only in *anāhata*, the next centre, that individuation begins, according to Jung. This *chakra*, located at the level of heart and lungs, is associated with the symbols of air, breath, and wind. Here we find a growing emancipation from the earth and the passions, the appearance of reasoning and thinking, and the emergence of the self. While *manipūra* is still associated with the downward movement of matter, *anāhata* is associated with the upward thrust of air. In *anahata* 'a new thing comes up, the possibility of lifting yourself above the emotional happenings and looking at them' (Jung, 1975: 30), and this means nothing less than the discovery of the self. But there are dangers here too, for though this chakra is associated with love and service towards others, it also carries with it the possibility of self-aggrandisement, for here 'you are likely to get [psychological] inflation', warned Jung, in which case 'you would then be an individualist [who is] a man who did not succeed in individuating' (p. 31). Once again, as in *manipūra*, the path of personal development is portrayed by Jung, not as rosy path towards sweetness and light, but as a hazardous upward climb with all its accompanying dangers and setbacks.

The world of the *vishuddha chakra*, located at the throat and symbolised by ether, is the world of subjective experience, of abstract thought, and mental

114

concepts. It means 'a full recognition of the psychical essences of substances as the fundamental essences of the world, and not by virtue of speculation but by virtue of fact, as experience' (Jung, 1976: 7). Coward suggests that it is 'the world of the psychologist, like Jung, who has come to know the reality of such psychic entities as ego, archetypes and self, not from someone else, but in his own experience' (1985: 121). It represents, then, a form of self-knowledge which is no longer bound up with the selfish needs of the ego, but has reached the more impersonal and impartial plane of the self. Perhaps, too, it suggests the idea, central to much of Jung's thinking, that the world can only be understood in the final analysis in psychic terms, summed up in such remarks as 'Existence is only real when it is conscious to somebody' (CW11.575).

There remain the *ājnā* and the *sahasrāra chakras*, situated between the eyebrows and at the top of the skull respectively. Jung has little to say about these. In *ājnā* we reach the point where 'the psyche gets wings . . . where you know you are nothing but psyche', and where 'the ego disappears completely' (Jung, 1976: 17). At the highest level of *sahasrāra*, we find ourselves 'beyond possible experience', where all dualities have disappeared and where the psyche has been absorbed into the one – *Brahman*. Clearly Jung believed that at these levels the Tantric system had nothing to say to the West. The notion of the loss of the individual self through its absorption into a higher unity, expressed in the Hindu doctrine of the identity of *Ātman* and *Brahman*, and summed up in the phrase 'thou art that', could not, if taken literally, be made sense of in terms of the Western conceptual framework. He maintained, with admirable consistency, that only that which is capable of being experienced can enter into our understanding of the world, and since the absorption of the self meant the virtual disappearance of the experiencing subject, then strictly speaking the state of total oneness cannot be experienced or understood. Indeed, not only is there nothing here to which the Western mind can relate, but any attempt to do so might carry with it the danger of the total identification of the subject with the unconscious. This is a matter to which we shall return in the chapter on 'Reservations and Qualifications'.

The complete cycle of the *chakras* – though with reservations concerning the final two – represents, therefore, the cycle of human psychological growth, 'The Seven Ages of Man'. The upward spiralling of the *kundalinī* serpent symbolises 'the urge of realization [which] naturally pushes man on to be himself' (Jung, 1975: 2). This is not for Jung just some blind force of nature at work, but rather the full realisation of the self, its individuation; it is that which alone renders life in any way meaningful. Many sadly fail to get very far along this path; there are plenty of people who, as he put it, 'are not yet born; they seem to be all here, but as a matter of fact they are not yet born; they are only in the world on parole' (Jung, 1975: 21). The Tantric path, with its vivid symbolism, helps us in the West, whose religious and metaphysical symbols have atrophied, to realise that 'The ultimate aim and strongest desire of all mankind is to develop the fullness of life which is called personality' (CW17.284).

115

It is important to emphasise here the notion of the 'fullness of personality'. In the Western religious and philosophical traditions one sometimes gets the impression that as one climbs the spiritual ladder, the lower rungs, and especially those associated with the body and the passions, are discarded as no longer of use, indeed as impediments to further development. This is not the way Jung saw it. The process of growth is something which, while transcending the past, absorbs, and carries it higher. The lower *chakras* are not simply rungs on a ladder, to be forgotten as soon as climbed beyond, but rather integral elements within the whole psyche at whatever stage; 'What you have arrived at', he insists, 'is never lost' (Jung, 1976: 18). This may be likened to Hegel's idea of sublimation where in the dialectic the initial stage is cancelled yet preserved and carried through, transformed, into the higher stages.

But despite these close parallels between the Tantric path and the path of individuation, Jung's dialogue with Kundalini reveals differences, and underlines his determination to translate its ideas into terms which harmonise with those of Western consciousness. We have already noted his reservations about the final two *chakras*. There is also a sense in which he turned the *chakra* system on its head in order to render it accessible to the Western psyche. Kundalini offers a path of enlightenment which begins deep down in the unconscious and rises up and beyond this into a state of super-consciousness in which the ego attains unity with the universal self. Jung, by contrast, 'starts on the surface of "unaware ego-consciousness" and then dives into the unconscious as the process of indivi-duation, of self-discovery, begins' (Coward, 1985: 116). 'In the East', Jung insists, 'the unconscious is above, while with us it is below' and hence, insofar as we try to understand it in our own terms, it is necessary for the Westerner to reverse the whole process (Jung, 1975: 12–13). This means that effectively Jung viewed the ascent towards the higher *chakras* as a path, not towards super-consciousness, but rather towards a greater integration with the unconscious.

At first sight this may appear to conflict with Jung's philosophical doubts about the logical possibility of identifying the ego with a higher self; might it not seem that by identifying the upward path as a move in the direction of the unconscious, he views it as tending towards the ultimate elimination of the conscious ego? His point here, however, appears to be not that the exploration of the unconscious leads towards the abandonment of the conscious ego, but rather that in its development the self embraces and integrates the unconscious. He describes this procedure elsewhere as the 'transcendent function' in which, as we noted earlier, the higher and lower constituents of the self come into dialogue, and thence into harmony, with each other. This involves what he called the 'lowering of the threshold' of consciousness to permit hitherto unconscious constituents to come into play and to be consciously integrated within the personality as a whole – i.e. the 'self'. The danger in Kundalini for the Westerner, therefore, is that it encourages the total immersion in the unconscious state, and hence the ultimate dissolution of individual consciousness in a cosmic *partici-pation mystique*; the trance-like state which Jung imagined to be the final goal of yoga can only lead to a loss of that function which is characteristic of the Western psyche, namely its rational consciousness, and to 'an artificial stultification of our Western intelligence' (CW11.933). In 1942 he wrote to a correspondent that '[in] the course of these [yoga] concentration exercises, the individual gets into a dream state, or autohypnotic condition, which removes him from the world and its illusions', and hence, since 'the goal of yoga is the void of deep sleep, yoga can never be the final truth for the occidental world' (*Letters I*, 1942: 311).

Thus, in spite of emphasis on the need for psychic balance, and hence on the need of the West to develop a more introverted disposition, Jung is wary of the possibility that Westerners, in adopting the methods of yoga, will dive headlong and unprotected into the unconscious, and thereby lose their grip, not only on rational consciousness, but on the objective world as well. He warns that '[if] a European tries to banish all thought of the outer world and to empty his mind of everything outside, he immediately becomes the prey of his own subjective fantasies' (CW11.939). This points once again to his belief in the wide differences between the two cultures. The Indian religious attitude, he insisted, 'is the diametric opposite of the Christian, since the Christian principle of love is extraverted and positively demands an object. The Indian principle makes for riches of knowledge, the Christian for fullness of works' (CW6.191).

What, in the end, then, can we learn from Kundalini yoga? *Not* the attainment of *Brahman*, the supreme state of bliss in which all discriminations between the self and the All have been dissolved; this would involve not a dialogue but a capitulation to the East's allures. In any case, according to Jung, this state of final perfection is not one that can be attained by the human psyche; opposites cannot be finally eliminated, the negative cannot ultimately be filtered out leaving the positive and enlightened principle in sole and exclusive command. The Tantric method, and the principles underlying it, certainly teach us that the psyche must be treated as an organic whole, rather than as a set of discrete forces, but this should not lead us to conceive it as an undifferentiated unity in which all opposition and discrimination has been eliminated – 'the dark night in which all cows are black', as Hegel ironically expressed the metaphysical monism of Schelling. What *can* be learned is that a path of enlightenment, negotiating on its way the various centres of the psychic organism, is available to those who seek it. Even though the final identification of $\bar{A}tman$ with *Brahman*, the universal Ground of being, is a conception inescapably foreign to the European mind, there remains the way itself, the redemptory exercise by means of which the human being seeks to realise selfhood.

To do this we need to develop our own Western yoga. There are, in fact, remarkable agreements, Jung believed, between the insights of yoga and the results of modern psychological research, and it is precisely upon these foundations that a new form of Western yoga might conceivably be built. 'True to our European bias', he claimed,

'we have evolved a medical psychology dealing specifically with the *kleshas* [i.e. the shadow side, the impediments to spiritual growth]. We call

117

it the 'psychology of the unconscious'. The movement inaugurated by Freud recognized the importance of the human shadow-side and its influence on consciousness.

(CW11.941)

It is on this foundation, which in turn rests on the whole Western cultural tradition, that a Western yoga might be constructed.

7

BUDDHISM

Jung's personal attachment to Eastern thought is most conspicuous in the case of Buddhism. From the days of the early development of his psychology right up to the time of his death the image and the ideas of Gautama Buddha and the traditions that stem from him were recurrent preoccupations. Furthermore, the warnings he frequently expressed concerning the adoption in the West of Eastern – especially yogic – practices are far more muted in the case of Buddhism, and late in life he felt confident enough to recommend its teachings as 'ways and means of disciplining the inner psychic life' (CW18.1577) without his usual reservations.

As I pointed out in an earlier chapter, Jung grew up in a cultural climate which was becoming increasingly open to ideas from the East, especially those of Buddhism which had, since its emergence into European consciousness in the middle years of the nineteenth century, succeeded in capturing the imagination of many European and American intellectuals. Pre-eminent among the philosophers drawn to Buddhism in the nineteenth century were Schopenhauer and Nietzsche, both of whom played a crucial role in the shaping of Jung's intellectual outlook. Each of these philosophers in his own unique way had sought a dialogue with the East, Schopenhauer as a way of amplifying his notion of the world as endless striving and suffering from which we need to seek some form of non-transcendent salvation, Nietzsche in articulating his search for a mode of authentic self-awareness. Jung's own psychological reflections on Buddhism were carried to much greater depths, however, and have provided a paradigm of inter-cultural cross-fertilisation that has an important place in the extraordinary development of interaction between the West and Buddhism in recent decades.

GENERAL APPROACH

Once again the central focus of attention is on the *self*. In his autobiography Jung described in vivid prose a powerful experience he underwent when visiting the stupas of Sanchi, where Buddha preached his 'fire sermon'. Overwhelmed by the

119

mood of the place, a mood assisted by a group of Japanese pilgrims chanting and processing round the stupa, he came to a new realisation of the essential nature of Buddhism. At that moment, as he recalled, he

> grasped the life of the Buddha as the reality of the self which had broken through and laid claim to a personal life. For Buddha, the self stands above all gods, an *unus mundus* which represents the essence of human existence and of the world as a whole. . . . Buddha saw and grasped the cosmogonic dignity of human consciousness; for that reason he saw clearly that if a man succeeded in extinguishing this light, the world would sink into nothingness. Schopenhauer's great achievement lay in his also recognising this, or in rediscovering it independently.

(MDR: 309)

Despite the oft-affirmed primacy of his attachment to Christianity, Jung saw in the Buddha an embodiment of the archetype of the self that was at once more intelligible and more complete than that of Christ, for while the humanity of the latter was confused by association with the transcendent Godhead, in the case of Buddha, who had married and who lived a full life-span, the image of a fully developed human person was more conspicuous. He became, Jung insisted, 'the image of the development of the self . . . a model for men to imitate', a guarantee that 'every human being could become an illuminate' (MDR: 309–10).

Jung's positive assessment of Buddhism becomes all the more clear if set in an historical context, for in the nineteenth century, largely as a result of the influence of Schopenhauer, Buddhism had acquired the reputation of being a somewhat negative, even a nihilistic, philosophy. Its appeal to the rationally minded of that epoch lay in the belief that it postulated no transcendent deity, that it advocated a sublime but inner-worldly ethic, and that its ultimate aim was the final dissolution of the individual consciousness in the eternal night of *nirvāna*.[1] Jung's views on this matter are representative of, and in some respects foreshadowed, the revolution that has taken place in Buddhist studies in the twentieth century and which has articulated a more positive and optimistic interpretation of its teachings, emphasising the way of healing and of life-enhancement. For Jung the Buddha's message was essentially about *self-healing*, in both senses of this ambiguous phrase: first, in the sense that it is concerned with the healing *of* the self, the attempt, as J. Marvin Spiegelman puts it, 'which aims at the transformation of the ego in order to help an individual to overcome the "dis-ease" of life brought about by impermanence' (Spiegelman and Miyuki, 1985: 172); and secondly, in the sense that it is concerned with the healing *by* the self – that is to say, not through the medium of an external agency, but through the agency of the autonomous individual. In other words, what he found was a method which was built on the self's capacity and urge to realise itself through its own efforts to seek individuation.

What led Jung to Buddhism, then, was not philosophy or comparative religion but primarily his professional interest as a doctor whose central concern was the treatment of psychic suffering. '[As] a doctor', he wrote towards the end of his life, 'I acknowledge the immense help and stimulation I have received from the Buddhist teachings' (CW18.1580). Buddha came to represent for him a teacher whose fundamental concern was not with theoretical matters but rather with the alleviation of pain and distress. What the study of Buddhist literature enabled him to do, he claimed, was 'to observe suffering objectively and to take a universal view of its causes', and to confirm his belief in the possibility of extricating human consciousness from what he called 'the entanglements of emotion and illusion' (CW18.1575). Once again his approach was shaped by his belief that in the West the traditional sources of psychic healing were drying up due the fact that 'Christian ritual has lost its meaning [and] the authority of religious ideas has collapsed' (CW18.1577). The discourses of the Buddha, by contrast, offer 'a helpful training . . . thus remedying an often regrettable defect in the various brands of Christianity' (CW18.1577).

A further appeal of Buddhism lay in its emphasis on *experience*. Christianity, in its traditional orthodox mode, has emphasised reliance on the authority of the Church and of scripture, and ultimately on faith in the saving power of Christ. Buddhism, by contrast, teaches a path which, in the final analysis, one must find and tread for oneself. True, there is the element of faith in the Buddha's teachings, but it is a matter, not of following these teachings slavishly, but of trying them out, as it were, for oneself. What makes emancipation from suffering possible, then, is not the saving power of another, not the acceptance of doctrine nor the pursuit of metaphysical speculation, not ritual observance, but rather the direct experience of the individual seeker. For this reason Buddhism has sometimes been designated, perhaps mis-leadingly, a form of empiricism, even a science. Jung recognised in this a clear parallel to his own approach. He frequently claimed that his own psychological work was based on 'empirical' facts, on direct personal experience, rather than on theory. Likewise the tendency of the psyche towards self-realisation and individuation constituted for Jung a form of *gnosis*, a direct experience of the inner world of the archetypes and an inner pathway of self-discovery.

Jung drew attention, however, to one important difference between the two ways of self-healing. While acknowledging and identifying with the Buddhist path towards enlightenment, and recognising in this a direct parallel with his own concept of individuation, he emphasised the fact that Buddhism held out the possibility of *complete* emancipation and enlightenment – a goal which he himself deemed to be impossible. Moacanin notes that 'Unlike Buddha, Jung does not perceive the possibility of an end to suffering. In his view happiness and suffering represent another pair of opposites, indispensable to life, and one cannot exist without the other' (1986: 85). Jung wrote that

Man has to cope with the problem of suffering. The Oriental wants to get rid of suffering by casting it off. Western man tries to suppress suffering with drugs. But suffering has to be overcome, and the only way to over-come it is to endure it.

(Letters I: 236)

If *nirvāna* means a state of illumination or bliss in which an individual is finally released from suffering, death, and all earthly bonds, an emancipation from the wheel of all arising, subsisting, changing and passing away, then for Jung this is a condition irreconcilable with the condition of being human. Just as he rejected the possibility of a state in which the conscious self is totally absorbed into the all-embracing oneness of *Brahman*, so too he could make no sense of a condition in which the dynamic interplay of psychic principles was superseded by a condition of complete and final psychic equilibrium. Life, according to Jung, is essentially a dialectical movement to-and-fro between opposites and has no final resolution, no Hegelian Absolute in which all opposites are reconciled. While it is true that the psyche *aims* towards the state of perfect equilibrium, it remains a boundary condition, not a realisable state: 'Complete redemption from the sufferings of this world is and must remain an illusion' (CW16.400).

THE TIBETAN BOOK OF THE DEAD

So far we have spoken of Jung's relation to Buddhism in general terms. We must now look in more detail at the dialogues he held with specific traditions and texts. It will be no surprise to readers to learn that Jung offered no systematic account of Buddhism. He clearly had an overall understanding of the varieties of Buddhist belief and practice in the various regions of Asia where it has developed, and recognised the distinction between *Hinayāna* and *Mahāyāna* Buddhism, the two great and in many ways divergent traditions into which Buddhism is divided. He had no understanding of Oriental languages, and his only direct acquaintance with Buddhism was with the *Theravāda* school in Sri Lanka, *Theravāda* being the only surviving school of the *Hinayāna*. In fact, however, he had very little to say about the theory or practice of the *Theravāda* school, a form of Buddhism which regards itself as closest to the original form of Buddhism, and which emphasises the liberation of the individual through the individual's own efforts. It is true that its emphasis on individual enlightenment is, as we have seen, analogous to his own psychological concept of individuation, but it is to the *Mahāyāna* tradition, especially the Tibetan Tantric and the Japanese Zen traditions, that he paid most attention.

Before discussing Jung's relationship with each of these in turn, it will be useful to say something about the *Mahāyāna* (the 'Great Vehicle') in general, and about the Tantric Buddhism characteristic of Tibet in particular. While the *Hinayāna* (the 'Small Vehicle') teaches that the world is to be renounced because it is a world of pain and sorrow, *Mahāyāna* teaches that this pain and sorrow arises from the illusory nature of our understanding. Its teachings, therefore, centre on the need to awaken from the dream-state. The path to this awakening leads to the understanding that all things are the offspring of mind, and that the true and universal essence of mind lies, like a dust-free mirror, at the basis of all phenomena. This essence, called the Buddha-nature, is present in all beings, which means that all beings can seek liberation from illusion, and hence from suffering, by cleansing the mirror-mind of its illusion-making patina. A feeling of compassion for all sentient beings pervades the *Mahāyāna* tradition. This means that the 'merits' attained by one being are available for all, and entails the *Bodhisattva* ideal according to which an individual will forgo the full liberation of *nirvāna* in order to assist in the salvation of others. Tibetan Buddhism, or Lamaism, is part of the *Mahāyāna* and was introduced from India in the seventh century CE. Inspired by the Tantric traditions of India, it places great emphasis on the methods of spiritual transformation. Perhaps most important in relation to Jung is the so-called 'esoteric' Buddhism, a 'secret' path taught only to initiates under the strict guidance of a lama, and whose methods include the use of *mandalas* (ritual diagrams) and *mantras* (ritual sounds). This path involves highly sophisticated mental disciplines, making use of techniques of visualisation in which the images of deities and *Bodhisattvas* are summoned before the mind's eye and contemplated in physical and symbolic depth.

In recent years the West has undergone a rapid induction into the Buddhism of Tibet. In many ways this represents the last major wave of Eastern philosophy to sweep over Western consciousness. Following its suppression by the Chinese communists and the exiling of the lamas, including of course the Dalai Lama, after the Lhasa Uprising in 1959, Tibetan Buddhism has become widely known in the West. Tibetan Buddhist centres have been established in many parts of Europe and America and have attracted widespread interest and following. Jung first became acquainted with this particular school in the inter-war years when Tibet was still a 'Forbidden Land' from which Westerners were strictly excluded, and its philosophical systems known only by tenuous and mostly unreliable repute.[2] A major step towards the opening up of the religious culture of Tibet occurred in 1927 with the publication of *The Tibetan Book of the Dead* by the American scholar W.Y. Evans-Wentz. In his Preface to the first edition, Evans-Wentz speaks of the need to 'reproduce Oriental ideas in a form which would be intelligible to the European mind', and in his commentary makes frequent reference to the many Occidental parallels with the 'various mystic or occult doctrines current in the Orient' (1960: xix). He ends with the hope that his English-language edition will serve 'as one more spiritual strand in an un-breakable bond of good will and universal peace, binding East and West together in mutual respect and understanding, and in love such as overleaps every barrier of creed, caste and race' (p. xxi).

The book itself, supported by these lofty sentiments, clearly had a major impact on Jung who, it will be recalled, was at about the same time being initiated into the Chinese alchemical secrets of *The Golden Flower*. In his own words:

'The Tibetan Book of the Dead' caused a considerable stir in English-speaking countries at the time of its first appearance in 1927. . . . For years, ever since it was first published, the *Bardo Thödol* has been my constant companion, and to it I owe not only many stimulating ideas and discoveries, but also many fundamental insights. . . . Its philosophy contains the quintessence of Buddhist psychological criticism; and, as such, one can truly say that it is of an unexampled sublimity.

(CW11.833)

He agreed to write a 'Psychological Commentary' for the German edition of 1935, an act of considerable professional courage at a time when he had barely established his own reputation as a psychologist independently of Freud. His approach to this task lay along the path of dialogue, similar to the kind we have already observed in the case of the two Chinese texts. Thus, impelled no doubt by the inspiration of Evans-Wentz, the stated aim of his Commentary was 'to make the magnificent world of ideas and the problems contained in this treatise a little more intelligible to the Western mind', believing that those who read it would 'reap a rich reward' (CW11.832).

A first glance at the text suggests that such a 'rich reward' is highly improbable. The book is essentially a book of instruction for the dead and the dying, and a guide for the soul of the departed in its passage of forty-nine days from death to rebirth. Its purpose is first to prepare the dying on how to approach the coming journey, thereby providing religious solace and comfort for the last moments. Then the text offers to guide the soul of the dead through the various stages of the coming journey, and anticipates in some detail the experiences likely to be met with on each stage of this journey. This involves confrontations with various spirits and deities, both terrifying and benign, spirits such as the Tormenting Furies who pursue the soul with tornados, snow, rain and terrifying hailstorms and whirlwinds, or the Divine Father-Mother who surrounds the soul with protecting rays of light. And finally it outlines the process whereby the soul is reborn into a new existence. The whole process is based on the continuous operation of *karma* in which the new life is generated naturally and necessarily from the old.

How is it possible to make sense of this in the context of a Western culture where not only is the idea of rebirth totally alien to its religious and philosophical traditions, but death itself is avoided and ignored as far as possible? As Evans-Wentz points out, 'in the Occident . . . the Art of Dying is little known and rarely practiced' (1960: xv), the only exception, according to Jung, being the Catholic ritual of the Mass for the Dead. Nevertheless, the very strangeness of this 'useless book', as Jung ironically describes it, can perhaps confront us with the inadequacies of our own civilisation. It may teach us, not only to confront death as an inescapable and necessary part of life, but also to re-examine the nature and scope of the human mind itself.

In the first place it confronts us once again with the central importance of the psyche. It demands what Jung called a 'great reversal of standpoint' in which we 'see the world as "given" by the very nature of the psyche' (CW11.841). Jung saw the Tibetan text as presenting us with a conception of the mind in which, by contrast with the typically Western view, the psyche is taken to be the fundamental datum of experience, the material world being in a sense a projection of it. *The Tibetan Book*

124

of the Dead, while on the surface a set of instructions for the dying, can be seen at a much deeper level to represent an 'insight into the secrets of the human psyche' (CW11.833), a book whose metaphysical statements are, Jung insisted, 'statements of the psyche, and are therefore psychological' (CW11.835).

This can be seen at several levels. In the first place the visions attributed to the dead soul are to be treated in effect as projections of the mind of the dead person, not as 'real' entities. The text itself, according to Evans-Wentz, suggests that the visions are purely illusory, arising from the previous incarnate existence (1960: 35). As we shall see shortly, Tibetan Buddhism has developed highly sophisticated methods of visualisation in which all kinds of symbolically complex figures are made use of in the process of psychic transformation, figures which Jung sought to interpret in terms of his theory of archetypes and the collective unconscious:

> the whole book is created out of the archetypal contents of the unconscious. Behind these there lie – and in this our Western reason is quite right – no physical or metaphysical realities, but 'merely' the reality of psychic facts, the data of psychic experience. . . . The world of gods and spirits is truly 'nothing but' the collective unconscious inside me.
>
> (CW11.857)

The question of reincarnation is left on one side by Jung. Here, as elsewhere, he was happy to remain agnostic about metaphysical matters, and to view the account of the figures that appear on the soul's journey as indicative of the deep psychological understanding evident in the Tibetan Buddhist tradition.[3] It points, in Jung's mind, to the fact that they, far more than the West, have understood that the psyche is a microcosmos with a life of its own, as rich and as fertile as the outer cosmos, and hence for Jung the story of an inner world peopled with strange and often terrifying figures made perfect sense from a psychological standpoint.

At another level Jung interpreted the *Bardo* as depicting the journey into the unconscious, an 'initiation process' which opens up the hidden strata of the psyche. This involves reading the text backwards, as it were, for rebirth into a new body represents not the end but the beginning of this exploration. In the West we have tended to remain at the level of adult consciousness, but starting with Freud we have now begun to look back at the realms that lie beneath that of conscious awareness and that were laid down in the repressive operations of the oedipal stage. But Freud did not go far enough, for he halted at the level of infancy. Some, such as Otto Rank, have gone back to the birth trauma, and some have gone back even further to conjectured traces of intra-uterine experiences. To press our investigations still further back is to risk entering the realm of metaphysics and the occult; a literal interpretation of the forty-nine-day journey of the soul would certainly carry this implication. But, as we have noted, Jung was determined to give the *Bardo* a strictly psychological interpretation, following, as he saw it, the spirit of the text itself. What lies beyond conception is that which we inherit from our past. In the East this is called *karma*; for Jung it is 'the inheritance of psychic characteristics such as predisposition to disease, traits of character, special gifts, and so forth'. Just as we have no difficulty in supposing that we inherit universal traits which are common to the human race, so too we may inherit 'universal dispositions of the mind . . . in accordance with which the mind organizes its contents' (CW11.845).

This line of exploration, then, leads to the notion of the collective unconscious, and to the theory of archetypes. This hypothesis involves the inheritance of 'an omnipresent, but differentiated, psychic structure . . . which necessarily gives a certain form and direction to all experience'. The archetypes themselves are 'organs of the pre-rational psyche', but they have no specific content; 'their specific content only appears in the course of an individual's life' (CW11.845). To repeat, for Jung 'the whole book is created out of the archetypal contents of the unconscious', and indeed 'The world of gods and spirits is truly "nothing but" the collective unconscious inside me' (CW11.857). This helps to explain why the experiences of the dead soul represented in the text are archetypal in nature, for they represent, not the individual *karma* of the particular dead person, but a universal, trans-subjective disposition.

The opening up of and surrender to the unconscious realm points to a third psychological level within the *Bardo*. The symbolic passage of the dead soul towards rebirth, which seems to take one beyond the level of everyday conscious, rational life, is in essence the struggle for selfhood and wholeness, Jung surmised. To achieve selfhood means liberation from the confines of the rational ego and the willing descent into the shadowy underworld that lies beneath the conscious surface. It means the integration of archetypal elements, some of them terrifying like the Eight Wrathful Ones, some benign like the Peaceful Deities, the confrontation with which is necessary for the soul's transformation. Jung sees in this transformation a close analogue to the practice of psychotherapy for here, too, what is demanded is first an opening of the psyche to the unconscious with all its unsettling fantasies and urges, and then a capacity to face and ultimately to integrate these elements. This, too, involves a sacrifice of – death of – the authority of the ego, and a willingness to face the dangerous uncertainty of psychic transformation, for 'No one who strives for selfhood (individuation) is spared this dangerous passage' (CW11.849). The journey of the soul from death to rebirth, therefore, represents not just the turn of the cycle of rebirth but the cycle of renewal that characterises the day-to-day spiritual quest.

THE TIBETAN BOOK OF THE GREAT LIBERATION

This spiritual quest is the key to the other Mahāyāna text for which Jung wrote a psychological commentary, *The Tibetan Book of the Great Liberation*, published in the introduction to Evans-Wentz's edition in 1939. The metaphysical implications of this work are less prominent than in the case of the *Bardo*, for it contains no mythical narratives to offend Western scientistic sensibilities, and hence Jung's hermeneutical struggles on this occasion are less strenuous. Nevertheless, the emphasis throughout the text on the fundamental reality of the world of mind is one which, though in agreement with Jung's own way of thinking, still confronts and challenges some of our most cherished assumptions.

The text itself is reputedly the work of Padma-Sambhava, a monk who, after wandering many years as a disciple under various teachers in India, Burma and Nepal, brought Tantric Buddhism to Tibet in about 747 CE. Its main purpose is 'to expound the method of realising the Great Liberation of *Nirvāna* by the yogic understanding of the One Mind' (Evans-Wentz, 1954: 196). The emphasis throughout the treatise is on the doctrine that the only reality is mind or consciousness, and that all things, including material reality, are mind-made. Furthermore, all minds, and hence all existing things, are manifestations of the Absolute or One Mind. The path of liberation, then, lies not in the external world, which must be seen for what it is – a sort of dream – but in the inner path of self-knowledge, and those who would attain wisdom, the full awakening of Buddhahood, must understand that all things, including one's own self, are illusory.

Jung's approach to the text rests on a premise to which we have already drawn attention as underlying his whole approach to the East, namely his belief that the materialist, extraverted psychological attitude of the West desperately needs its complementary opposite from the East. To recap: in the West we have since the Enlightenment, according to Jung, increasingly marginalised mind and consciousness, seeing them as epiphenomena, not realities in their own right. But for Jung the very reality of the world as far as we are concerned depends on the presence within it of the knowing subject. One of Jung's central arguments, reiterated at many points in his writings, is that consciousness is not merely a freakish and accidental byproduct of the material world, but in a very crucial sense is the very condition of its existence; it is indeed 'the greatest of all cosmic wonders' (CW8.357), 'the world's pivot' (CW8.423), for 'without consciousness there would, practically speaking, be no world, for the world exists as such only in so far as it is consciously reflected and consciously expressed by psyche. Consciousness is a precondition of being' (US: 46). A view such as this involves a complete *gestalt* switch in our understanding of the world, a 'great reversal of standpoint'.

Our problem in the West, according to Jung, lies in our failure adequately to integrate mind into our world-view, a situation which has led to a debilitating conflict between science and religion, one which has not taken place in the non-Christian world of the East. This conflict involves a fundamental misunderstanding on our part, however, for materialism is not a 'fact' but rather an hypothesis, and a metaphysical one at that – an hypothesis which is no more self-evidently true than the notion that the world is constituted by spirit. 'Matter is an hypothesis', Jung insists. 'When you say "matter" you are really creating a symbol for something unknown, which you may just as well call "spirit" or anything else' (CW11.762). The materialist is metaphysician despite himself. It is a mistake, therefore, to suppose that science has decisively falsified a religious world-view. Conversely, religion is equally at fault for maintaining a dogmatic pre-critical (i.e. pre-Kantian) position in which it clings to the literal meaning of its doctrines, trying 'to retain a primitive mental condition on merely sentimental

127

grounds' (CW11.763). Just as science hypostasises matter, so religion hypostasises mythical figures and forces.

To alleviate such intellectual cramps it is necessary to recognise the extent to which reality is structured by mind. Thus, for example, philosophical investigation is by no means a 'perfect and unconditioned instrument', but rather is 'a function dependent upon an individual psyche and determined on all sides by subjective conditions'; indeed, Jung comes very near to an idealist position when he argues that

> it is dawning upon us to what extent our whole experience of so-called reality is psychic; as a matter of fact, everything thought, felt, or perceived is a psychic image, and the world exists only so far as we are able to produce an image of it.

> (CW11.766)

This was probably a reference to certain extraordinary ideas that were emerging in physics in the inter-war period which seemed to run sharply against traditional materialist views, and were summed up in the famous remark by the physicist James Jeans that the universe is 'nearer to a great thought than to a great machine'. Elsewhere in his writings Jung, through his friendship with the physicist Wolfgang Pauli, had noted the extent to which the new physics had brought consciousness back into the world-picture of science, and pointed the way to a reconciliation between the materialist and idealist positions.

Such insights undoubtedly lay at the back of his Commentary on *The Tibetan Book of the Great Liberation* where he discovered remarkable corroboration for these modern speculations. In that text he found that mind is accorded a central role, that the text 'bases itself upon psychic reality, that is, upon the psyche as the main and unique condition of existence' (CW11.770). Its typically introverted attitude, so alien to the Western mind, enabled it to explore the inner workings of the psyche in a remarkably sophisticated way a thousand years before similar explorations were undertaken by Western philosophy, and to discover the extent to which our attitudes to the world are shaped, not so much by the world outside, as by our own mental dispositions. In the text he discovered the belief that everything is rooted in consciousness, and thus all external appearances, even of the most solid-looking objects, are the offspring of mind. By contrast our Western obsession with the extraverted standpoint, at any rate until the time of Kant, has blinded us to the need to turn the eye inwards and to examine the contribution that the mind makes to the construction of the world.

Furthermore, Jung believed, the treatise enables us to see that introspection is not to be viewed as the morbid, life-denying, withdrawal from the real world, but rather a necessary condition for self-liberation. As he wryly expressed it: 'If introspection were something morbid, as certain people in the West opine, we should have to send practically the whole East, or such parts of it as are not yet infected with the blessings of the West, to the lunatic asylum' (CW11.823).

Despite Jung's inclination towards a form of philosophical idealism, however, he was certainly not advocating an abandonment of the whole Western scientific outlook. The East, with its supposed detachment and inertia, was equally, if oppositely, biased. Eastern thinking, as expressed in the *Great Liberation*, points to a way out, not by inviting a capitulation to its introspective allures, nor by borrowing its ideas, but by seeking a more balanced view in which the demands of both matter and spirit, of extraversion and introversion, are equally met. He claimed that

> the two standpoints, however contradictory, each have their psychological justification. Both are one-sided in that they fail to see and take account of those factors which do not fit in with their typical attitude. The one underrates the world of consciousness, the other the world of [mind]. The result is that, in their extremism, both lose one half of the universe; their life is shut off from total reality, and is apt to become artificial and inhuman.
>
> (CW11.786)

Once again, then, Jung's approach to the text was psychological. Whatever metaphysical assumptions may lie beneath it, these are beyond his competence, he claimed, and so 'it is necessary to bring down its lofty metaphysical concepts to a level where it is possible to see whether any of the psychological facts known to us have parallels in, or at least border upon, the sphere of Eastern thought' (CW11.788). He was well aware that this approach to the *Great Liberation* had its limitations, that it was partial at best, for as a sacred text arising from a remote culture it was bound to transcend the limitations of a purely scientific study. His aim was 'simply to bring ideas which are alien to our way of thinking within reach of Western psychological experience' (CW11.788). Thus, for example, the gods mentioned in the text are treated as 'archetypal thought-forms', their peaceful and wrathful aspects interpreted as mutually complementary psychic opposites (CW11.791). The Eastern teaching of non-duality, of the fundamental unity of all things, which is evident in the text, expresses the idea that mind has its roots in what Jung calls 'the instinctual matrix', the unconscious ground on which the variegated individual conscious life rests (CW11.800). And finally the 'self-liberation', which is the ultimate goal of the method taught in the treatise, brings Jung back to the heart of his own teaching, which is the path of individuation.

ZEN BUDDHISM

The question of self-liberation was also uppermost in Jung's mind when discussing Zen, the final Buddhist tradition that we shall deal with here. Of all the *Mahāyāna* schools, Zen approximates most closely to the simple, unadorned spirit of the *Theravāda*. The exotic spirit-world of Tibetan Buddhism, with its *Bodhisattvas*, its colourful rituals and its sophisticated psychology, are far distant from the almost puritanical and antinomian tendencies to be found in the Buddhist schools that dominated China and Japan. But it was also, Jung believed, close in spirit both to aspects of Western Christian culture, such as the conversion experience and the mystical tradition, and to his own psychotherapy. It was these correspondences which led him to believe that 'Zen is a true goldmine for the needs of the Western psychologist' (*Letters I*: 128).

What drew Jung to Zen was its invitation to transcend rational thinking and words, and its reliance on the immediacy of experience rather than on theories or written teachings. This is not to say that either Jung or Zen rejected the need for rational thinking or for the written word, yet for both there was a point at which the understanding and transformation of the psyche could only proceed along a path that went beyond words. Evidence for this is to be seen, on the one side, in Jung's emphasis on the primacy of the mental image, and, on the other, in Zen's use of the *kōan*. Both have been accused of irrationalism, but this label only makes sense insofar as they both emphasised the limitations, rather than the indispensability, of the intellect and its products. Jung's sympathy for the strangeness of Zen concepts and its tendency to block verbal definitions and abstract explanations was no doubt linked to his diffidence concerning the possibility of rational formulations of his own conception of the human psyche. He frequently emphasised the primacy of experience and the subordinate role of theory, and was at pains to admit the inadequacy of his own intellectual formulations. This inclination and its relevance to his interest in Zen is brought out in a revealing conversation with a student, Ira Progoff. Progoff asked Jung how he might state the essence of his method in such a way that would fit his own truest feelings and regardless of how others would misunderstand or misinterpret it. Jung's reply was 'It would be too funny. It would be a Zen touch' (quoted in Moacanin, 1986: 48).

The origins of Zen, according to tradition, are to be found in the Buddha's Flower Sermon, in which he held up a flower to a gathering of disciples without uttering a word. This simple gesture sums up eloquently the spirit of direct seeing and instant transformation which is at the heart of Zen. More than other Buddhist schools it emphasises the uselessness of ritual and of intellectual analysis, and teaches a way towards self-realisation (*satori*) and enlightenment that is summed up as 'direct pointing to the human heart'. The two surviving Zen schools, *Rinzai* and *Soto*, emphasise the methods of meditative absorption and the *kōan* respectively, the former involving the practice of 'just sitting', the latter involving the use of paradox to hasten the attainment of enlightenment. The history of Zen Buddhism, which derives from the *Ch'an* Buddhist tradition established in China in the sixth century CE, is a complex one, but Jung treats Zen as a single phenomenon, and makes no reference to its historical origins or to the varieties of its constituent schools.

As with the Taoist and the Tibetan texts we have been discussing, Jung's interest in Zen Buddhism dates roughly from its earliest introduction into the West. By contrast with these other cases, however, his interest in Zen was aroused, not by an original text, but by Daisetz Suzuki's *Introduction to Zen Buddhism* which was published in Germany in 1939, and for which Jung was invited to write a foreword. Suzuki was trained in Zen in his native Japan, but travelled widely in the West, and produced throughout his long life a series of books on Zen which, from the first volume of *Essays in Zen Buddhism* published in 1927, provided the chief source of the understanding of Zen in the West. He lectured widely in America where he became recognised as the leading authority on Zen. He was not in the accepted sense a scholar, however, and cannot be described as a 'pure' interpreter of this philosophy for he was greatly influenced by the American psychologist William James – an influence which led him to accentuate the psychological aspect of Zen. Jung, too, was impressed by James whom he met in America in 1909, and it is important to bear the link between these three in mind when considering Jung's own attempt at a psychological interpretation of Zen.[4]

In approaching this subject, Jung once again began by dwelling on the strangeness and apparent incomprehensibility of Eastern concepts. He spoke of the 'exotic obscurity' of Zen, and while admitting that some of the sayings of Western mystics border on the grotesque, Zen discourse tends to 'sound like the most crashing nonsense' (CW11.882), and the central concept of *satori* 'is practically impossible for the European to appreciate' (CW11.877). Nevertheless, he was convinced that Zen is not mere 'mumbo-jumbo', and that a 'proximity of understanding', however inadequate, can be attempted. Certainly he was dealing here with something that was not philosophy in the orthodox Western sense, but the key lay, in the first instance, in the recognition that Zen is not offering a system of thought but a certain kind of *experience*. Many Westerners in approaching Zen might imagine it to be something highly complex and sophisticated that could only be understood after years of study and meditation, but perhaps this is a mistake – perhaps *satori* is a perfectly natural occurrence, something intrinsically simple, the signficance of which is within the grasp of any human being, of whatever culture. This idea of direct experience is illustrated by Jung in the following example quoted from Suzuki's book:

> A monk once went to Gensha, and wanted to learn where the entrance to the path of truth was. Gensha asked him, 'Do you hear the murmuring of the brook?' 'Yes I hear it', answered the monk. 'There is the entrance', the Master instructed him.

> (CW11.878)

Like the gesture of the Buddha's Flower Sermon, this example cannot be further explicated for it points to something that can only be made sense of through direct experience.

The second key for Jung was to be found in the idea of *self-knowledge*, which is itself the key to individuation, the peculiarity of Zen lying in the unique method it offers for attaining this goal. To be sure, the key of self-knowledge does not open the door to complete illumination, but it does suggest a way in which the apparent differences between Zen and Western consciousness can be transcended. Self-knowledge has not been a central theme in the Western tradition, Jung maintained, but definite intimations of it are to be found in Christian culture.

Thus, in the mystical tradition of the West we find many examples of attempts to wrench oneself free from bondage to an incomplete state of consciousness, one that is exclusively attached to the ego, and

> its texts are full of instructions as to how man can and must release himself from the 'I-ness' of his consciousness, so that through knowledge of his own nature he may rise above it and attain the inner (godlike) man.
>
> (CW11.890)

In the writings of Meister Eckhart, the great German mystic, for example, there is a clear statement of the need to transform narrow consciousness into a god-like state which seems, so Jung believed, like an echo of the Zen *satori* experience. This experience, whether in Eckhart or in Zen, is not a discovery in the normal sense – not a matter of seeing something new, but of *seeing differently*. Mysticism has often been associated in the West with the discovery of a transcendent reality beyond normal everyday experience. But it has another sense, one that joins East and West, namely that of a new way of seeing. In this sense it is like the Christian notion of faith in which the world, though remaining the same, becomes 'wholly other', in which by suddenly emptying oneself, and by letting go of egocentricity, the world is transformed. As Jung puts it: 'A new man, a completely transformed man, [appears] on the scene, one who has broken the shell of the old and who not only looks upon a new heaven and a new earth, but has created them' (CW11.892). A similar sense of personal transformation, involving a 'break-through of total experience', and a 'way of release to wholeness', can, according to Jung, be found in such modern masterpieces as Goethe's *Faust*, Nietzsche's *Thus Spoke Zarathustra*, and the writings of William Blake (see CW11.905).

It is through modern psychotherapy, however, that hermeneutical mediation is most effectively transacted, and, as with the Tibetan texts we have been examining, the most evident comparison is between Zen and analytical psychology. Jung saw Zen meditation not as some strange and esoteric activity but as part of the natural healing process whereby the psyche is able to integrate the unconscious into the conscious aspects of the self, a process central to the analytical endeavour. Insofar as meditation allows unconscious material to become integrated at the conscious level, it is parallel to techniques such as active imagination or dream analysis in which contact is made with the archetypes of the collective unconscious. Modern psychotherapy, he tells us, is based on the principle that 'the unconscious contents bring to the surface everything that is necessary in the broadest sense for the completion and wholeness of conscious orientation' (CW11.899), a method and a goal which parallels that of Zen meditation. Of course the parallel is by no means exact, and Jung voices his usual warnings concerning the undesirability of Zen practices for the European, but in both we can see the disciplined pursuit of self-transformation, of a 'way of release' to wholeness.

The comparison between Zen and psychotherapy is especially evident in relation to the *kōan*, a spiritual practice which provokes more than the usual degree of suspicion and scepticism in the Western mind. Jung offers the following example of this method:

> A monk once asked the Master: 'Has a dog a Buddha nature too?' Whereupon the Master replied 'Wu!' As Suzuki remarks, this 'Wu' means quite simply 'bow-wow', obviously just what the dog itself would have said in answer to such a question.
>
> (CW11.894)

Now at one level this is clearly 'crashing nonsense', at best a joke to Western ears. But a more sympathetic reading might interpret this sort of exchange as an attempt to provoke the novice into breaking through the barrier of the intellect which normally provides an effective screen against fresh insight. We surround ourselves with a wall of conventional views, cemented together by our linguistic inheritance, which prevents us from looking honestly into our own natures. Consciousness, Jung insists, 'is inevitably a world full of restrictions, of walls blocking the way. . . . No consciousness can harbour more than a very small number of simultaneous perceptions. All must lie in shadow, withdrawn from sight' (CW11.897). The Zen kōan, he believed, represented a dramatic method of breaking through from the conscious to the unconscious level, a 'demolition of rational understanding' which enables one's inner potential to be realised in a special moment of illumination. Practice and self-discipline are of course essential for the attainment of this illumination, but in the end it comes, not as a consequence of a set of procedures or of a rational thought sequence, but spontaneously.

The hermeneutical method employed here might seem, then, to draw this peculiar ritual out of its cultural context and begin to make sense of it in universal human terms. Though there is something singular about this whole phenomenon, something unique to Asia and at first glance alien to the Western mentality, it does in fact give expression to a type of universal religious experience, which in Christianity takes the form of 'conversion'. It also parallels the long and laborious climb of the patient in analysis who, after seemingly pointless mental clamberings over nonsensical dreams and fantasies, suddenly emerges onto a summit and can 'see' for the first time, a moment of self-discovery which cannot be predicted or rationalised.[5]

Finally, this means the attainment of wholeness, of *individuation* in Jung's term. Late in his life he wrote that the 'secret passion which keeps Zen and other spiritual techniques alive through the centuries is connected with an original experience of wholeness' (*Letters II*: 602). The experience of totality is a rare thing in any culture and one which demands the utmost of the seeker: 'The attainment of wholeness requires one to stake one's whole being. Nothing less will do', Jung warns (CW11.906). But it is also, in the final analysis, something that transcends the power of words and eludes the strenuous efforts enjoined by our methods. One of the most characteristic features of Jung's psychology was his belief that the unconscious, the irrational or shadow side of our nature, is not something evil or threatening, but is perfectly natural and, with encouragement, contains within itself the power of self-healing. It is this respect for the inner self, which has the strength to 'let go', to avoid the manipulations of the rational ego, that drew Jung so strongly to Zen, and perhaps to Eastern philosophy as a whole.

MANDALAS

We have seen that the theme of psychic wholeness and integration permeates Jung's dialogue with Eastern philosophies. It appears in the alchemical symbolism of *The Secret of the Golden Flower*, in the synchronistic world-view of the Taoists, and in the spiritual path of Kundalini yoga. In his study of the *mandala* symbolism it becomes the central focus of attention, for in this image he found expressed most succinctly the very unity of psychic life. As an archetypal idea it was, as he put it, 'a reflection of the individual's wholeness, i.e. of the self' (CW11.230).[6]

The discovery of the mandala symbol came at a crucial and turbulent period in Jung's life, the period when, following his split with Freud, he underwent his 'confrontation with the unconscious'. He expended much labour in subsequent years in investigating the varieties of mandala images, ranging from the dreams and fantasies of patients to the symbols and rituals of the world's religions and mythologies, but it was in the crucible of his own inner experience that the significance of these images was initially forged. The discovery made, indeed, an important contribution to his recovery. During the period of crisis from 1912 onwards, in which he felt 'totally suspended in mid-air', his imagination was invaded by ever more lurid and frightening fantasies. Some had an apocalyptic quality, seeming to presage a political disaster in Europe; others involved a descent into the bottomless abyss of his own unconscious, or a confrontation with biblical-like figures. His method of coping with these fantasies was to express them outwardly in drawing, painting, and in building models with stones, and it was while thus engaged that he found himself creating regular, symmetrical images which he later identified as mandalas. He gradually came to realise that these images were nothing less than images of the wholeness of the personality, 'cryptograms concerning the state of the self which were presented to me anew each day', and in which he saw 'the self – that is, my whole being – actively at work' (MDR: 221). Each of the many mandala drawings he did at this time were steps leading back to a single point, to the centre, and he came to the realisation that 'in finding the mandala as an expression of the self I had attained what for me was the ultimate' (MDR: 222). The realisation of the self became for him the goal that could make sense of life, and the mandala constituted its most perfect symbol.

The use of the term 'mandala' to refer to his experiences at this period is, however, a little anachronistic, for it was only subsequently that he became acquainted with the Oriental versions of it, and came to the view that the mandala represents one of the oldest religious symbols of humanity. His first published discussion of this term appears in 1929 in his Commentary on *The Secret of the Golden Flower*. There he noted that 'Mandala [in Sanskrit] means "circle", more especially a magic circle', and went on to argue that mandala symbolism is to be found in many different cultures, including Christian, Egyptian, and American Indian, though the most beautiful examples are to be found in Tibetan Buddhism. The 'golden flower' itself is a mandala symbol since, looked at from above it appears as a regular geometric pattern, and expresses the idea of growth towards integration and unity. He also discovered at this stage that mandala images frequently occurred in the dreams and fantasies of his patients, and that mandala drawings are often produced by the mentally ill (CW13.31).

In 1937, in his lectures on psychology and religion, he offered the following brief account of Tibetan Buddhist mandalas:

> These consist as a rule of a circular padma or lotus which contains a square sacred building with four gates, indicating the four cardinal points and the seasons. The centre contains a Buddha, or more often the conjunction of Shiva and his Shakti, or an equivalent *dorje* (thunderbolt) symbol.
>
> (CW11.113)

The primary function of these images is to act as a kind of cosmological map, to provide a symbolic guide to the structure of the world, both human and divine, in which each devotee will have to undertake his or her life's journey. They also have a more immediate practical significance in terms of the conduct of this journey, for they act as one of the chief aids to the discipline of meditation: 'They are yantras or ritualistic instruments for the purpose of contemplation, concentration, and the final transformation of the yogi's consciousness into the divine all-consciousness' (CW11.113). The origin of such images lay, he conjectured, not in Lamaist dogma, but in dreams and visions, and indeed, the 'true' mandala is, strictly speaking, not an observable image at all, but 'is always an *inner* image which is gradually built up through (active) imagination' (CW12.123, my emphasis).

The transformational character of the mandala is symbolised as 'the union of all opposites, and is embedded between *yang* and *yin*, heaven and earth; the state of everlasting balance and immutable duration', a state which in Chinese alchemy is called the 'Diamond Body' (CW9i.637). In the Tantric tradition it is viewed as a method of identifying with the deity and escaping the world of illusion. In Jung's summary:

> The goal of contemplating the processes depicted in the mandala is that the yogi shall become inwardly aware of the deity. Through contemplation, he recognizes himself as God again, and thus returns from the illusions of individual existence into the universal totality of the divine state.
>
> (CW9i.633)

In the West, with the exception of certain unorthodox traditions such as the Gnostics, the divinity is typically experienced as a being who is external to man. In the East divinity is experienced as lying *within* the self, as the central point of the inner cosmos, and hence the mandala symbolises 'divinity incarnate in man' (MDR: 367).

Mandalas can also, Jung insisted, take the form of a ritual dance or of a temple building. A ritual dance of this kind is shaped by a regular symmetrical pattern of movement, and may mark out, or be conducted within, a sacred place, a *temenos* or magic circle, in which the divine presence is experienced. The same geometrical patterns can be observed in many temple structures in the East, which are also based on the figures of the square and the circle. These, likewise, can be considered to be mandalas, and indeed, as he pointed out, the drawn mandalas themselves can be viewed as the plan of a temple precinct (CW12.166). He cited the example of the great temple of Borobudur in Java (CW18.409 and MDR: 308), the ground plan of which is a circle within a square, the circle itself being not a building but a huge sculptured hemispherical mound called a stupa. These stupas (known as dagobas in Sri Lanka) – which are to be found throughout South-East Asia and were originally constructed to house sacred relics – can be seen as three-dimensional versions of the mandala, conveying the same symbolism of wholeness and cosmic-spiritual integration. Like the drawn mandalas, stupas are also objects of mental concentration, not through being contemplated but through the process of circumambulation whereby the devotee proceeds round the stupa in a spiral pathway which leads symbolically towards the centre and to enlightenment. As J.M. Lundquist notes: 'The stupa is the most characteristic three-dimensional representation of the mandala [and] indeed, within Buddhism, the erection of a stupa was prescribed as one of the chief means of attaining Buddhahood' (1990: 116).[7]

The 'discovery' of the Oriental mandala image was interesting enough in itself, and no doubt has wide implications for our understanding of Oriental religious belief and practice. But Jung's attempt to make sense of this image as a universal, archetypal, phenomenon by means of a whole network of analogical links to a wide range of cultural phenomena, West as well as East, modern as well as ancient, was nothing less than a hermeneutical *tour de force*. The most fully documented examples were derived from the dreams and fantasies of his patients, many examples of which are reproduced and analysed in the *Collected Works* (see CW9i.525–712, and CW12.122–331). They all share the characteristics of a regular symmetrical structure, often roughly circular in shape and with north–south and east–west axes, and a centripetal tendency which forces the attention towards the centre. For Jung they had deep psychological significance and represented 'a kind of ideogram of unconscious contents' (CW9i.622). Jung was careful to point out that his patients were very unlikely to have had access to the comparative material drawn from other cultures since in many respects he was introducing this to Europe for the first time, and in order not to prejudice the examples produced by his patients he took the precaution of waiting for thirteen years before publishing his preliminary findings (CW9i.623).

In addition to these examples, Jung collected a very wide range of mandala-like figures from a variety of different historical epochs and cultural traditions. Within the Christian tradition he noted a number of mandala-like motifs in the representation of Christ, indicating, he believed, the idea of psychological and spiritual wholeness, and drew attention to several specific examples from Christian mystics such as Jacob Boehme (CW9i.20 and CW13.31), Hildegard of Bingen (CW18.1225), and Brother Nicholas of Flüe (CW9i.12). Comparisons were also drawn with the tradition of Mediaeval European alchemy with its emphasis on the unification of opposites and its cosmological conception of the *unus mundus*, the unitary cosmos in which the opposites are reconciled; for the alchemist, these ideas, considered psychologically, are 'exemplified in mandala symbolism, which portrays the self as a concentric structure, often in the form of a squaring of the circle' (CW14.776). And ranging even further afield, he drew attention to the mandala-like sand-paintings of the Navajo and Pueblo Indians (CW9i.700-1), to palaeolithic cave paintings in Rhodesia (CW13.45), and to ancient magic circles (CW11.157).

What, then, was the aim of this hermeneutical exercise? What sense can be made of this diverse range of examples? Clearly the aim was not that of pure anthropology or history. It will be evident that Jung's aim was psychological. What he hoped to uncover through the accumulation of such data was evidence of the underlying archetypal structure of the human psyche, and confirmation of his belief that this structure applied universally and, as such, was part of the inheritance of mankind. As with his studies of Chinese alchemy and Kundalini yoga, his purpose in studying the mandala symbols of the East, therefore, was not to recover and revivify long-lost metaphysical beliefs, but rather to search out the psychological significance that lay beneath them – a significance which, he believed, provided 'one of the best examples of the universal operation of an archetype' (CW9i.623), namely the archetype of the *self*. This meant that '[for] our more modest psychological purposes we must abandon the colourful metaphysical language of the East' and concentrate instead on the process of psychic transformation, which he saw as the shifting of the psychological centre of personality from the ego to the self (CW9i.638).

We have already taken note of the idea of the self in Jung's thought, along with the related idea of individuation, and have frequently emphasised the key role that this concept played in Jung's model of the psyche. The self, to recap, is the totality of psychic function, 'the sum total of [man's] conscious and unconscious contents' (CW11.140). It is not a static entity but 'a dynamic process', 'an active force' whose essence is one of continual transformation and rejuvenation (CW9ii.411), and whose natural course of development is to bring its diverse elements into some kind of unity. This unity, he insisted, is not that of undifferentiated oneness, but rather a harmony, a balance sought through the interplay of opposing but complementary forces.

In the light of this, it is not surprising that Jung saw the mandala as, in Anthony Stevens' words, 'an ancient and ubiquitous expression of the self' (1982: 290). The mandala symbol offers an outward and tangible expression of an archetypal God-image which, Jung believed, is present in the psyche universally and represents the fundamental human need to integrate and give sense to the disparate aspects of human experience. From a psychological standpoint this means the

137

function that integrates the personality as a whole, which is the self. In this symbol, therefore, the theological and the psychological are brought together as an image of wholeness. As an archetypal idea it is 'a reflection of the individual's wholeness, i.e. of the self' (CW11.230). This wholeness is, as we have seen, not one of undifferentiated simplicity, but rather arises out of the interactions and tensions between opposing but complementary elements. Let us now see how this is represented in the actual mandala symbol.

This symbol represents, first, an image of psychological diversity and opposition, and brings into play all aspects of human psychic life, the bad as well as the good, the shadow as well as the light. In its most developed Tibetan form it contains at least three separate and distinct spheres of life. The first, the outer ring, Jung notes, 'consists of fire, the fire of *concupiscentia*, "desire", from which proceed the torments of hell', and where are depicted the horrors of the burial ground. This could be seen as referring to the instinctual, unconscious life, containing what Jung called the 'shadow', namely those aspects of the self of which we are ashamed or which are often too powerful or frightening to be confronted directly. Then comes a kind of temple or monastery courtyard which 'signifies sacred seclusion and concentration'. Here Jung identifies, symbolically, the various psychic functions – thinking, feeling, sensation and intuition – which go to make up the conscious life of the individual. And finally at the centre of the mandala there is a further circle in which sits a figure, usually of the Buddha, sometimes of Shiva in embrace with his consort Shakti, and which represents the state of timeless spiritual perfection (CW9i.630–1).

As well as difference, the total image represents at the same time the striving for balance and unity in which opposites are reconciled. Though in its most common form the Tibetan mandala is a static image, nevertheless it symbolises a dynamic process of spiritual growth. The disparate elements of which it is constituted, though in a sense lying opposed to one another, are not situated outside of each other in mutual exclusion but stand in complementary fashion within the balanced symmetry of the whole, like opposing themes within musical counterpoint which seem to run contrary to each other yet blend together to make a harmonious whole.

In traditional religious terms this represents the path of enlightenment in which the adept passes through various phases of development in order to achieve *nirvāna* or unity with *Brahman*. Translated into psychological terms this means the same as individuation, namely the full realisation of the self. In a striking cross-fertilisation of analogies, Jung suggests that '[if] a mandala may be described as a symbol of the self seen in cross section, then the tree would represent a profile view of it: the self depicted as a process of growth' (CW13.304). The basic motif of the mandala image, therefore, is one of psychic integration and wholeness in which the various elements strive to attain selfhood and in which

[there] is the premonition of a centre of personality, a kind of central point within the psyche, to which everything is related, by which everything is

arranged, and which is itself a source of energy. The energy of the central point is manifested in the almost irresistible compulsion and urge to *become what one is*.

(CW9i.634, Jung's emphasis)

This becoming-what-one-is 'is an individuation process, an identification with the totality of the personality, with the self' (CW18.271).

The mandala image is not only a *symbol* of wholeness and healing, but can be actively employed as a means towards that end. Jung first discovered this in his own case and later confirmed this discovery through the spontaneous production of similar images by his patients. The mandalas drawn by his patients suggested to Jung, not just a representation of a state of psychic wholeness, but rather the striving to overcome inner chaos, and the search for some form of integration. Just as, for the yogi, the mandala offers a means of overcoming the opposites of spirit and matter, so, for his patients, the use of mandala drawings expressed a need to resolve psychological tensions, and acted as 'an antidote for chaotic states of mind' (CW9i.16). In working through such images he came to recognise that his patients' drawings could be interpreted as an attempt to bring into play and into mutual interaction elements from both the conscious and the unconscious that had hitherto remained unreconciled and a source of mental suffering. The mandala drawing enabled them to express these unreconciled oppositions and to bring them to the level of consciousness where they could be worked through and perhaps reconciled. Thus, following on from 'chaotic dis-ordered states marked by conflict and anxiety', they serve, he argued, 'to produce an inner order . . . [and] express the idea of a safe refuge, of inner reconciliation and wholeness' (CW9i.710). He went on to claim that

The fact that images of this kind have under certain circumstances a considerable therapeutic effect on their authors is empirically proved and also readily understandable, in that they often represent very bold attempts to see and put together apparently irreconcilable opposites and bridge over apparently hopeless splits.

(CW9i.718)

He emphasised that this is not an automatic healing process – neither a remedy that can be induced through repetition or imitation of images derived from an external source, nor something that can be applied through rational reflection. Rather it is 'evidently an *attempt at self-healing* on the part of Nature, which does not spring from conscious reflection but from an instinctive impulse' (CW9i.714, Jung's emphasis).

This argument represents a special case of a viewpoint which goes to the heart of Jung's whole psychology, namely that religious symbolism in general expresses a deep need for healing and wholeness. Despite the almost endless variety of its manifestations in human history, religious beliefs, images and rituals arise, he believed, from a universal psychological need, namely the need for meaning and purpose. Contrary to Freud, who spoke for the modern rationalist tradition of the West, Jung saw religious beliefs and practices, not as superstitious or whimsical fantasies, nor as ethnic curiosities, but as manifestations of a universal, unconscious, archetypal predisposition. Every religion, he believed, 'is a spontaneous expression of a certain predominant psychological condition' (CW11.160). Where Freud had understood religion in pathological terms, as 'the obsessional neurosis of mankind', Jung viewed it as 'man's greatest and most significant achievement, giving him the security and inner strength not to be crushed by the monstrousness of the universe' (CW5,343). This is not to say that he denied any transcendent significance or truth to these beliefs, but rather he felt the necessity to take an agnostic attitude in order to understand such beliefs psychologically; 'to treat a metaphysical statement as a psychic process is not to say that it is "merely psychic"', he argued (CW11.448), but merely to indicate the limits of the scientific method.

From a psychological standpoint, therefore, the 'truth' of the mandala images that he discovered in Oriental cultures signified a remarkable and striking transcription onto visual and ritual terms of an underlying psychological need, one which was at the heart of all religious endeavour, namely the need for completeness and wholeness. While all relgious symbolism expresses this need in one form or another, the mandala, with its evident symmetry, its unity-in-diversity, its idea of circumambulation, and its sense of progression towards completeness, represented for Jung one of the most perfect symbols of the religious quest of mankind. Its attempt, in symbolic fashion, to 'square the circle' of psychic life makes it *par excellence* the 'archetype of wholeness'.

Part III

EPILOGUE

8

RESERVATIONS AND QUALIFICATIONS

Jung has become a prophet of the Orient in many people's eyes, a powerful advocate for Eastern wisdom in a post-Christian era. However, this reputation is not entirely apposite. In the last few chapters we have seen evidence of Jung's efforts to build a hermeneutical bridge with Eastern thought, but at the same time we have noticed that his enthusiasm for the East was marked by well-defined limits. To be sure, he frequently acknowledged 'the value of Oriental wisdom' (MDR: 304), and emphasised its importance in his own intellectual development. At times he cannot praise the East too highly – 'this spiritual achievement of the East [is] one of the greatest things the human mind has ever created' (CW11.876) – and often seems to rank it above Western culture, using it, as we have seen, as a tool for criticising, even for undermining, the European cultural tradition.

Yet at the same time he was careful to distance himself from it. His writings on this subject are full of reservations and qualifications, and often read more like debates with himself than fully worked-out conclusions. Repeatedly he warned of the dangers for the Westerner in approaching the East too closely, and we are frequently told that Eastern spirituality cannot simply be taken over and absorbed by us. It is 'foreign' to our history, to our culture, to our very psychological make-up, and he was especially dismissive of movements such as Theosophy which sought to merge East and West in a global, syncretistic philosophy. 'You cannot mix fire and water', he sternly admonished: 'The Eastern attitude stultifies the Western and vice-versa' (CW11.772). He was critical, too, of some of the fundamental doctrines of both yoga and Buddhism, and appears at times to be dismissive of the philosophical assumptions behind their teachings. This is a rather paradoxical situation, and in this chapter I shall examine these reservations and qualifications, and seek to understand their implications for his attempted dialogue with the Orient.

JUNG'S DISTANCE FROM THE EAST

Jung was firmly convinced that in some sense the West needed the East. We have drawn attention to his belief that the Western psyche is unbalanced, too inclined

143

towards the externalities of rationalised power and ego control. The 'introverted' East, too, is unbalanced according to Jung, but that was not his primary concern. His aim was, in effect, the cure of the sick Western psyche. He was deeply concerned with what he saw as the loss of traditional religious symbols which had long served as a container for human emotions and aspirations, the atrophy of which was the source, not only of the mental suffering he witnessed in his consulting room, but of the appalling barbarity into which civilised Europe had lapsed in the twentieth century. In the face of this crisis many turned towards the East, hoping to discover there a replacement for the god that had failed them. Jung fully understood and sympathised with the infatuation with Eastern spiritual disciplines, but in the end he saw the necessity for Europeans to position themselves firmly within their own culture, to find the cure from within their own traditions. The danger with this infatuation, as Jung saw it, was that it failed to strike at the root of the disease, which lay not elsewhere but in ourselves. Too often he observed Westerners rushing headlong to the East, grasping with typical Western insatiability at its supposed treasures, but failing to look within and to seek a solution inside themselves. His whole concept of individuation, the natural tendency of the psyche to seek wholeness, is an unfolding from within, not an acquisition from without.[1]

Whether we think in terms of an individual or a culture, such an endogenous unfolding cannot take place in isolation, however. Just as patients in their search for psychic integration need to engage in a dialogue with the therapist, so too does a culture. The psychological value of the hermeneutical process applies as much to the world at large as it does to the intimate interaction between patient and therapist. To understand Jung's reservations about the East we need, then, to recall some of the characteristic features of the hermeneutical process. It demands, first, a recognition of one's own historical situation and a realisation of the distance between oneself and the other; it requires a readiness to be open to the other, but not to be absorbed by it, a recognition of the prejudices and limitations that lie on both sides of the dialogue, and an ability to be both other- and self-critical. Dialogue is not mutual absorption but mutual exchange, and as such does not imply uncritical admiration. Above all it means the opening up of the self in a way that precludes the loss of one's identity, but guarantees an enhancement of one's being.

Let us look first at the question of *distance*. To engage in a fruitful dialogue with another one needs, of course, to be open, but this in its turn means insisting on the gap that lies between. Put it this way: you cannot meaningfully converse with another unless you recognise the otherness of that person. There is no doubt that Jung, for all his enthusiasm, deliberately kept his distance from the Orient. His account of his travels to India and Sri Lanka gives the reader the sense of someone who was quite deliberately refusing to be seduced by what he called 'the allurements of the oderous East', not because he disliked it, but because saw an inclination in himself to like it too much. There was, indeed, one incident, to which we have alredady referred, where he was momentarily overcome by the atmosphere of the stupas at Sanchi, but for the most part he seems to have been acutely conscious of his own Europeanness and of the foreignness of that which surrounded him. Significantly, Jung took with him as reading matter for his voyage a volume of European alchemy, the *Theatrum Chemicum* of 1602. For many travellers to the East this might seem a strange choice; why not a history of India, or a study of Indian philosophy or religion? The answer lies in his remark that the alchemical work belonged 'to the fundamental strata of European thought that was constantly counterpointed by my impressions of a foreign mentality and culture' (MDR: 304), thereby helping him to maintain his critical distance from the culture that impinged so vividly upon him.

One consequence of this outlook was that he was not in the least tempted by the attractions of syncretism – the blending together of the outlooks of East and West into a single universal *Weltanschauung*. Jung has sometimes been reproached with supporting syncretistic tendencies through his encouragement of interest in the East. Thus, for example, the Dutch theologian Willem A. Visser't Hooft accused Jung of 'the importation on a mass scale of exotic religious systems', and of 'contributing directly or indirectly to the creation of religious eclecticism in which the most diverse religious conceptions are assembled without any possibility of real spiritual judgement' (quoted in Wehr, 1987: 459–60). This represents a serious misunderstanding of Jung. In his approach to the East he emphasised the inescapable differences between Eastern and Western ways of thinking, and he must therefore be seen in marked contrast with many thinkers in the first half of this century who sought to construct a world philosophy which would integrate and transcend the provincial philosophies of Eastern and Western cultures respectively. A representative example is the Indian philosopher S. Radhakrishnan who spoke of a 'cross-fertilization of ideas and insights . . . taking place in the deeper fabric of men's thoughts', and looked forward to 'a world society with a universal religion of which the historical faiths are but branches' (1939: 347–8).[2]

By contrast Jung's outlook was fundamentally pluralistic. He consistently refused to countenance a 'Jungian' system, and espoused an epistemological relativism which calls into question the possibility of a single pontifical perspective on the world. The purpose of his dialogue with the East, therefore, was not that of absorbing and integrating Eastern thought into a super-philosophy but rather of healing the one-sidedness of Western culture by forcing it to recognise the need to open itself out to its complementary opposite. For him the East could lead the West to the rediscovery of the inner cosmos, of the worlds of the imagination, of intuition, of the unconscious, but only in its own terms and with its own methods.

This interpretation is reinforced by the fact that Jung was highly critical of several central Eastern concepts. Two stand out for special mention: the question of the self and the ego, and the related question of suffering. We shall consider each in turn.

THE SELF, EAST AND WEST

Jung was convinced that his conception of the ego and its relation to the self bore a close analogy to a central theme of Indian yoga philosophy. To recap briefly: the Indian concept of $\overline{A}tman$ formed, in his view, 'an exact parallel to the psychological idea of the self' (CW16.474). In both cases the aim was to transcend the limits of the conscious rational ego and to allow the emergence of a sense of its interconnectedness with a wider and deeper reality. For Jung, it will be recalled, the self represents the realisation of the fullest potential of the human psyche, the attainment of wholeness through the transcending of opposing tendencies within it. In contrast with the psychoanalytic tradition, he saw the ego, not as an absolute monarch ruling the forces within the psyche, but as an integral part of a dynamic system. Yoga philosophy likewise teaches the transcendence of the ego, the need to attain a higher self in which the painful strivings of the ego are transformed, a state called *nirdvandva* where the mind is no longer divided against itself through the demands of opposing principles, but experiences the pure consciousness of spirit. 'In India, as with us, the experience of the self . . . is a vital happening which brings about a fundamental transformation of personality' (CW16.219).

But at this point a chasm opens up between the two, one which Jung saw no way of bridging. The ultimate goal of yoga was not merely the integration of the ego into the higher self, but rather a state of complete absorption (*samādhi*) in which the ego, to all intents and purposes, ceases to exist. 'There is no doubt', Jung insisted, 'that the higher forms of yoga, in so far as they strive to reach *samādhi*, seek a mental condition in which the ego is practically dissolved' (CW11.775). The techniques of yoga, he believed, aimed at the attainment of a trance-like state in which the ego becomes absorbed into the unconscious and where consequently the self-conscious subject disappears. The goal of yoga is identity with '"universal consciousness" [which] is logically identical with unconsciousness . . . a state in which subject and object are almost completely identical' (CW9i.520).

The first problem is a cultural one: the yogic way of absorption is not suited to the Western psyche. The Eastern mind, Jung supposed, 'has no difficulty in conceiving of a consciousness without an ego' (CW11.774), for it is less egocentric than ours. The Western psyche, by contrast, has a strongly developed sense of the self-conscious rational ego, and any tendency towards assimilation by the unconscious can lead to dangerous inflation: 'It must be reckoned a psychic catastrophe when the ego is assimilated by the self', he warned (CW9ii.45). Presumably the Eastern psyche, with its less highly developed ego, will float quite happily in the sea of the unconscious, content to be carried to a destination that lies beyond itself. The more developed Western ego by contrast, resting on a sea of unconscious contents which have been severely repressed, is in danger of being drowned in this sea and thereby taking on its violent potentialities; according to this view, Hitler represents a good example of someone whose ego became too fully identified with his unconscious, with catastrophic inflationary consequences. Jung believed that a better way for Western man to transcend the ego and attain to selfhood was through the process of active imagination, a technique whereby unconscious contents are brought to the sur- face and assimilated in a controlled way. The question of cultural differences between East and West raises more general issues which we shall pursue shortly.

The second problem here is one of logic: in the final analysis Jung simply cannot make sense of this idea. While the Eastern mind appears to have no difficulty in conceiving consciousness without an ego, Jung, on the contrary, could not 'imagine a conscious mental state that does not relate to a subject, that is, to an ego'. For him, '[if] there is no ego there is nobody to be conscious of anything' (CW11.774). In order that a higher self should be realised there must be an individual consciousness that does the realising:

> There must always be somebody or something left over to experience the realization, to say 'I know at-one-ment, I know there is no distinction'. One cannot know something that is not distinct from oneself. Even when I say 'I know myself', an infinitesimal ego – the knowing 'I' – is still distinct from 'myself'.

> (CW11.817)

Stated in this way, therefore, the Indian doctrine of non-duality, of the ultimate obliteration of the distinction between subject and object, is quite simply a contradiction in terms. If there is no subject to know the world, then the non-dual position simply cannot be stated as an object of knowledge. Jung's position remains finally and obdurately pluralistic: 'In this as it were atomic ego, which is completely ignored by the essentially non-dualistic standpoint of the East, there nevertheless lies hidden the whole unabolished pluralistic universe and its un- conquered reality' (CW11.817).

This reluctance to go the whole way East and adopt a monistic position is evident also in another respect. In yogic philosophy the individual human mind or consciousness is a manifestation of a higher consciousness, not, in the final analysis, a reality in its own right. The material world, too, though not an illusion in the crude sense of the term, is also a reality which is not absolute but is dependent on a higher reality, *Brahman*. Jung saw things the other way round, maintaining that consciousness arises, phylogenetically (in terms of the species), from the unconscious, which in turn is the evolutionary product of the biological world. As Faber and Saayman put it: '[Jung] ascribed a pivotal role to the evolutionary process as a factor influencing human behaviour and his theory thus contains a biological thrust' (1984: 170). This 'evolutionary process' and 'biological thrust' can certainly not be identified with Darwinism, for Jung maintained something like an emergent theory and sought to avoid any kind of biological reductionism. Nevertheless, in spite of the idealist tendencies in Jung's thinking, his theory of the psyche cannot be identified with the idealism of yogic philosophy. Although, as we have seen, he insisted that the psychic world cannot be reduced to the world of nature, but is a kind of microcosm in its own right, he

147

saw it, from an evolutionary standpoint, as an emanation from the natural world, not from the universal mind.[3]

A consequence of all this for Jung was that full self-realisation can never be attained, and here again the gap between yoga and himself is very apparent. Swami Ajaya points out that for Vedānta philosophy – that is the main Hindu school – 'the assimilation of the ego by the self, rather than being a psychic catastrophe, results in a state of illumination', a state of 'pure consciousness' (1984: 141). But according to Jung, the unconscious can never become fully luminous to the ego, and complete self-realisation can never be attained. As we explained above, he taught that the fundamental structure of the psyche involved a polarity between complementary opposites, and hence conflict was of its very essence. The psychic life involves a dialectical movement to-and-fro between opposites, it has no final resolution, it can look forward to no Hegelian Absolute in which all contraditions are resolved: 'The life of the unconscious goes on and continually produces problematical situations. . . . There is no change which is unconditionally valid over a long period of time. Life has always to be tackled anew' (CW8.142). In short, 'Complete liberation means death' (*Letters I*: 247).

This view is fundamentally at odds with yoga, and also with Buddhism, for both hold out the hope of an ultimate transcendence of the ego and consequently the final conquest of suffering. By contrast with this, Jung wrote that 'Complete redemption from the sufferings of this world is and must remain an illusion' (CW16.400). This does not mean that we can do nothing about suffering; psychotherapy is after all devoted to its alleviation. In the end, however, we can only deal with suffering by facing it and living through it. Thus, in spite of his claim that Buddha was a more complete human being than Christ, on the question of suffering he clung to his Christian heritage. In a letter to an acquaintance in 1938 he wrote that, while the East sought to eliminate suffering by 'casting it off', and the West sought to suppress it with drugs, the only way to overcome it was that of Christ, namely to endure it (*Letters I*: 236). In many ways this is reminiscent, too, of Nietzsche's refusal to escape from suffering into an illusory world, and his demand that we face suffering and thereby seek to overcome it. This attitude is well illustrated in the following passage from Jung's autobiography, which serves as a useful summary of these past few paragraphs:

> The Indian's goal is not moral perfection, but the condition of *nirdvandva*. He wishes to free himself from nature; in keeping with his aim, he seeks in meditation the condition of imagelessness and emptiness. I, on the other hand, wish to persist in the state of lively contemplation of nature and of the psychic images. I want to be freed neither from human beings, nor from myself, nor from nature; for all these appear to me the greatest of miracles. Nature, the psyche, and life appear to me like divinity unfolded – and what more could I wish for? To me the supreme meaning of Being can consist only in the fact that it *is*, not that it is not or is no longer.
>
> (MDR: 306)

It is perhaps significant that the one Indian whom Jung appeared to respect without reservation was not the famous holy man Shri Ramana Maharshi, whom he deliberately avoided on his visit to India, but rather one of the Maharshi's disciples, a simple family man and primary school teacher who surpassed his master in wisdom because 'he had "eaten" the world', finding wisdom and holiness in the discharging of his everyday duties, not in the scaling of spiritual heights: 'He has found a meaning in the rushing phantasmagoria of Being, freedom in bondage, victory in defeat' (CW11.953).

PHILOSOPHICAL ASSUMPTIONS

This fundamental disagreement with Indian philosophy reflected Jung's general belief that, in conducting a dialogue between East and West, it was necessary to place its metaphysical assumptions into abeyance. While the Orient has much to teach us in terms of psychic introspection, its philosophical stance can, if taken literally, stand in the way of a fruitful exchange. This is partly due to Jung's belief that at certain crucial points yoga philosophy was simply mistaken, that, as he put it 'Eastern intuition has overreached itself' (CW11.818). Indian metaphysical speculations, lacking a firm empirical grounding, are based on pre-Kantian assumptions about the virtually limitless scope of human knowledge, and this led to the contradictions we have just noted in which claims are made about the self which go beyond the bounds of possible knowledge. Yoga in its traditional form is not really psychology but metaphysical speculation which suffers 'a curious detachment from the world of concrete particulars we call reality' (*Letters II*: 438).

Jung's scepticism concerning Eastern metaphysics was, however, the consequence of a more general methodological standpoint which he adopted. Jung has sometimes been identified with the Christian faith, or perhaps with a peculiar Gnostic version of it. However, he was always careful to attempt to separate his subjective and personal beliefs from his 'official' scientific convictions. 'As a responsible scientist', he wrote, 'I am not going to preach my personal and subjective convictions which I cannot prove' (CW18.1589). There is no place in psychology for matters of faith or doctrine since these must always transcend our rational understanding. As a psychologist, therefore, he would not allow himself 'to make statements about the divine being, since that would be a transgression of the limits of science' (*Letters I*: 384). Nevertheless, the fact of religious belief was of crucial significance for his understanding of the human psyche. Where Freud had treated the phenomena of religion as bordering on the patho- logical, a sign of the childish dependence of mankind, Jung saw them as con- stituting the very core of the healthy human psyche. For him the essence of religion lay not in beliefs and doctrines but rather in a certain kind of inner experience, creeds being merely codified, organised, and ossified forms of what was fudamentally a special sort of inner experience.

In his approach to religious belief, therefore, he sought to lay to one side its metaphysical assumptions and to concentrate his attention on the *phenomenology* of belief. 'Our psychology is, therefore, a science of mere phenomena without any metaphysical implications', he wrote (CW11.759). 'I quite deliberately bring every-thing that purports to be metaphysical into the daylight of psychological under-standing . . . [and] strip things of their metaphysical wrappings in order to make them objects of psychology' (CW13.73). Thus, for example, in dealing with the doctrine of the Resurrection he addressed himself, not to its historical or theological signifi-cance, but rather to its symbolic meaning as 'the projection of an indirect realization of the self', an image pointing towards psychological integration and wholeness (CW18.1567).

He took precisely the same approach to the belief systems of the East. Here, too, he attempted to set on one side all metaphysical claims, treating them with agnostic indifference, and concentrating his attention on their psychological nature and significance. We saw earlier that in dealing with the concept of *karma*, for example, he was careful to avoid any presumption concerning the doctrine of rebirth, treating it instead as an expression of the collective unconscious, a notion for which he claimed nothing but empiricist credentials. We saw too how, in his Commentary on *The Tibetan Book of the Dead*, he transformed the experiences of the dead soul in its passage from death to rebirth into psychological terms, and prefaced his introduction to *The Tibetan Book of the Great Liberation* with the disclaimer that 'Psychology . . . treats all metaphysical claims and assertions as mental phenomena and regards them as statements about the mind and its structure' (CW11.760). And we saw in his discussion of the *I Ching* that he took a strictly agnostic attitude to its pronouncements, describing his approach as 'psychological phenomenology', and insisting that 'nothing "occult" is to be inferred. My position in these matters is pragmatic' (CW11.1000). This dis-tancing from the truth-claims of Eastern thought, as well as his hermeneutical intentions, is made clear in a letter of 1935 where he wrote that

I am first and foremost an empiricist who was led to the question of Western and Eastern mysticism only for empirical reasons. For instance I do not by any means take my stand by the Tao or any yoga technique, but have found that Taoist philosophy as well as yoga have very many parallels with the psychic processes we observe in Western man.

(*Letters I*: 195)

Sometimes, though, Jung took matters a bit further. So far we have emphasised the fact that he dealt with Eastern ideas from a psychological point of view, taking a strictly agnostic attitude to any claims to objective truth about the world beyond the psyche. There he acted like an anthropologist who studies, say, the religious beliefs of a culture, while endeavouring to take no position on their truth or validity. At times, however, he took a more radical stance, appearing to claim that metaphysical assertions are *nothing but* psychological claims. In his Com-mentary on *The Secret of the Golden Flower*, for example, he wrote:

My admiration for the great philosophers of the East is as genuine as my attitude towards their metaphysics is irreverent. I suspect them of being symbolical psychologists, to whom no greater wrong could be done than to take them literally. If it were really metaphysics that they mean it would be useless to try and understand them. But if it is psychology, we can not only understand them but can profit greatly by them, for then the so-called 'metaphysical' comes within the range of experience.

(CW13.74)

This suggests a stronger claim than one that simply places metaphysical beliefs in agnostic parentheses. It appears to argue that metaphysical statements are impossible altogether. This is borne out by the following quotation from the same source:

Every statement about the transcendent is to be avoided because it is only a laughable presumption on the part of a human mind unconscious of its limitations. Therefore, when God or the Tao is named an impulse of the soul, or a psychic state, something has been said about the knowable only, but nothing about the unknowable, about which nothing can be determined.

(CW13.82)

Perhaps, then, Eastern philosophers are really psychologists in metaphysical clothing. The suggestion here is not that we as psychologists can interpret their ideas in our own terms, but rather that their claims *really are* psychological ones, that when yoga philosophy appears to be making claims about 'universal consciousness' it is really making claims about the psyche. This is in effect an example of *reductionism*. It takes not the form that 'A can be treated as B', but rather that 'A really is nothing but B'. Now Jung has often been accused of psychologism – namely, of treating religious statements in general as if they were nothing but statements of the psyche – and we shall return to this charge in the next chapter; it may well be the case that Jung himself was ambivalent on this question and allowed himself to be swayed now one way, now the other. But here we need to emphasise once again that Jung's dialogue with Oriental thought was far from one of unqualified admiration, but involved a rigorous exchange, and sometimes trenchant criticism and opposition – not so much a gentle conversation, perhaps, as a sustained argument.

This rigorous and forthright confrontation with the Orient is evident in his attitude to its practices, as much as to its theories. Admirers of the East, and of Jung's contribution to its opening towards the West, are often surprised and even hurt to discover that not only was he less than enthusiastic about the adoption by Westerners of practices such as yoga, but that he went out of his way positively to discourage them. As I noted earlier, his commentaries on Eastern texts are peppered with remarks like 'I wish particularly to warn against the oft-attempted imitation of Indian practices' (CW11.933), and 'a direct transplantation of Zen to our Western conditions is neither commendable nor even possible' (CW11.905).

Westerners who, in ever-increasing numbers, were seeking to adopt Eastern practices are accused of being 'spiritual beggars', of wanting to cover up their nakedness with the 'gorgeous trappings of the East', of 'breaking into Oriental palaces', and of applying Eastern ideas 'like an ointment'. Encouraging statements like 'Study yoga – you will learn an infinite amount from it' are immediately countermanded with the stern warning: 'but do not try to apply it' (CW11.868).

Given his claim that the West had much to learn from the East about the inner workings of the psyche, and that its introspective orientation provided a much-needed counter-balance to the predominantly extraverted attitude of the West, should he not have concluded that its methods of psychic investigation could profitably be developed in the West too? Given his belief that Oriental philo-sophy provides an outstanding method of psychic healing, should we not expect Jung, a self-appointed psychic healer, to be eager to convey its benefits to his own culture 'which sickens with a thousand ills'?

JUNG'S ENCLAVISM

To answer these questions we need to understand that Jung adopted a modified form of *Enclavism*. Enclavism, it will be recalled, is the view that cultures, societies, nations are relatively encapsulated entities with a specific identity of their own. In its extreme form this leads to the conclusion that no communication is possible between cultures; each is locked within its own linguistic and conceptual boundaries, and meanings cannot be conveyed from one to the other. Jung, of course, never adopted this extreme position, for his whole hermeneutical approach was based on the assumption that, however strange a foreign culture may seem, there are ways of engaging in a fruitful dialogue with it. However, he also took the view that, while it is possible to understand and learn from an alien culture, there are severe constraints on our capacity to adopt its world-view and practices.

This view in its turn was based on the belief that cultural identity grows from deeply rooted psychological factors. Jung's primary concern as a psychologist was with the individual; indeed he took the view that the indvidual is a funda-mental ontological category, something that cannot be reduced to anything else. Society he viewed as something derivative, a collection of individuals rather than a category in its own right: 'nations are made up of individuals' (CW10.45), he wrote, and this led him to adopt an attitude of extreme suspicion towards all collectivities which, in his view, posed a threat to the integrity of the individual. He was especially concerned about the erosion in the modern Western world of the individual's capacity for self-reliance and responsibility, and with what he saw as the tendency for persons to become social functions and tools of the state.

Nevertheless, during the inter-war period he began to take a close interest in social and political questions, and to embark on the intellectual enterprise of applying psychological concepts in a broader way to whole societies, cultures and nations. In addition to ego-consciousness and the collective unconscious,

Jung identified *collective consciousness*, which comprises the beliefs, attitudes, and world-view of a given society or group. He argued that, though individuals are born with an inherited potential for psychic growth, which he called the collective unconscious, this potential could only be brought to realisation by the influence of the culture of a particular society. The peculiar organisation of the psyche, he believed, 'must be intimately connected with environmental conditions' (CW8.324), and to understand human psychology 'it is absolutely necessary that you study man also in his social and general environments', and consider 'different kinds of societies, different kinds of nations, different traditions' (quoted in Evans, 1979: 151). Thus in addition to those collective aspects of the psyche which are associated with archetypal inheritance, Jung also identified a level of collectivity which arises from the social and cultural context in which the individual psyche develops. It is important to emphasise that for Jung the collective unconscious has nothing at all to do with race, it is 'a pattern peculiar to mankind in general', and hence has 'nothing to do with so-called blood or racial inheritance' (CW18.79); it is inherited along with bodily organs and behavioural reflexes, and hence at this level 'you are the same as the Negro or the Chinese' (CW18.93). The collective consciousness, on the other hand, is a cultural manifestation and hence varies from one society or culture to another.

Jung had a strong sense of the role of history in shaping the human psyche, and the importance of the study of history in psychology – 'Without history there can be no psychology', he remarked – and as Ira Progoff noted, Jung realised at an early stage in his work 'that he would not be able to understand his material unless he studied man on a canvas large enough to include the history of the human race as a whole' (1953: 4). By contrast with Freud's 'bias against the past', as Philip Rieff put it, Jung's whole way of thinking was suffused with history. As a young man he had been deeply impressed by the work of two fellow Baselers, the great historian of the Ancient and Renaissance worlds, Jacob Burckhardt, and J.J. Bachoven, the historian of mythology. He was very conscious of his own personal and cultural roots, and was aware of the way his own thinking had evolved from that of his predecessors, and in all his writings displayed great sensitivity to historical precedents, influences, and comparisons concerning his own ideas. The psyche itself he saw as essentially historical for '[man] carries his whole history with him [and] in his very structure is written the history of mankind' (CW6.570). For this reason we can only hope to understand ourselves and come to terms with our present condition if we relate to the past whence we have sprung.

In the light of this we can understand why it was that Jung insisted that 'Eastern mentality is fundamentally different from ours', for it is the product of a different history, has emerged from quite different cultural conditions, has been shaped by a different climate, a different topography. The Eastern spirit is based upon its own peculiar and unique history, for its peoples have experienced an unbroken development going back thousands of years, and hence have a cultural identity – a collective consciousness – that is quite different from our own. The religious teachings of India constitute the essence of several thousand years of history, and though we can learn a lot from Indian thought, it remains something foreign to our Western mentality. However much we may admire and be inspired by a text such as *The Secret of the Golden Flower*, or the teachings of *kundalinī*, they remain something 'foreign to our organism' (CW13.5), 'a foreign body in our system' (Jung, 1975: 9).

For this reason we should beware of seeking to adopt the ways of the East, for this would be merely attempting to imitate a culture which was not our own. Is it appropriate, he asked, that we should

> put on, like a new suit of clothes, ready-made symbols grown on foreign soil, saturated with foreign blood, spoken in a foreign tongue, nourished by a foreign culture, interwoven with a foreign history, and so resemble a beggar who wraps himself in kingly raiment, a king who disguises himself as a beggar?
>
> (CW9i.27)

To do so would be to play our own history false, like the Theosophists who cover themselves with 'the gorgeous trappings of the East', and who feign a legacy 'to which they are not the legitimate heirs' (CW9i.28).[4] We cannot simply transplant ideas and practices from one tradition to another. While we can learn from the many parallels that can be drawn between East and West, we cannot simply discard our own history, which is built deeply into our psyches, and adopt the practices of another tradition. 'Western man cannot get rid of his history as easily as his short-legged memory' (CW11.802). The organic metaphor plays a strong role in Jung's thinking:

> Anyone who believes that he can simply take over Eastern forms of thought is uprooting himself, for they do not express our Western past, but remain bloodless intellectual concepts that strike no chord in our inmost being. We are rooted in Christian soil.
>
> (CW9ii.273)

Arguments concerning differential development as between cultures have sometimes been employed in the West since the nineteenth century to denigrate and marginalise non-European cultures. It is important to emphasise once again that Jung's approach was quite different from this. His attitude towards the East was often laudatory, even at times deferential, and he was careful to balance his critical attitude towards yoga with expressions of admiration, as in the following passage:

> If I remain so critically averse to yoga, it does not mean that I do not regard this spiritual achievement of the East as one of the greatest things the human mind has ever created. I hope my exposition makes it sufficiently clear that my criticism is directed solely against the application of yoga to the peoples of the West. The spiritual development of the West has been along entirely different lines from that of the East and has therefore

produced conditions which are the most unfavourable soil one can think of for the application of yoga.

(CW11.876)

Thus, according to Jung, the urge to 'take over Eastern forms of thought' typifies an endemic weakness in the Western psyche, the desire to appropriate, to control, to manipulate. The desire to adopt Eastern ways and attitudes is indicative of what we would nowadays call Western 'consumerism' with its tendency to turn everything, including spirituality, into a commodity that can be acquired and exploited. The spirituality of the East is not something that can be acquired in this way; we cannot simply shake off our culture like an outdated fashion in clothes, for it has its roots in a totally different tradition. With heavy irony he insisted that 'yoga in Mayfair or Fifth Avenue, or in any other place which is on the telephone, is a spiritual fake' (CW11.802), and can only succeed in producing 'an artificial stultification of our Western intelligence' (CW11.933).

With our consumerist tendencies, the spiritual goodies of the East have become like drugs: they give us a temporary sense of release and enlightenment, they give us a delightful feeling that we have transcended our painful condition, but in the end they leave us with all our problems unsolved. In effect they become a means not of tackling our condition, but of avoiding it. How typical, Jung laments, of Western man! Our 'imitative urge', misleads us into 'snatching at such "magical" ideas and applying them externally, like an ointment', thus enabling us to avoid facing up to ourselves. People will do anything, he concluded, no matter how absurd,

> to avoid facing their own souls. They will practise Indian yoga and all its exercises, observe a strict regimen of diet, learn theosophy by heart, or mechanically repeat mystic texts from the literature of the whole world – all because they cannot get on with themselves and have not the slightest faith that anything useful could ever come out of their own souls.

(CW12.126)

THE RISKS OF YOGA

Our meddling, acquisitive attitude towards the East carries with it even greater risks. Jung repeatedly warned that our whole psychological constitution, with its extraverted tendency and its strongly developed sense of ego-consciousness, is unsuited to yogic practices, and the unthinking adoption of these practices could have unfortunate, even dire, consequences. On the one hand, it could lead to a strengthening of will and consciousness which could exacerbate the split between the conscious and the unconscious, and prevent the integration of these two sides of the personality. On the other hand, he warned of the dangers of releasing unconscious contents, without appropriate safeguards, which could swamp the conscious psyche and lead to severe psychoses, because the unconscious world, like the world of microphysics, contains within itself explosive forces of

155

unexpected magnitude. The trance-like states sought in yoga, and the powerful methods of Tantric yoga, were especially to be feared. Here there was a real danger, he believed, that psychotic states could be induced which in turn might easily lead to a real psychosis. There is no doubt that Jung recognised in certain yogic states patterns of behaviour which reminded him of the psychotic behaviour he had observed in schizophrenic patients at the Burgholzli Hospital, and in his discussion of the *The Tibetan Book of the Dead* he spoke of it as 'a danger that needs to be taken very seriously indeed' (CW11.847). These dangers are fully recognised in the East by those who practise and teach these techniques, but while they have developed methods – which have deep cultural roots – for coping with these dangers, we in the West are virtually defenceless against the storms that might erupt unexpectedly from the depths of the unconscious.[5]

Does this mean, then, that in the final analysis Eastern techniques are of no value in the West? Jung drew back from so drastic a conclusion. 'Study yoga – you will learn an infinite amount from it', he repeatedly urged; but at the same time 'do not try to apply it' (CW11.868). Yoga can inspire and motivate us, but we shall not be true to ourselves if we merely seek to imitate it. To be true to ourselves, and to our cultural heritage, we must seek a path of spiritual develop-ment which comes from our own inner resources. Jung insisted that by pursuing Eastern methods, by taking on board Oriental philosophies, we are in effect obstructing the path towards our own development, we are substituting some-thing alien for our own authentic experience. 'Too much Oriental knowledge', he wrote in a letter concerning the *I Ching*, 'takes the place of immediate experi-ence, and thus blocks the way to psychology' (*Letters I*: 139). Hence, spiritual renewal for the West must come not from foreign borrowings, nor, as he expressed it, from a 'Tibetan monastery full of Mahatmas' (a reference perhaps to the fantasies of the Theosophist Madame Blavatsky), but from within our own cultural and spiritual traditions. 'We must get at the Eastern values from within and not from without, seeking them in ourselves' (CW11.773).

We must, then, 'build on our own ground with our own methods' (CW11.773). But what grounds and what methods are available to us? We are frequently told by Jung that the West almost entirely lacks the tools with which to engage in an inner exploration. Since the early Christian Gnostics, the only equivalent of yoga in the Western Christian tradition is to be found in the *Spiritual Exercises* of Saint Ignatius, but this work can hardly provide the basis for a spiritual renewal in the twentieth century.

There are two sorts of answers suggested by Jung. The first urges, predictably, that any way forward for the West must arise from the indigenous culture, namely the Christian traditions of the West, that it must grow from the roots of our own history and culture. This is not something that can be invented and put into practice overnight, but will require a long and difficult gestation period. Never-theless he predicted that 'In the course of the centuries the West will produce its own yoga, and it will be on the basis laid down by Christianity' (CW11.876). The second answer relates more specifically to the methods that have been developed by Freud and himself in the field of psychotherapy. According to Jung, these come closest in the modern Western world to the techniques of yoga; his own method of active imagination, in which a patient pursues a narrative fantasy under the supervision of a therapist, is offered as an especially suitable model for the Western psyche.

Neither of these suggestions was elaborated in detail; they remained little more than promissory notes for the future, and we shall examine in the next chapter the question of the extent to which either of these answers is satisfactory. On the face of it they appear to be rather mouse-like offspring from such an arduous hermeneutical labour, and they will provide a convenient starting point at which to begin looking at the whole question of the adequacy of Jung's treatment of Eastern spirituality.

9

CRITICISMS AND SHORTCOMINGS

The project for a 'Western yoga' points to an ambiguity we have noted again and again in Jung's approach to the thought of China and India. On the one hand, he was full of enthusiasm for the East, praising its exalted wisdom, seeking to draw on its inspiration, even in some ways seeking to imitate it, and describing yoga as 'one of the greatest things the human mind has created' (CW11.876). On the other hand, he emphasised its distant, even alien, character, drawing a sharp boundary between the psyches of East and West, and warning the inquisitive Westerner against thoughtlessly overstepping it. As Moacanin (1986: 92) puts it:

> At times Jung is speaking in favour of Eastern traditions, praising their ways of approaching the psyche and their intuitive wisdom, which the West lacks, and at other times he warns Westerners against the dangers of embracing a system that is foreign to their culture.

This ambiguity is especially evident in his *Foreword* to Suzuki's *Introduction to Zen Buddhism* where he speaks of the desirability, even the urgency, of exploring the ways of the East, yet at the same time is careful to underline the 'exotic obscurity' of Zen, and to caution his Western reader against its unsuitability for them. The obvious excitement and curiosity for Eastern ways and ideas he experienced on his trip to India, is balanced by a determination to keep his distance from 'all so-called "holy men"', and to cling to his 'own truth' (MDR: 305). Yet reiterated claims about the fundamental cleavage between the psyches of East and West are contradicted by statements like: 'there is only *one* earth and *one* mankind, East and West cannot rend humanity into two different halves' (CW8.682).

The ambivalence of Jung's approach was evident in the issues discussed at the end of the previous chapter. There we saw that, while Jung was convinced that the West needed some sort of yoga, some kind of spiritual path that would lead us out of our current psychological bondage to extraverted materialism towards a more balanced and harmonious way of being, he maintained that we must create our own yoga, shaped by our own Christian traditions, rather than imitate the ways of the East.[1] Now at one level this seems a sensible prescription, for the idea of creating one's own path rather than following another's carries with it an attractive moral assumption about autonomy and self-reliance; his somewhat derogatory references to the idea of the 'imitation of Christ' rings sympathetic chords in the ears of the modern age with its concern for the virtues of authenticity and self-realisation. But if we begin to question at a deeper level we might well begin to wonder why it is necessary, in this context, to engage with the East at all. If its culture, its ideas, its ways of spiritual growth are so entirely alien to our own, what benefit is there in embarking upon a dialogue with it? If there lies an insurmountable gulf between East and West, how can the one possibly learn from the other?

His reservations and warnings have indeed gone largely unheeded. The enthusiasm in the West for Oriental wisdom, the pursuit of its ideals, the study of its writings, the imitation of its practices, have increased at an exponential rate since the time that Jung was writing on this subject. Of course, he could hardly have been expected to foresee the cultural implosion which followed the Second World War, and the development thereafter of what amounts to a global culture. What is surprising, however, is that he did not grasp the possibility that the dialogue which he in many ways initiated might grow and develop in ever more fruitful ways, and that there might be considerable beneficial effects to be gained by adapting and even adopting the ways and ideas of the East. It is true that there are dangers, as he rightly pointed out, in the *'unthinking'* adoption of Eastern practices, but all the evidence suggests that by and large the yoga techniques of Buddhism, Hinduism and Taoism can be successfully integrated into Western culture, and that their effects can be beneficial. The project for 'creating our own yoga' has to all intents and purposes already begun in a thousand different ways through the adaptation of Oriental methods to the circumstances of the modern world, for example in such fields as health, psychotherapy, personal growth, and professional training. Moreover, the past few decades have witnessed an extraordinary proliferation in the West of centres and institutes teaching a wide range of yoga techniques from *Tai Chi* and *Kendo* to Transcendental Meditation and *Zazen*. These have plainly filled a widely felt need, and while such techniques are not without their risks, they have greatly enriched our cultural life and and have plainly provided for many individuals the opportunity for spiritual and personal growth.

CULTURAL IDENTITY AND CULTURAL PREJUDICE

Let us pursue the question of change in the cultural climate. The first thing to note is that much has happened since Jung's era to render the whole notion of *'our'* culture questionable, if not obsolete. Owing to the ever-increasing interpenetration of peoples, the growing ease of travel, and the ever-widening availability of electronic means of communication, the idea of a cultural tradition with which individuals can exclusively identify themselves, and which permits an easy discrimination between 'my' culture and 'your' culture, has less force in our own age than in Jung's. It is true that ethnic self-awareness and inter-ethnic rivalry have appeared to be on the increase in recent years; enclavism is all too literally on the march once again. But the notion that ethnic divisions, however keenly felt, correspond to clear-cut cultural or psychological identities is much less plausible now than it was fifty years ago. Indeed the whole tendency of the world that we call 'modern' is away from a sense of community and belonging-ness and towards feelings of *anomie* and alienation, a world in which there is a breakdown of traditionally close social relationships and a growth of individual isolation and cultural rootlessness.

Moreover, as we emphasised in an earlier chapter, the fact is that, throughout our history, peoples and their ideas have perpetually inter-penetrated and interacted. As G.E.R. Lloyd points out, strange mentalities do not belong exclusively to 'other' cultures but are also in our midst (1990: 40). Thus, for example, the idea of a simple monolithic Western Christian culture, stretching back to antiquity like a single unbroken thread, is something of a myth, for it is more like a tangled web than a single thread – a web which includes many competing traditions and in which must be included the activities of heretical occultists, Gnostics, and the like, as well as other more unorthodox strands. Christianity itself, which Jung recognised as the essential ingredient of the European psyche, was originally an Oriental religion, brought into Europe by Jews such as Peter and Paul and adopted by the Romans as a religion alien to their indigenous cults – cults which can now be seen to have not completely died out. Similarly, in the East the missionary activities of the Buddhists, especially in China – a country usually seen as one of the most encapsulated of cultural enclaves – offer an intriguing example of the creation of cultural symbiosis. Jung himself was an intrepid explorer of marginalised cultures and belief systems, in some ways a model of openness towards unorthodox ideas and cults lying alongside but out of tune with the central themes of what he saw as his own culture. An instructive illustration of this tendency is to be seen in his extended dialogue with mediaeval alchemy which, despite its patently outsider status in the context of Western Christendom – it derived originally from Egypt, and was regarded at the very least with suspicion by the Church – was viewed by Jung as a model of the process of individuation. It is therefore all the more surprising that when dealing with the East–West dialogue he appears to be unhappy with the idea of cultural inter-penetration, treating it as marginal and suspect, albeit psychologically interesting.

How are we to account for this seeming paradox? In spite of the notorious lack of consistency in Jung's writings, the issue here is more than one of ambiguity or ambivalence. To see this we must consider again the question whether Jung, for all his heroic attempts to transcend cultural boundaries, was not himself an exponent of a vicious form of enclavism.

In his attempt to draw attention to the fundamental differences between East and West, which I discussed in the last chapter, Jung often characterised these differences in ways which now appear to us somewhat naive. At one level he seems to have fallen for popular stereotypes, employing phrases such as 'the mysterious Orient', 'the baffling mind of the East', 'the unfathomableness of

India', 'the dreamlike world of India', and 'the odorous East', and his repeated refrains concerning 'the strangeness' and 'the incomprehensibility of the Eastern psyche', can be read as echoes of distorting attitudes and shibboleths which have for a long time been all too common in the West. In hermeneutical terms it does of course make sense to create some kind of initial distance between inter-locutors, but phrases such as these carry a huge weight of prejuduce which can only serve to frustrate the whole attempt at dialogue.

At a deeper level this emphasis on difference can easily become hypostasised and turned into a full-blown psychological theory. As we saw, Jung often sought to explain the apparent chasm between East and West in terms of underlying psychological differences, differences which are deeply rooted in our respective traditions. Not content with this, he went further and argued that these differences can be formulated in terms of binary distinctions. The most common of these involved the use of his distinction between the *extraverted* and the *introverted* psychological types. The West, with its concern for the practical demands of life, its empirical science, its technological prowess, its political activism, represents a typically extraverted point of view. The East, with its spiritual sophistication, its concern with the inner world of consciousness, its quietistic acceptance of life, offers the opposite introverted point of view. He spoke, too, of the mania of the Western mind for objectivity, of its egocentricity, of its greed and rapacity. By contrast with these features, he saw the East as less egocentric than the West, as possessing a profounder understanding of life, as having an altogether gentler and more passive disposition. The Western mind has an upward tendency symbolised in the skyward thrust of the Gothic style of church architecture, whereas the Oriental mind tends to stay closer to the earth and 'turn back into the maternal depths of nature', a feature to be found symbolised in the Hindu temple. And finally, the Western psyche represents the most exquisite development of rational consciousness, whereas in the Eastern psyche we can observe by contrast a fascination with the unconscious depths of the mind.

The search for distinctive psychological characteristics between different cultural communities and historical epochs, and the use of psychological con-cepts to explain cultural and historical phenomena, may not in itself be an objectionable undertaking. Psycho-history, for example, is now a recognised field within historical studies, and Jung may be viewed as having made an important early contribution towards its development. His general contention that 'Psychological differences obtain between all nations and races, even between the inhabitants of Zurich, Basel, and Bern', differences which are parallel to those that obtain between individuals (CW10.1029), is unexceptionable as a preliminary conjecture awaiting further elaboration. Nevertheless, there is little doubt that Jung's employment of this methodology in practice was at the very least overly simplistic, and at worst offensive to the parties concerned.[2]

For a start, there is the frequent over-simplification of the differences between East and West, typified by remarks such as: 'The West is always seeking uplift, but the East seeks a sinking or deepening' (CW11.936), and in speculations such as 'the mind of the Far East is related to our Western consciousness as the unconscious is, that is, as the left hand to the right' (CW18.1484). Conjectures such as these are, to be sure, not without heuristic value, but left unanalysed and unqualified they are grossly inadequate and misleading.[3] Also, they are frequently based on inadequate scholarship, as for example Jung's assertion that 'Critical philosophy [is] foreign to the East' (CW11.759), which fails to take account of dialectical traditions in Indian philosophy such as that of the Buddhist *Mādhyamaka* and the development of Buddhist logic. As the Indian philosopher B.K. Matilal complains: 'too often the term "Indian Philosophy" is identified with a subject that is presented as mystical and non-argumentative, that is at best poetic and at worst dogmatic. A corrective to this view is long overdue' (1986: 4–5).[4]

Furthermore, even leaving aside the obvious complexities within the European context, the tendency on Jung's part to lump all Asian religions and philosophies together is insensitive to the vast differences between India and South Asia on the one side and China and Japan on the other, and indeed to the differences that are to be found within these separate regions themselves. As I argued earlier, the civilisations of China and India, along with their ways of thought and behaviour, show rich internal variety, and though the religious and philosophical systems of Asia have overlapped and inter-penetrated, they represent a wide spectrum of world-views and values. Few would wish to deny that there are psychological variations between peoples of different cultural backgrounds, and even that these variations could in some way be systematised, but it is implausible, to say the least, to suggest that the complex and rich cultural heritages of Asia, or for that matter of Europe, are expressions of a single psychological type.

It is true that in his writings on this subject Jung concentrated his attention for the most part on a variety of specific texts and ideas, from both East and West, treating them in detail and in depth, and in general was sensitive to cultural and psychological differences. As I have frequently emphasised, Jung was in many ways a pluralistic thinker and a self-confessed empiricist who stood against the tendency to over-simplify and to construct grand theories. For example, he spoke of the need to understand the human psyche from a variety of different perspectives, and warned that '[the] greatest danger that threatens psychology is one-sidedness and insistence on a single standpoint' (CW10.1053). In a lecture given in Germany in 1933 he remarked that 'It was one of the greatest experiences of my life to discover how enormously different people's psyches are' (CW10.285). It is all the more surprising, therefore, that he allowed himself to be drawn into the game of psychological stereotyping, and felt impelled to sum up the mind of the East in sweeping generalisations.

There is evidence here of the influence of the once popular French anthropologist, Lucien Lévy-Bruhl, who was frequently mentioned by Jung in his writings, and who taught that there are categorical differences between the mentality of primitive and modern Western peoples. The thinking of the former are 'prelogical' and characterised by a tendency towards mysticism and the absorption of the individual mind in what he termed the *participation mystique*. This he contrasted with the supposed analytical habit of thought of scientific Western man. Now, while Jung certainly took exception to the implication in Lévy-Bruhl's theory that there is some kind of innate difference between the intellectual powers of primitive and modern man, nevertheless the idea of pervasive mentalities and the notion of the *participation mystique* clearly influenced his outlook in general and his understanding of the Oriental mind in particular. He made strenuous efforts to reject any attempt to establish an order of merit or value between East and West, but he was often trapped into making comments and observations which, though no doubt well intended, appear to us now as naive, and even dangerous. Thus, for example, he spoke of the Eastern intellect as 'childish' compared with the Western intellect (CW13.8), and though he qualified this remark by denying that this had anything to do with intelligence, the suspicion must remain in the mind of the reader that he was implicitly ranking the Western mentality above the Eastern. And again, he claimed to have observed that an Indian, 'inasmuch as he is really Indian, does not think', but rather he 'perceives the thought', going on to say that in this respect he 'resembles the primitive' (CW10.1007). Our worries about these remarks are not entirely removed by the qualification that 'no offence is intended', nor by the subsequent discussion in which he argued that the liberation of Western consciousness 'from the burden of irrationality and instinctive impulsiveness' has led to 'many relapses into the most appalling barbarity' and to a diabolical misuse of science and technology (CW10.1008–9).

The whole question of differential mentalities and of national psychologies is a minefield, and Jung himself stepped into this minefield in the 1930s, namely at the time of his most intense interest in the East. In 1933 Jung accepted an invitation to become president of the International General Medical Society for Psychotherapy, an organisation based in Germany but including sections from other countries, and which enjoyed the approval of the Nazis who had come to power in that same year. Although Jung had sought to mitigate the consequences of anti-semitic legislation for the Society, and strove to maintain its international character, as editor of the Society's journal he made certain injudicious remarks concerning the psychological differences between Jews and Aryans which led to accusations of racism and anti-semitism. While allowing that the Jews, like the Chinese, with their three-thousand-year-old civilisations, enjoyed 'a wider area of psychological consciousness than we', he hazarded that the Jewish race as a whole 'possesses an unconscious which can be compared with the "Aryan" only with reserve', that 'it has been a grave error in medical psychology up to now to apply Jewish categories – which are not even binding on all Jews – indiscriminately to Germanic and Slavic Christendom', and that the Aryan unconscious 'has a higher potential than the Jewish' (CW10.353–4).[5]

Now it is easy to lift such remarks out of context and to misunderstand the general drift of Jung's argument which, ostensibly at least, sought to rescue psychotherapy from what he saw as the dogmatic and narrow approach of Freud

163

and his followers, an approach which he claimed was not representative of 'European man'. Nevertheless the remarks were not only offensive and insensitive in the light of the Nazis' anti-semitic ideology, but betray once again an overly simplistic conception of national psychology. They betray a willingness to contrast the collective psyches of Jews and gentiles respectively in a way that overrides not only enormous individual variations but also the complexities of history and of cultural evolution. This point is a central contention of Andrew Samuels who believes that psychologists should resist the temptation to indulge in national typologies and be content instead to contribute to a multidisciplinary endeavour in this field. Jung got into trouble, he believes,

> less because of his politics than because of his ambition to become a psychologist of nations. . . . [His] mistake was to expand his role as a psychologist to the point where he could seem to regard the nation as an exlusively psychological fact to be observed solely from a psychological point of view.
>
> (Samuels, 1992: 24)

In his own defence Jung argued that the attempt to differentiate between Germanic and Jewish psychology 'implies no depreciation of Semitic psychology, any more than it is a depreciation of the Chinese to speak of the peculiar psychology of the Oriental' (CW10.1014); hence he claimed to 'express no value-judgements, nor do I intend any veiled ones' (CW10.1031). But the comparison with the Chinese is revealing, for, however blameless were Jung's conscious intentions, his talk of 'the peculiar psychology of the Oriental' is as objectionable as his talk of the peculiar psychology of the Jews.

Part of the problem here lay, as I have suggested, in Jung's failure to address adequately the whole cultural and historical context in which religious and philosophical ideas arise. As in his studies of European alchemy, he paid little heed to the social, political, and economic environment in which these ideas flourished, and there was on the whole little attempt on his part to recover the meaning of the texts he studied by examining their place within the relevant cultural matrix. He approached these texts as if they provided an unmediated, albeit imperfect, insight into the Eastern psyche, a direct illumination of the Oriental mind. I argued in Chapter 3 that it is a mistake to tie ideas so closely to the cultural matrix that cross-cultural communication then appears impossible. But at the same time it is equally a mistake to ignore the cultural setting almost completely. This omission on Jung's part certainly sits ill with his own stated commitment, discussed in the previous chapter, to the need for historical awareness in psychology, and with his belief that 'it is absolutely necessary that you study man in his social and general environments' (quoted in Evans, 1979: 151). Statements such as these have a clear hermeneutical ring about them, and no doubt Jung would have concurred in principle with Gadamer's assertion that 'the meaning of the part is always discovered only from the context, i.e. ultimately from the whole' (1975: 167), but his actual practice with regard to Eastern texts and ideas does not always confirm this.

This whole approach sometimes gives Jung's studies of Eastern thought a somewhat disembodied quality. His understanding of the East was essentially *textual*, and a rather rarified and desanitised one at that. His oft-repeated image of the Indian mind as concerned with an unswerving vision of the transcendent whole – an attitude which conspicuously contrasted with the predatory inclinations of the European mind – is a case in point. Now this idealisation may suit the needs of some of his readers who simply want to transpose Oriental wisdom into their own terms, but it inadequately serves Jung's own ambition to comprehend 'the peculiar psychology of the Oriental', and to build a 'bridge of understanding' between the two sides. The exalted image of the East which frequently – though not, it should be added, exclusively – emerges from Jung's writings does indeed represent a refreshing antidote to Western arrogance, and is a welcome corrective to some of the distorted perceptions Europeans have had of their own civilisation and its place in world history. But at the same time it may, in its turn, represent a subtle form of cultural imperialism. As I noted above, Jung was acutely aware of what we would now call the 'consumerist' nature of much Western interest in the East, the fact that it desires to put on 'the gorgeous trappings of the East . . . like a new suit of clothes', and to 'imitate its ways unthinkingly'. But there is a danger that his own approach to the East falls into the same trap, a danger that the East becomes an ideal, unreal object controlled and manipulated for our own purposes, a vision which is effectively blind to the real East, deaf to its real voice.

This subtle, rather *un*-hermeneutical, form of appropriation is not new in history, of course. In Chapter 2 I described the way in which, first, the Enlightenment *philosophes* and, later, the German Romantics projected onto the Orient – Confucianism and the Vedanta respectively – idealised images of their own political and spiritual needs. Their 'discovery' of the East, though real enough in one sense, was also at a deep level an act of creation, the fashioning of some ideal 'other' which provided them with the means to execute their own projects. In Nietzschean terms it might be described as a manifestation of the 'will to power'. A similar point has been made by P.C. Almond concerning the European attitudes in nineteenth-century Britain where Buddhism became in effect a textual object, the upshot of which, he argues, was that '[through] the West's progressive possession of the texts of Buddhism, it becomes, so to say, materially owned by the West; and by virtue of this ownership, ideologically controlled by it' (1988: 24).

In the light of this we might once more raise the general question whether in these circumstances anything that might properly be called a dialogue could take place. Can there be a genuine dialogue where one side is in virtually total control, where in Halbfass's words, 'the European "mode of thinking" has already achieved planetary domination' (1988: 169)? Perhaps, as he goes on to suggest, there can for the present be no escape from the despotic global presence of European thought, that 'in the modern planetary situation, Eastern and Western "cultures" can no longer meet one another as equal partners [since they] meet *in* a Westernized world, under the shape of Western ways of thinking' (*ibid.*), and hence there can be no possibility of a genuinely global forum for intellectual exchange. No doubt all translation involves a measure of appropriation, but in the passage of ideas from East to West, where the languages and cultures of the latter have assumed the status of world domination, may we not be witnessing something less like an innocent conversation and more like an imperial annexation?

Now while these large issues go well beyond the scope of this book, nevertheless they inevitably raise questions about Jung's own project in seeking to encompass Asian – and other non-modern and non-European – modes of thinking within a theory of universal archetypes. It will be recalled that his first major literary invasion of Oriental territory was his Psychological Commentary on *The Secret of the Golden Flower*, an expedition which, so he claimed, enabled him not only to construct a bridge between East and West but to confirm his theory that the human mind is innately conditioned towards certain universally identifiable modes of thinking and experiencing – the archetypes. There is a certain naïvety here which assumes that an enterprise such as this can be carried out without regard to the social and political circumstances. This naïvety was evident in the way in which he felt confident in raising questions about 'Semitic psychology' in the 1930s, seemingly regardless of the wider political implications for such questions in Nazi Germany at that time. The question of Eastern thought and its relation to a universal psychological theory is certainly more subtle and less direct, but it points to similar underlying issues which are avoided by Jung. His lapse into stereotypes and the use of terms like 'childish' and 'primitive' when speaking about Eastern thought and peoples may involve less immediately contentious issues than those concerning Semitic psychology, but the fact of the matter is that, as we saw above, Jung himself made a connection between talk about Jewish and about Oriental psychology, yet drew the wrong conclusions from it. The disclaimers that he 'implies no depreciation', and that 'no offence is intended' by such locutions, sound hollow to our ears which are now more attuned to picking up clues to sub-texts and to hidden ideological meanings. It is easy, indeed, to be critical with hindsight, and rather anachronistic to subject Jung to bombardment with critical ordnance that has been developed since his day, but it is important to bring such issues into play, if only for the sake of estimating the contemporary relevance of Jung's 'dialogue' with the East. I shall return to this subject in the final chapter.[6]

THE ADEQUACY OF JUNG'S METHOD

These issues have implications for the claim made earlier that Jung's approach was essentially *hermeneutical*. Here a number of issues arise. The first is whether Jung's approach allows sufficient space for the East to speak for itself. I indicated in an earlier chapter that, according to Gadamer's hermeneutical model, any dialogue with the textual past must take account of the historical situation both of the text itself and of that of the reader of the text; in the case of the former this means allowing the text to speak for itself; in the case of the latter it involves the recognition of one's own agenda and one's own pre-judgements. Now the problem with Jung's approach, it could be argued, is that it pays too much attention to the latter and too little to the former. It is fully conscious that it starts out from the spiritual needs of 'modern man', and the clinical needs associated with the development of psychotherapy, and hence that it is drawing ancient Oriental texts into modern Western discourse. Thus, for example, the construction of a grand dichotomy between extraverted and introverted mentalities, and the search for some kind of psychological balance between the two, may make good sense, and indeed be highly beneficial, within the context of Western history and Western needs. But to draw the East wholesale, willy nilly, into this narrative is to turn the dialogue into a monologue, and to render the East merely a figment of Western imagination. Gadamer urges that 'To interpret [a text] means precisely to use one's own preconceptions so that the meaning of the text can really be made to speak for us' (1975: 358). But he also speaks of the need to open oneself up to the other person, and of 'the reciprocal relationship . . . between interpreter and text, corresponding to the mutuality of understanding in conversation' (p. 349).

The question that Jung's methodology raises is whether it adequately facilitates this opening up, this mutuality. His insistence on engaging with the strange mind of the Orient via the concepts and practices of analytical psychology is highly suggestive, but may in the final analysis be self-defeating. It is true, as I argued in Chapter 3, that we cannot simply shuffle off our culturally shaped conceptual apparatus and penetrate the meanings of foreign texts with no presuppositions whatsoever; Gadamer's hermeneutics teaches us that our prejudices and pre-judgements represent an essential component of all meaningful exchange. But at the same time it can be argued that Jung clings too firmly to his own cultural territory, protesting too much that we must 'build on our own ground with our own methods', that we should not 'sacrifice . . . our own nature', or allow ourselves to be 'torn from our roots'. In spite of his own often-repeated willingness to learn from the East, with claims such as that 'the *Bardo Thödol* has been my constant companion [to which] I owe not only many stimulating ideas and discoveries, but also many fundamental insights' (CW11.833), he felt it necessary to distance his readers from such texts with phrases like 'foreign to our organism' and 'a foreign body in our system'. The very eloquence of such phrases, and the frequency of their occu rence, leaves the reader with the sense that in the final analysis we are locked within the prisons of our own local mentalities.

This leads to a second question which touches on a central and distinctive feature of his hermeneutical approach. Jung's attempts to span the gulf that divides the present from the past, the West from the East, are based very largely on the postulation of *analogies*, a method which, as we noted in Chapter 3, he also employed in his work as a psychotherapist. Thus, for example, the transcultural manifestation of the mandala image is postulated by drawing analogies between patterns and diagrams found in different media in different cultures. *Karma* is compared to archetypes. Kundalini yoga is compared to individuation.

The Tibetan account of the passage of the dead soul is likened to psychological transformation. *Satori* is likened to a psychological breakthrough. Now drawing analogies such as these is in itself quite unexceptionable; in general the possibility of human discourse depends on such a semiotic function, and to grasp the meaning of a term often takes the form of drawing an analogy with one that is better known. But Jung's intentions go further than this. His quest for analogies is in fact a quest for underlying psychological identities or essences. He hopes that by demonstrating the analogical connections between concepts from remote cultures he can penetrate through to the archetypal foundations on which the psyche itself is built.

The trouble here is that the drawing of analogies is a notoriously inexact science which, at its worst, is capable of delivering any desired conclusion whatsoever. As is often noted, anything can be compared with anything, and analogies can be drawn almost at will between any pair of terms. The sheer weight of analogies drawn by Jung is undoubtedly impressive, not least because of the extraordinarily wide range of cultural sources, both East and West, from which they are culled. But in the end the reader is left wondering what, if anything, has been proved. Questions can be raised, for example, concerning the close analogies drawn by Jung between the spiritual methods of the East and the practice of psychotherapy. There has been a tendency – one that goes well beyond Jung – to identify psychotherapeutic with spiritual aims, and as Jacob Needleman has wryly commented: 'The shrinks are beginning to sound like gurus, and gurus are beginning to sound like shrinks' (quoted in Claxton, 1986: 296).

This is not the place to discuss the general issue concerning the compatibility between psychological and spiritual growth. However, as far as Jung is concerned, it is necessary to ask whether Eastern spiritual practices are being squeezed unnaturally to fit into his own model of psychological development. There may indeed be some broad analogies between, say, the discipline of Kundalini and the path of individuation, but from this it cannot be inferred that they represent, at a fundamental level, one and the same process. Those approaching the matter from a religious point of view, such as Martin Buber, might well be concerned that the transcendent nature of religious experience – its relationship to an essentially 'other' – means that it is inherently different from one that is properly termed 'psychological'. Approaching the matter from a different angle, Coward, for example, while admitting that 'Jung's reinterpretion of Kundalini yoga in terms of his own psychological theory is an exceptional *tour de force*', suggests that by subsequent standards of scholarship Jung's distortion of the *chakra* system would be unacceptable, and that his inaccurate description of the conceptual structure of Kundalini yoga would do nothing more than 'provide a colorful, if at times confusing, backdrop against which Jung could develop his own thinking about the ego, the emotions and the self' (1985: 123). Thus, while modern students of comparative psychology or religion might find suggestive the drawing of similarities such as these between Eastern and Western thought and practice, it is another question whether they can be deemed to be in any useful sense 'the same thing', or whether any theoretical edifice can be erected thereon.

At one level Jung's search for a common language in which to communicate with foreign or with lost cultures is admirable, for it widens the possible dimensions of human sympathy, and enhances our sense of the commonality of the human race. But at another level the methodology employed lends itself to special pleading and to indulgence in wishful thinking. Our admiration for Jung's courage in confronting these 'alien' texts in the way that he did, therefore, must be tempered by caution in accepting the authenticity of the details of his 'discoveries'.

This inevitably leads us to the question of the validity of Jung's actual interpretations. There is nothing in the hermeneutical or the dialogical approach as such which guarantees correctness, nothing which certifies that Jung's interpretation of particular Eastern texts was sound. It is a central tenet of Gadamer's that the task of interpreting a text or historical event can never be completed and indeed is necessarily always in the process of revision. It will be recalled that, according to Gadamer, there is no interpretation which is timelessly true or correct 'in itself', and that the inevitable historicity of the interpreter means that historical understanding is always under-way, never finished, for it 'depends on constantly new assimilation and interpretation' (1975: 358). In the light of this it is to be expected that the readings which Jung offered in the 1930s will now appear in certain respects inadequate and dated. Thus, for example, the translations used by Jung have now been improved in many respects, and in general the scholarship in this area has advanced considerably beyond that which prevailed in Jung's day.

This whole issue of the drawing of parallels between Western psychology and Eastern spiritual teachings has been raised in a highly critical way by R.H. Jones. He does not wish to deny in principle the legitimacy of attempts to translate terms from one religious tradition to another, such as the use of the term *mantra* to refer to Christian evocations of the name of Jesus. However, according to him, Jung fundamentally distorted Eastern texts by drawing parallels which are essentially inappropriate, and most significantly by substituting his own theoretical constructs from analytical psychology as equivalences for Eastern religious concepts (1979: 142–4). According to this argument, what Jung failed to appreciate was the difference between his own conceptual framework and that of the Eastern traditions he was dealing with – a failure which resulted in a systematic distortion of the latter. For example, the idea of individuation, a theoretical concept that is central to Jung's system, cannot easily be transposed into Eastern terms in the way that he believed. In the first place, individuation implies *self*-liberation whereas many (though not all) traditions in India and East Asia are based upon belief in the power of *others* to bring this about (p. 145). In the second place, individuation involves the quest for a balance between the conscious and the unconscious, and hence presupposes the impossibility of abolishing the conscious ego, whereas yoga is concerned with the transcendence of ego-consciousness and the purification of the self from all worldly defilements (p. 148).

169

This relates to a further and more fundamental misunderstanding on Jung's part, according to Jones, namely his identification of the 'higher' consciousness of Indian philosophy with his own concept of the collective unconscious, a misunderstanding which, as we shall see shortly, arises from Jung's inability to imagine a conscious mental state that does not relate to a subject or ego. The crucial point at which the concepts of 'enlightened mind' and 'collective un-conscious' diverge is, according to Jones, that the former is in some sense a *conscious* state of mind, whereas the state of *samādhi* is a 'state of awareness without self-awareness . . . a state which . . . Jung cannot conceive' (1979: 147). Here again, Jones claims, Jung is conspicuously trapped in the net of his own conceptual system, his failure to grasp the full meaning of the idea of enlighten-ment arising from his failure to be sufficiently aware and critical of his own theoretical assumptions and those of the culture from which he sprang. Jones does not mention the hermeneutical tradition here, but his criticism could easily be seen, not so much as a rejection of this approach as drawing attention to Jung's failure to live up to its demands.

THE ADEQUACY OF JUNG'S UNDERSTANDING

The adequacy of Jung's attempts to draw analogies between Eastern and Western concepts raises the thorny question of translation. The translations employed by Jung were, in most cases, the results of pioneering efforts of Wilhelm and Evans-Wentz in his own day, or were the work of Max Müller in a previous era, and it is hardly surprising that improvements have been made in the intervening period. The sino-logist A.C. Graham, for example, while acknowledging the historical importance and sympathetic nature of Richard Wilhelm's translations, admits that by the standards of recent scholarship they are somewhat 'free', and that they could 'benefit from the advances in Classical Chinese grammatical studies over the last half century' (1989: 358n). This point is made more trenchantly, and more specifically in relation to Jung, by Thomas Cleary who, in the Introduction to his new translation of *The Secret of the Golden Flower*, comments that

> Although Jung credited *The Secret of the Golden Flower* with having clarified his own work on the unconscious . . . what he did not know was that the text he was reading was in fact a garbled translation of a truncated version of a corrupted recension of the original work.
>
> (Cleary, 1991: 3)

More in-depth and wide-ranging questions in this regard have recently been raised by John Reynolds, and it will be useful to look at his arguments in some detail.

In his new edition of *The Tibetan Book of the Great Liberation*, retitled *Self-Liberation Through Seeing with Naked Awareness*, Reynolds argues that the Evans-Wentz translation used by Jung is fundamentally flawed, and that, 'Misled by this translation, Dr Jung had no way to know what the Tibetan text was actually talking about' (1989: 108). For a start, Evans-Wentz himself, though an important innovator in this field, was not a Tibetan scholar, his training at Oxford being in Celtic folklore, having come to Indian studies via theosophy, and indeed as he himself freely admitted he had no knowledge of the Tibetan language and had only spent a few months in Tibet. For his translation he relied on a rough rendering made by a Tibetan Lama which he reworked and edited, largely on the basis of a knowledge of Hindu Vedānta philosophy filtered through the lenses of his theosophical beliefs. Naturally Reynolds places no blame on Jung for this, and is at pains to express his admiration for both men's efforts in awakening the West to the historical and philosophical significance of Tibetan Buddhist litera- ture. But at the same time he draws attention to a number of misunderstandings perpetrated by Jung on the basis of this faulty translation. Thus, for example, he points out that Jung's identification of the expression 'Mental Self' with his own concept of the self is based on Evans-Wentz's mistranslation of *prajñāparamītā*, which means 'the perfection of wisdom or the wisdom which has gone beyond', a term which, Reynolds assures us, has no psychological connotation but rather refers to an insight which 'goes beyond all metaphysical concepts and mental constructions' (1989: 145).

In effect, therefore, 'what Dr Jung was commenting upon in his "Psycho- logical Commentary" was not the psychic reality of the East but the psyche as represented by Evans-Wentz' (1989: 108). Inevitably, Reynolds believes, this led Jung to a number of conclusions regarding Tibetan Buddhism 'which are reflec- tions more of prejudice than of insight' (p. 106), prejudices which were not just a matter of simple mistranslation. Amongst these misunderstandings are: Jung's tendency to think of Orientals as typically inhabiting a sort of dream-world, by contrast with the 'definite and tangible' world inhabited by Westerners; his equation of the unconscious of Western psychology with the 'Superconscious' or 'Cosmic Conscious' of the East, 'suggesting that the principal difference between them is that we Westerners strive for individual awareness and autonomy, while the Oriental does not' (p. 107); and his insistence that the Buddhist notion of non-duality (*samādhi* and *advayajñāna*) could be equated with his idea of the conjunction of opposites, a construal at variance with both Buddhism and Vedānta (p. 108). Nevertheless, it must be added that Reynolds recognises the importance of Jung's endeavours in this field, and goes on to speculate that, had Jung enjoyed the opportunity of dealing more directly with the texts and practi- tioners of Tibetan Buddhism, he might well have revised his views 'of the unsuitability of Western people practising "Eastern" methods of meditation and spiritual development' (p. 114).

This raises the whole question of the adequacy of Jung's grasp of the nature of Eastern spiritual practices. Peter Bishop, for example, argues that Jung did not fully appreciate Buddhist meditation, seeing it in terms of concentration and absorption, as a trance-like state in which one withdraws from the world and surrenders to the unconscious (1984: 49–50). Roberts Avens also criticises Jung for his belief that 'meditation [is] a one sided attempt to withdraw from the world, dissolving the ego and leading back to an indefinite experience of oneness and timelessness' (1980: 80). This sort of criticism is not entirely accurate since, in his discussion of Zen meditation, Jung specifically attibuted to *Zazen* the aim of refining consciousness rather than eliminating it: 'It is not that something different is seen, but that one sees differently', he claims, and spoke of *satori* as an 'illumination', a 'revelation', and as an insight into the self (CW11.891, and *passim*). Nevertheless, it is true that his accounts of meditation generally emphasise the loss of rational, conscious awareness and the withdrawal from the external world, from the body and the senses. Thus he spoke of yoga as 'a method by which libido is "systematically introverted"', causing the subject to 'sink into the unconscious', its ultimate aim being the dissolution of the ego into the universal Ground – *Brahman* (CW6.190–2). And elsewhere he spoke of the goal of yoga as 'the void of deep sleep', an 'autohypnotic condition, which removes [one] from the world and its illusions' (*Letters I*, 1942: 311), and as involving 'the condition of imagelessness and emptiness' (MDR: 306).

Now while it may be the case that this accurately represents some aspects of Eastern yoga and meditation practice, it fails to do justice to the whole range of such practices to be found in Asia, and tends at the same time to perpetuate certain rather unfortunate myths and stereotypes concerning Eastern religions. Many Buddhist practices have the aim not of putting adepts to sleep but precisely of waking them up. This has already been noted in the case of Japanese *Zazen*, but it is also to be found in the method of *vipassanā* where the aim is often referred to as 'clarity of seeing', and in the method of 'mindfulness' in which consciousness is not dissolved but rather trained to concentrate on a single object, either internal or external. These and other practices, such as those associated with the *Vajrāyana* tradition, incorporate a whole range of mental exercises in which the mind is taught, not to eliminate itself, but rather to refine itself, to achieve a state of clarity and purity in which the world is not so much avoided as confronted without illusion or self-deception. Mokusen Miyuki, for example, challenges the view that Eastern religions typically aim at the dissolution, or at least the depotentiation, of the ego, citing the case of the Pure Land tradition of Buddhism which 'aids the individual to strengthen the ego through the integration of unconscious contents' (Spiegelman and Miyuki, 1985: 137–8). In a similar vein, Herbert Guenther asserts that 'the point of meditation is not to develop trance-like states; rather it is to sharpen perceptions, to see things as they are' (1975: 27).

Jung's refusal to experiment with yoga methods inevitably led to a self-imposed limitation on his capacity to sympathise with and to make sense of Eastern religious thought and practice, and it is interesting to speculate whether, had he been more aware of the variety of meditational techniques and had he been prepared to experiment with them, as he was with the *I Ching*, his judgement as to the suitability of yoga for the Westerner would have been less harsh. We saw in the last chapter that he had grave misgivings about the adoption in the West of yoga techniques, and such misgivings may have been justified to some extent; unprepared, immature, and ill-directed exposure to yoga constitutes a psychological danger. But while he was wise to warn against the consequences of the 'unthinking', i.e. the undisciplined, adoption of Eastern practices, his failure to encourage or to anticipate the growth of a responsible and disciplined practice of yoga must be seen as a serious shortcoming in his bridge-building enterprise. There are today many individuals and organisations which have taken these arts seriously and which practice and teach them in a serious and responsible way, and it is difficult to imagine that Jung could have maintained his disapproval had he been able to witness developments during recent decades.

Jung's reservations about what he saw as the task of dissolving the conscious ego were not just practical ones. He was not only concerned with the possibly harmful consequences of such practices for the Westerner, but, as we have seen, actually believed that they rested on some kind of conceptual mistake. He maintained that '[if] there is no ego there is nobody to be conscious of anything' (CW11.744), and hence an egoless state is not a higher state of the individual but one in which the individual is obliterated entirely. 'There must', he insisted, 'always be somebody or something left over to experience the realization [of egolessness]' (CW11.817).

Several critics have seized on this as pointing to severe limitations in Jung's understanding of Eastern thought, and to his inability to emancipate himself from Eurocentric categories, in particular from the duality of subject and object. According to Alan Watts, Jung, like Freud, clung to the idea of the substantiality of the ego, in spite of his recognition of its relativity in relation to the whole of the psyche. He argues that Jung's reluctance to allow the possibility of an egoless state is the consequence of little more than 'a mere convention of syntax' – the subject–predicate structure of Western languages, and his insistence on a strong ego structure is the consequence of the Western 'struggle against nature' which in turn is 'the necessary condition of civilization' (1973: 106). He sees Jung's aversion to ego-absorption as manifesting a predominant Western prejudice, namely the belief that the advance of the human race requires the emergence of ego-consciousness from the level of bestiality and primitive unconsciousness, and that any regression to this state is full of dangers both for the individual and for society, dangers all too evident in Nazi Germany. The Eastern view of the transformation of the ego, according to Watts, should not be understood in this way. It does not involve a return to some earlier state 'of the swamp and the cave' from which we need to be emancipated, but rather an elevation into a higher state in which the ego is not abolished but sublimated. One of the consequences of Jung's failure fully to emancipate himself from Western prejudices, he adds, is that 'the voice of the Protestant conscience' still speaks loudly within him, and urges him to reject the temptation to believe that the human spirit is capable of rising above its pains and troubles, and that it can therefore, as in the East, allow the conscious ego a sabbath from perpetual strife.

In a similar vein, and in a book with a similar title to that of Watts, Swami Ajaya argues that Jung, while enlarging on Freud's concept of the psyche by exploring the depths of the collective unconscious, fails to penetrate further into the broader perspective offered by yoga psychology. Jung's advance beyond Freud lay in his recognition of the importance of the world of archetypes, but 'he remained absorbed with comprehending the ideal forms [of the archetypes] and could not envision a meaningful state of consciousness beyond that' (1984: 157). He recognised the importance of the withdrawal of projections, namely the realisation that many of our obsessions and fears are illusions created from within our own minds, but failed to carry this a stage further by allowing that the archetypes themselves are creations of the mind. Buddhist and Vedānta psychology, according to Ajaya, 'goes beyond Jung and other dualistic thinkers; it asserts that the entire universe, including the inner world of archetypes, is a projection of the unified and undifferentiated consciousness' (p. 160). Yoga psychology 'goes on to explore those modes of experience found above the realm of archetypes' (p. 307).

What this criticism amounts to, then, is not so much that Jung misrepresented yoga philosophy, but rather that, despite his admiration for Indian psychology and his stated affinity with it in certain respects, he failed to carry his own psychological speculations far enough, a limitation evident also in Jung's reluctance to elaborate on the higher *chakras*. Yoga pointed the way, not back to the collective mentality of 'primitive' people, but rather to a higher form of consciousness in which duality of subject and object is transcended. The state of 'pure consciousness' that this entails is not one in which the individual subject has been abolished, but rather one in which the divisions that we mark out on the face of the world, such as that between the self and the not-self, are seen to be projections, and hence illusions. In the final analysis Jung remained wedded to a dualistic outlook, one which denied the possibility of fusing subject with object in some higher unity.

Whether one believes this to involve a misunderstanding on Jung's part, or alternatively an insight on his part into the metaphysical confusions of Indian thought, depends on philosophical judgement. On the one side, it could be argued that within any system of philosophy yoga involves a fairly straightforward contradiction; on the other hand, it could be argued that Western philosophy itself is limited and needs to take account of experiences that are incompatible with Western logic. Whichever view one might wish to take here, it is apparent that a thread of recent thinking can be traced which sees Jung's interpretation of Eastern thought as limited to the extent that it fails to go beyond the conceptual framework of orthodox European understanding. Moacanin, taking note of Jung's reluctance to conceive of the possibility of achieving total non-duality, turns the argument back on Jung by pointing out that his own concepts 'are often irrational and paradoxical', and that transpersonal experiences of non-duality 'are not unknown in the Western tradition too' (1986: 94).

A more fully developed example of this sort of criticism is to be found in the writings of the transpersonal psychologist, Ken Wilber. Like Watts and Ajaya he believes that Jung, while making significant advances over Freud, failed to draw the appropriate lessons from his Eastern explorations, and remained within the compass of what Joanna Macy has called 'the skin-encapsulated ego'. Wilber allows that Jung did indeed recognise the transpersonal or numinous dimension, that our egocentred understanding of the human person must be placed within the wider horizon of the self, and that the self in turn must be seen as the domain of the archetypes of the collective unconscious. The problem, Wilber believes, is that Jung then goes on to confuse the higher self with pre-personal structures. He makes no distinction between a *lower* collective unconscious and a *higher* collective unconscious, and hence fails to allow for the possibility of the evolution of the self to a higher level. Because Jung tends to identify the archetypes with certain collectively inherited archaic-mythic images, there is no place in his scheme for what Wilber takes to be a truly transpersonal experience, namely one in which the self realises a state of unity with the 'ground of being', without at the same time becoming absorbed to the point of obliteration (1990: 225 and 255).

Transpersonal psychologists such as Wilber have tried to persuade us that in addition to the physical and the mental realms of being, we need to recognise a third and higher realm, namely the spiritual (1990: 91ff). In this they claim to be offering nothing new but to be rediscovering for the modern world ideas which have long lain at the core of the 'perennial philosophy', and which have returned to the orbit of Western consciousness via the East. They involve what Wilber calls 'higher levels of consciousness' where dualisms created by the illusion of the ultimate reality of the ego are transcended. Jung is frequently seen as having facilitated this rediscovery of lost knowledge of the spiritual, and his recovery of ideas from the East is seen as having made a significant contribution to this process. However, considerations such as those we have been discussing suggest a different view. Perhaps Jung was not the great champion of spiritual values, the prophet of spiritual renewal that he is sometimes made out to be. Perhaps he was in fact a *reductionist*, despite his own frequent claims to the contrary. It is true that he rejected what he saw as Freud's attempts to reduce the psychic world to the level of sexual desire, and to see the products and manifestations of the human psyche as nothing but the sublimation of instinctual drives. But at the same time Jung himself could be accused of reducing the spiritual to the *psychic*, and thereby of failing to grasp the full significance of the philosophical systems of the East. Statements like 'The world of gods and spirits is truly "nothing but" the collective unconscious inside me' (CW11.857) would seem to support this claim.

The accusation of reductionism, which is made by Ajaya, Wilber, Reynolds, and others, relates to the more general question of Jung's supposed *psychologism*. This means, roughly, the tendency to reduce religious and spiritual experiences to the intra-psychic level, to claim that statements about God, spirit, the transcendent, etc., are really statements about the psychological reality of the archetypes. One of the first to level this accusation was Martin Buber who, in his book *The Eclipse of God*, warned that Jung's proclaimed phenomenological stance was deceptive, that he was in fact advocating 'the religion of pure psychic immanence', and as a modern Gnostic who emphasised knowledge over faith he was denying the reality of a transcendent God (1957: 83–4). We might also cite here the more recent accusation by R.H. Jones that Jung has simply substituted his own theoretical constructs for 'equivalent' religious concepts, and thereby has systematically distorted the intentions of Eastern thinkers (1979: 141ff).

Jung consistently denied such accusations. His method, he claimed, was that of the psychologist and the empirical scientist, not the theologian or the philosopher, and hence he neither affirmed nor denied the existence of realities corresponding to mental phenomena. In reply to Buber he insisted that knowledge of transcendent realities was a matter of faith, and 'unfortunately I cannot boast of this possession. . . . What I have described is a psychic factor only, but one which exerts a considerable influence on the conscious mind' (CW18.1505). This sentiment is echoed in his Commentary on *The Tibetan Book of the Great Liberation* where he asserts that his psychology is 'a science of mere phenomena without any metaphysical implications' (CW11.759).

This sounds liberal enough, and would appear to allow space for the believer to make assertions that go beyond the purely psychological. However, as I argued in the previous chapter, Jung appears at times to be making a stronger claim than one of agnosticism. Thus, in the Commentary on *The Secret of the Golden Flower* he demands that 'Every statement about the transcendent is to be avoided because it is only a laughable presumption on the part of the human mind unconscious of its limitations' (CW13.82), and in the same work he goes as far as to suggest that Eastern thinkers themselves did not intend their claims about a transcendent reality to be taken literally: 'I suspect them of being symbolical psychologists, to whom no greater wrong could be done than to treat them literally' (CW13.74). The problem is that Jung wanted to leave open the possibility of making metaphysical assertions, while at the same time offering us a psychological theory which purports to close the door to them. As Aziz puts it: 'It is one thing for Jung to say that he is solely concerned with the study of the phenomenology of religious experience, and yet another thing to assert that religious experience ultimately derives from the archetypal level of the psyche' (1990: 48–9).

This difficulty takes us back to the paradox with which we began this chapter, namely Jung's ambivalent attitude towards the East. He has led us to believe that Eastern philosophers have something important to say to us, that they have sustenance to offer the spiritually starved West, yet at the same time his method appears to bar us from progressing beyond the level of psychologically inherited archetypes. The mysterious Orient, properly transposed into the terms of analytical psychology, makes perfectly good sense, but beyond that it must be treated as nothing but a projection of the collective unconscious mind. But if that is the case, we must ask once again what value is to be derived from turning to the East; should we not stay at home and work on our own archetypes, and leave the East in peace?

Part of the problem lies in the fact that there has been a radical reinterpretation of Eastern, or rather more specifically Indian Vedānta, thought since Jung's day. During the period in which he was developing his ideas the Western view of Indian philosophy was dominated by the nineteenth-century neo-Kantian, neo-Romantic view of the East. Schopenhauer had been a ruling influence in this regard, not only on the general perception of Vedānta and Buddhism in the late nineteenth and early twentieth centuries, but also on Jung himself for, as we noted earlier, Schopenhauer was a major factor in the shaping of Jung's philosophical outlook. It was characteristic of this earlier view to see Indian philosophy as based on the belief that the world is an illusion and that the ultimate aim was to penetrate the veil of *māyā* to the eternal timeless world beyond. Recent scholarship has come to interpret Indian thought more in terms of ways of seeing, in terms of modes of understanding rather than in terms of illusion and reality. The sense of a world to be transcended has been replaced with the idea of a world that needs to be viewed without distorting illusions, the sense of a world infinitely 'beyond' by a world which is 'here' if only we could open our eyes to see it.

This problem is evident too when considering Jung's interpretation of Zen Buddhism. It will be recalled that it was through the medium of D.T. Suzuki's writings that he became acquainted with Zen, and when discussing this in Chapter 7 we noted that, as a result of the influence of William James, Suzuki adopted, at least in his early writings, a distinctly psychological approach to Zen. Now without disparaging Suzuki's enormous achievement in facilitating the passage of Zen ideas to the West, it must be recognised that, while this approach was no doubt very congenial to Jung and made his hermeneutical task that much easier, it must also have given it a certain bias. As the historian of religions, Heinrich Dumoulin, notes, there is in this and other respects a one-sidedness in Suzuki's approach which has not been endorsed by all other Zen scholars. Thus, for example, the *Soto* school of Zen, which emphasises the importance of meditation, is hardly discussed by Suzuki who pays most attention to the paradoxical and suprarational traits of the *Rinzai* school with its emphasis on the practice of the *kōan*. It is only in more recent years that Zen scholars and teachers have begun to rectify this imbalance and to emphasise the importance of sitting meditation, and also to compensate for Suzuki's earlier psychological interpretation by seeking to emphasise the essentially religious nature of Zen Buddhism.

Of course, Jung could not be expected to have anticipated recent developments in Oriental scholarship, or to have bettered the translations that were available in his day, and it would be naïve to assume that the contemporary interpretations and translations represent the final word on the subject. Furthermore, many of the more substantive criticisms elaborated above carry a considerable weight of theory which many would wish to challenge; the criticisms of transpersonal psychologists, for example, rest on metaphysical assumptions which are highly contentious. Nevertheless, the problems we have encountered in this chapter leave us with nagging questions about the relevance of Jung's Eastward explorations in our own day. From a purely historical point of view it is important when trying to assess Jung's contributions to the East–West dialogue to take full account of their historical relativity, namely to see them in the context of his time and culture, and not simply to judge him in retrospect. However, because of Jung's continuing presence in modern consciousness and his perduring influence well after his death, we cannot treat him as a purely historical figure. In the concluding reflections of this book I shall take up the question of the contemporary relevance of Jung's Eastern dialogue, a task which will provide an opportunity to reconsider some of the negative views expressed in the present chapter.

10

CONCLUSIONS

JUNG'S ACHIEVEMENT

Where does Jung's dialogue with the East stand in relation to modern thought, what value does it have for us today, and how can it be read by the rising generation? It is certainly true that his accounts of Taoism, Yoga and Buddhism were frequently faulty, either due to the inadequacy of the translations at his disposal, or, more significantly, to his eagerness to exploit Eastern ideas in the shaping of his own theories. He failed for the most part to convey an adequate picture of these traditions, and often saw them within the distorting mirror of European discourse which served to perpetuate some of the standard cultural prejudices of his day. It might seem – in the light of these and other criticisms outlined in the previous chapter, and especially in view of his notoriously ambivalent attitude to the East – that Jung's Oriental explorations must be confined to the history books, to be treated as nothing more than an interesting, if peripheral, episode in the history of ideas.

As a contribution to the history of ideas, Jung's engagement with Eastern thought certainly represents a significant undertaking, one that must be assessed in a frame wider than that of analytical psychology. As I have emphasised, he was not a uniquely original explorer in the remoter seas of the East–West passage of ideas, and his contributions must be set firmly within the context of an historical development that has been continuing for several hundred years at least. He learned from and stood on the shoulders of many giants who, from the Age of Enlightenment onwards, sought to place European thought within a wider, global horizon, and thereby to subject it to penetrating criticism. His own special achievement lay, first, in his attempt to illuminate contemporary psychological questions by means of a detailed comparison with religious and philosophical ideas from China and India, and, secondly, in his attempt to confront what he saw as the crisis of Western culture by engaging in a dialogue between the cultures of East and West.

At a purely personal level this represented a remarkable exploit. It must not be forgotten that at the time when Jung was engaged in this dialogue he was not yet

179

a respected, or even a widely known, figure, and was in need of establishing his own reputation as a psychologist independently of Freud; even as early as 1909 he had been warned by Freud that if he pursued his comparative studies in mythology he stood in danger of being dismissed as a mystic. Furthermore, his own theories were taking shape in an intellectual climate which was hostile to the general psychological point of view he was advocating – a climate where positivism and scientism were allied with an aggressive Eurocentrism, and he therefore took a great professional risk in exploring publicly ideas which were not only marginal to European interests but which were widely despised, or at the very least ignored, in intellectual circles. The image of Jung in the inter-war period is sometimes portrayed as that of someone who was bent on gaining a position of power within the European, and especially the German-speaking, psychotherapeutic community, but this view seems to be contradicted by his willingness to be seen engaged in conversation with ideas and traditions, Western as well as Eastern, that were widely deemed beneath consideration, and as little more than superstitious relics of bygone ages.

Following Freud's original warning, Jung frequently had to parry the accusation of 'mystic', and his interest in Eastern religions has frequently been cited in evidence by his accusers. However his rejection of the central tenet of Eastern mysticism, summed up in the Upanishadic phrase 'thou art that', points to an entirely different judgement. It should be evident by now that this epithet completely misrepresents Jung's hermeneutical dealings with Eastern ideas and texts, for not only did he seek to stand outside the conventional wisdom of the West, but he also kept a discrete distance from the Orient. Whatever his personal 'will-to-power', Jung's intellectual development in this period certainly demonstrates his determination to be his own man, and to tackle unconventional issues in an unconventional way, a habit that has undoubtedly led to misunderstandings of his work. The East was a prize to be won, but only on his own terms. Though powerfully drawn to its spiritual and psychological ideals, which as I suggested in Chapter 4 may have played some role in his own individuation process, he refused to become intellectually or personally identified with it, but stood his distance from it, as indeed he did in certain crucial respects from Christianity. This was partly the natural reaction of someone who disliked identifying himself with a system, whether his own or another's, but it was also due to his deep reservations concerning a central aspect of Eastern philosophy, namely the search for transcendence of all dualities, and hence of all oppositions and tensions.

His Eastern interests have also earned him other labels, such as 'reactionary', and have supported the view that Jung was engaged in defending all kinds of superstitions and dubious metaphysical beliefs. It should be clear to the reader of this book that this accusation, too, is misplaced. Jung's interest in the past was motivated by his concern for the present, and what he sought from 'outworn creeds' was not the refurbishment of old faiths but the construction of a new sense of meaning, a new path of self-discovery, one compatible with a modern outlook; here we might recall as an example his attempts to link Chinese cosmological ideas with modern physics via the concept of synchronicity. What he was concerned with in his dialogue with the East was the recovery of what Lundquist has called the 'usable past' (see Barnaby and D'Acierno, 1990: 120). His historical and archaeological explorations, especially of the despised and the marginalised, and his engagement with what Foucault has termed 'subjugated knowledge', were premised firmly on present concerns, first as a catalyst in the construction of his own psychological theories, and second in the confrontation with the moral dilemmas he believed needed to be faced in a post-Christian world. This exploit earned him few friends in that period. The belief in progress and in the inherent superiority of science and of Western modes of knowledge and practice had achieved almost the status of infallible doctrine in the early part of this century, and Jung's bold and outspoken opposition to this belief was echoed by few contemporary voices.

JUNG'S INFLUENCE

In the context of the intellectual and cultural climate of the inter-war years, then, Jung's dialogue with the East represented a singular and in many ways courageous intellectual exploit, one which deserves a place in the annals of the intellectual history of that period. These exploits, however, cannot be seen as confined to his own historical situation but have a wider significance, which makes him still an important figure in our own day. Like Nietzsche, who was such a powerful influence on him, he saw his task as directed towards the future, sometimes even speaking of his task in prophetic tones, and it is therefore appropriate that we should seek to judge him in that dimension as well.

The most obvious point of departure in a discussion of Jung's contemporary relevance lies in the extraordinary proliferation of cultural and intellectual contacts with the East that has occurred since his day, ranging from the spiritual quest of New Age wisdom-seekers to the formalised dialogues of theologians, philosophers, and psychologists. The popular enthusiasm increasingly evident in recent years for various forms of Buddhism, for meditation, yoga, and Eastern medical and therapeutic techniques has been complemented by a conspicuous new openness towards Eastern thought and traditions on the part of academics from a variety of disciplines, and matches, in both intensity and intention, the mania for China and India that occurred in the Enlightenment and Romantic periods respectively. Now, we need hardly remind ourselves that much of this development, especially that which involves the quest of individuals for enlightenment, has taken place in spite of Jung's cautionary warnings, and there can be little doubt that he would have had harsh words for those who in recent decades have made of the East a weapon with which to attack all things Western and Christian. Nevertheless, it is clear that he read the signs of the times with uncanny accuracy, seeing in the burgeoning interest in the East not passing fads but expressions of a deep and urgent need. 'The East', he remarked in 1931, 'is at the bottom of the spiritual change we are passing through today', a spiritual change which arises not from the evanescent need to escape into the exotic, into 'a Tibetan monastery full of Mahatmas', but rather 'from the depths of our own psychic life' (MM: 250).

His hermeneutical engagement with the East, furthermore, was not one which merely anticipated contemporary concerns, but was one which can still provide us with a usable model and indeed still contributes to contemporary debates. As Barry Ulanov put it in a recent book: 'Jung's explorations of Eastern thought and religion, strong, unquenchable, alternately sober and gleeful, have stirred responses almost as far-ranging and full of feeling as his psychological investigations' (1992: 46). It is sometimes pointed out that, over a wide cultural and intellectual range, confrontation with the East, or even indifference, has been replaced by dialogue, and there can be no doubt that Jung's pioneering work has played a part in this development. The exact degree of Jung's influence is hard to determine since so many intellectual and historical factors can be seen to have a bearing on it. Certainly he is frequently referred to in this context, especially within religious and anthropological studies, even if his specific views and writings are not often examined in detail. A list of writers who have engaged, not always uncritically, with Jung's ideas in this field in one way or another is a long and distinguished one and would include names such as Arnold Toynbee, Mary Douglas, Rodney Needham, Paul Tillich, R.C. Zaehner, Ninian Smart, Mircea Eliade, Joseph Campbell, and Alan Watts.

Brief comment on two of these will suffice. The historian Arnold Toynbee in his massive study of civilisations made much of his debt to Jung, especially his idea of the collective unconscious, and sought in his later years to build his own bridge of understanding between East and West. Like Jung he was concerned with the spiritual malaise of Western civilisation which in his opinion urgently needed the complementary qualities of the 'inward-turning religions' of the East. Jung's presence can be found equally, if more ambivalently, in the writings of R.C. Zaehner, Professor of Oriental Religions and Ethics at Oxford University. He drew widely on Jung's ideas because they 'seem to illumine much in Oriental religion that had previously been obscure', and like Toynbee drew on Jungian language and on the theory of the collective unconscious as a methodological framework within which to make sense of the universal phenomena of mystical experience. While the Catholic Zaehner strongly disagreed with Jung over the question of the reality of evil and over other aspects of Jung's theories, he applauded the latter's psychological interpretation of Buddhism, and was as sceptical as Jung of the value to Westerners of the imitation of Eastern spiritual techniques.[1]

As these two examples suggest, Jung's influence in the context of the East–West dialogue can be detected especially in the field of comparative religion and in studies of mythology, and his ideas continue to be drawn into discussions of the phenomenology and psychology of religious experience, though the historian of religions E.J. Sharpe suggests that the debt of scholars to Jung in this field has not always been adequately acknowledged and his contributions have frequently been overlooked. We have already noted the significance of the *Eranos* conferences, that extraordinary series of gatherings on the shores of Lake Maggiore, inspired both by Jung's archetypal theory and by his enthusiasm for the religious experience of Asia. The list of participants includes the names of many who were at that time or who were later to become leading figures in the field of comparative religion, and the *Eranos-Jahrbuch*, published from 1933 onwards, has become an important source-book for the student in that field. The conferences never gave birth to a 'Jungian' school of comparative religion, but the presence of his thought is discernable in many thinkers in that area.[2] Amongst these the writings of Joseph Campbell have perhaps done most to popularise a Jungian view on the universal significance of myth. Another participant was the distinguished historian of religions, Mircea Eliade, who like Campbell has taken a close interest in Asian cultures. He was especially appreciative of Jung's seminal influence, writing that

> when Jung revealed the existence of the collective unconscious, the exploration of those immemorial treasures, the myths, symbols, and images of archaic humanity, began to resemble the techniques of oceanography and speleology. . . . Similarly, archaic modes of psychic life, 'living fossils' buried in the darkness of the unconscious, now became accessible to study, through the techniques developed by depth psychologists.
>
> (Quoted in Sharpe, 1975: 211)

The tendency of scholars to overlook, or even to dismiss, Jung's work is not confined to this field but is a common factor. This is partly the consequence of a general difficulty that many readers experience with Jung's writings, due to what is seen as a pervasive stylistic obscurity and a lack of a systematic working-out of his ideas. Even his close colleague Aniela Jaffé commented that 'it cannot escape the attentive reader that the application of concepts and terminology is not always carried through consistently [and] occasional contradictions and obscurities arise' (1983: 27). This suspicion may also be due to the perception of Jung as an amateur who not only ranged widely over subjects in which he was not formally qualified, but – the worst sin of all – did not hold an appropriate academic post. This problem is especially apparent in regard to his writings on the East which, however replete with brilliant insights, do not comprise a systematically worked-out position, and are not raised on the foundations of standard scholarly rigour. There has also, of course, been the frequently laid charge of mysticism arising from his interest in some of the more marginal aspects of human experience, and not least from his interest in Eastern thought.

In the light of such attitudes it is not surprising that beyond the field of comparative religion his influence has most obviously been felt in spheres which lie on the fringes of academic respectability. Conspicuous amongst these are humanistic and transpersonal psychology, and other related 'alternative' fields such as gestalt psychotherapy and psychosynthesis, where the themes of self-actualisation, personal growth, and altered states of consciousness predominate (I leave on one side for the moment the explicitly Jungian schools of analytical and archetypal psychology). These emerged independently of Jung, and often in reaction against both Freudian and Behaviourist models, but they have come increasingly in recent years to recognise Jung as both precursor and as ally, and their influence is now at least as great as that of more orthodox psychotherapies. Stanislav Grof, a leading exponent of transpersonal psychology, argues that it was Jung who effectively challenged the philosophical foundations of the Cartesian model of the psyche and can thereby claim the title of 'the first modern psychologist' and 'the first representative of the transpersonal orientation in psychology' (1985: 187–8). Humanistic psychology, it should be noted, often claims the status of an entirely new paradigm resting on the principles of personal growth and self-actualisation rather than the mechanistic theories of behavioural psychology or the psychodynamic model of Freud. Transpersonal psychology, which is closely linked to humanistic psychology and with which we became acquainted in the previous chapter, emphasises the gradations of consciousness which lead beyond everyday levels and aspire to spiritual states experienced by mystics in many of the world's religions. In these and other related fields there is an emphasis on the importance of Eastern psychology, and in the construction of new models of the human person they have attempted to integrate within a new synthesis the insights of yoga, Zen and Taoism with Western philosophies and techniques. As the philosopher Warwick Fox notes, transpersonal psychologists 'have generally felt it necessary to look to Eastern thought as a source of conceptual language, theoretical method, and practical guidance' (1990: 299), and in doing so have followed the lead of Jung. Of special importance in all these fields has been the use of techniques of visualisation, which explore the therapeutic use of waking dreams and fantasies. Jung's influence here has been crucial, and, as we saw earlier, his development of these techniques was closely related to his study of similar methods advocated in ancient Taoist and Buddhist traditions.

Particular mention should be made of two therapists of the 'alternative' tradition whose ideas have been developed in close association with those of Jung and who have sought to forge links with Asian philosophies. The first is Roberto Assagioli, the founder of psychosynthesis. He was influenced by both Freud and Jung and, surprisingly, managed to remain on good terms with both men. Theosophy had a major impact on his intellectual formation, and the world's mystical traditions, including Jewish as well as Asian, played an important part in shaping his distinctive view of psychic development, with its emphasis on spiritual growth and its concepts of 'superconsciousness' and the 'higher self'. Assagioli, while acknowledging agreement with some aspects of Jung's model of the psyche, pointed to an important difference between them since, unlike Jung, he drew a clear distinction between 'archaic' unconsciousness, including the collective unconscious, and higher states of consciousness where qualities of love, self-transcendence, and ecstasy emerge. In the light of discussions in the previous two chapters it might appear that Assagioli's model is better able to accommodate some of the more sublime forms of Eastern religious experience than Jung's. The second is Swami Ajaya (formerly Allan Weinstock). He has made extensive use of Jung's ideas in his attempt to construct a 'unifying paradigm' which seeks to integrate Western psychotherapy with the teachings of yoga, though, as I noted in the previous chapter, he, like Assagioli, felt that Jung's account of the psyche did not allow him to make sense of the higher forms of consciousness postulated in Indian yoga.

As in the case of comparative religion, Jung's influence on alternative psychology is oblique, and it is impossible to disentangle the influence of his Oriental writings from that of his general psychological theories. His interpretation of yoga in psychological terms, and his attempt to strip away metaphysical trappings in order to uncover a concept of the self which makes sense in modern Western terms, is a factor in common, as is his central belief in the non-derivative reality of the psyche. Common, too, is the recognition of the importance for personal growth of kinds of experience and states of consciousness which transcend the everyday and go beyond rational ego-consciousness. Grof takes special note of Jung's 'willingness to enter the realm of the paradoxical, mysterious, and ineffable [which] included . . . an open-minded attitude towards the great Eastern spiritual philosophies [and] the *I Ching*' (1985: 190). Nevertheless, the precise interpretations offered by Jung, especially those closely tied to the idea of the collective unconscious, have not been closely followed, and both Grof and Wilber make clear their differences from Jung's position. Thus, while Jung stands on the edge of these fields, his influence is recognised and his ideas weave their way in and out of the literature.[3]

The second such 'fringe' area where Jung's ideas have played a role concerns debates surrounding the formulation of new ecological or holistic paradigms, and in related attempts to reconcile religious with scientific world-views. The quest for a holistic paradigm has arisen from a number of sources, and has brought together ideas and conjectures from a variety of disciplines including quantum physics, systems theory, and ecology. It takes various forms, but its common denominator is a desire to get beyond the dualistic and mechanistic models associated with the Cartesian–Newtonian paradigms, and to articulate a world picture which allows for an integration of all phenomena within a single quasi-living whole. This involves an attempt to recover some aspects of the pre-modern paradigm which sees the world as an *unus mundus*, as a single ensouled being. It has also led to the discovery of the contemporary relevance of ancient Eastern cosmological ideas.

Jung's own contribution to this endeavour is not insignificant. As Andrew Samuels points out, 'Jung anticipated many of the philosophical consequences of developments in modern physics which have changed the way we look at such basic concepts as time, space, matter, and cause and effect' (1985: 100). This transformation of outlook can be characterised as a move from reductionism to holism, and, as we saw above, the idea of wholeness was a central point of contact between Jung and the Eastern philosophies. We saw that with his concept of synchronicity he sought to move beyond the purely psychological realm and, by linking his ideas of the psyche with the elusive ideas of modern physics, to sketch the outline of a holistic world-view. In this way his dialogue with Eastern philosophy has made an important contribution to debates about the articulation of what to many is seen as a more ecologically benign view in which modern science and traditional wisdom can be combined within a new cosmology. Linked with this, it has contributed as well to 'green' thinking which has increasingly turned towards the East for models and for inspiration. Out of these speculations there remains to be harvested a rich crop of ideas that address some of our most urgent needs.[4]

This brief summary of the influence of Jung's thinking concerning the East would not be complete without reference to his own school of analytical psychology. Here the Oriental aspect of his thinking has played only a marginal or indirect role, its implications being reflected only dimly through the mirror of the theories of individuation, the collective unconscious, and the archetypes. The reluctance of Jung's immediate followers to investigate and develop this aspect of his work may, as I suggested earlier, have resulted from the need to gain respectability for the new movement, and in more recent years there has been little indication that analytical psychologists have been willing to ignore Jung's dire warnings and to make use in analysis of the methods of yoga or the *I Ching*.

The interest amongst Jungians in Eastern ideas, if not Eastern practices, is most in evidence in the archetypal school of analytical psychology, associated principally with the name of James Hillman. Here the emphasis is on the archetypal underpinning of the psychic life, and on the creative inner imaginal world of the person – ideas which Jung found to be a bridge between his own work and the ancient teachings of China and India. According to Roberts Avens, a leading exponent of this school who has taken a close interest in Asian thought, 'The East, even in its most metaphysically lofty flights, has been practising the imaginal path', and he argues that '[the] imagination is the common ground of both Eastern and Western spiritualities' (1980: 9–10). He sees the characteristic Eastern attitude towards images as 'embodied in the Taoist principle of action through non-action (*wu-wei*) . . . [and] in the Eastern systems of meditation [where] one is advised to watch the psycho-mental flux without interfering with it' (1980: 36), a feature which is close in spirit to Jung's method of active imagination. Like Jung, though, Avens is wary of copying Eastern techniques as such, and has expressed deep concern that the Western infatuation with ideas and practices uprooted from the East and absorbed out of context can lead only to a form of 'spiritual materialism'. He echoes Jung's warning that people will practise Indian yoga only because of the lack of faith that anything good can come from their own souls – a view expressed also by Hillman who believes that, by turning to the Orient, Westerners are indulging in a 'tender-minded humanism' and are avoiding their own shadow, i.e. the pathological element that is an essential if painful component of every human psyche. In the East this element

is rooted in the thick yellow loam of richly pathologised imagery – demons, monsters, grotesque Goddesses, tortures, and obscenities. . . . But once uprooted and imported to the West it arrives debrided of its imaginal ground, dirt-free and smelling of sandalwood, another upwards vision that offers a way to bypass our Western psycho-pathologies.

(Hillman, 1975: 67)

Mention should also be made of the fact that across a wide spectrum of psycho-therapeutic theory and practice in recent times there has been an evident willing-ness, outside of the sphere of Jung's influence, to engage in some sort of dialogue with Eastern philosophies. The most conspicuous example is that of Erich Fromm whose essay on Zen and psychoanalysis (first published in 1960) develops themes which had already been adumbrated by Jung. Like the latter, Fromm was concerned to draw parallels between Western psychotherapy and Eastern spiritual practices, and argued that Zen Buddhism 'can have a fertile and clarify-ing influence on the theory and technique of psychoanalysis' (1986: 108). He was especially interested in the Zen goal of *satori*, or enlightenment, which he directly compared with the Freudian therapeutic aim of 'making the unconscious conscious'. Like Jung, Fromm was deeply concerned with the wider implications of psychotherapeutic thinking, as evidenced in such books as *The Sane Society*, but it should be added that he was no admirer of Jung whom he criticised, *inter alia*, for treating *satori* as somehow opaque to the European mind.[5]

THE FRUITS OF DIALOGUE

Whatever the degree of influence, Jung's whole methodology, which we have outlined in some detail in the course of this book, is one which fits in many ways with the dialogical mood of recent times. His hermeneutical method, albeit practised implicitly and with little knowledge of the precise philosophical tradi-tion from which it sprang, offers a way of approaching the sometimes obscure texts and ideas of the East in the creative and open-ended mode of dialogue. As I have pointed out on several occasions, the dialogical mode of discourse is not to be construed as a cosy and undemanding chat, but is a procedure which stretches intellectual and moral resources, and requires a high degree of honest self-criticism. The results, moreover, are not to be counted in a tally of conclusions or truths finally arrived at, but in terms of a widening of sympathies, a broadening of horizons, and a deepening of our humanity. Here are some facets of Jung's dialogue with the East which may bear out this assessment.

For a start there is its historical awareness. We have seen that this had its limitations, for Jung took little notice of the social or economic conditions surround-ing the texts or ideas he was examining, and was not always inclined to question the possible hidden ideological motives lying beneath his essentially European project. For all his good hermeneutical intentions, Jung is still vulnerable, as we saw in the previous chapter, to the charge of 'Orientalism' – namely, that the East with which he claims to be in conversation is, in the final analysis, something of his own making, a fiction conjured out of his own peculiarly Western needs. But in spite of this limitation he demonstrated a capacity to recognise and to take account of the factors of difference and distance in the formation of historical judgement. This awareness helped to warn him against the naïve assimilation of ancient Oriental texts as if they were written in a timeless present, or as if they were written for the benefit of the European reader, and although he was quite explicitly in search of the underlying psychological bonds that tie mankind together, he was at the same time aware of the conceptual and philosophical differences which divide them. He was also aware of the relativity of his own historical situation, seeing it not in privileged terms, licensing him to speak with some supra-historical authority, but as an ever-moving and ever-reconstituted perspective. Consequently his project of building a bridge of understanding always remained a modest one which avoided any claims to complete understanding and emphasised the provisional and essentially incomplete nature of the enterprise.

This historical perspective encouraged him to challenge some of the pre-judices of his day concerning the supposed pre-eminence of European culture, and to recognise the necessity for rethinking European culture and history in a wider context. In his book on synchronicity, Jung pointed to Galileo's collision with the prejudices of his own age when he claimed to discover the moons of Jupiter with his telescope, and observed that we likewise need 'the courage to shock the prejudices of our age if we want to broaden the basis of our under-standing' (SY: 47). His work in this regard represents an intriguing re-enactment of the endeavours of earlier thinkers in the eighteenth and nineteenth centuries to hold up the East as a mirror for the West's critical self-examination, and to encourage a free encounter with other traditions in order to reawaken, in J.L. Mehta's words, 'the sense of vast alternatives, magnificent or hateful, lurking in the background, and awaiting to overwhelm our safe little traditions'. Such an expansion of awareness, Mehta continues,

> is not merely a prime necessity for the survival of civilization; it is the only safeguard against the dogmatism which paralyses self-criticism and halts the emergence of novelty in the patterns of conceptual experience, con-gealing tradition into a lifeless burden.
>
> (Mehta, 1985: 128)

While many thinkers in the West have busied themselves devising historical or philosophical frameworks with the implicit intention of demonstrating the inherent superiority of the West over the East, Jung devised a scheme which saw them as equal but complementary. As we saw, he was emboldened to point out that Europe is after all only a little peninsula of Asia, and that the European consciousness is 'by no means the only kind of consciousness there is [but] is historically conditioned and geographically limited, and the representative of only one part of mankind' (CW13.84). This enabled him to attempt an even-handed approach to the relationship between Christianity and Eastern religions. Thus, in his well-known debate with Martin Buber he urged the need to treat with equal seriousness the religious experience not only of Jews and Christians but also of the devotees of Islam, Buddhism and Hinduism 'who have the same living relationship to "God", or to Nirvāna and Tao, as Buber has to the God-concept peculiar to himself' (CW18.1507). And in speaking of the world-view of the North American Indians, he castigated 'that megalomania of ours which leads us to suppose, among other things, that Christianity is the only truth, and the white Christ the only redeemer' (MM: 246). It is true that he consistently identified himself as a Christian, and was acutely aware of his own roots in the history and traditions of Europe, but at the same time he was able to detach himself from this to some extent and to recognise the essentially plural nature of human experience and knowledge. He was able, too, to support this approach with a methodology which emphasises the sheer richness and variety of cultural forms, as well as arguing for their underlying unity.[6]

This pluralistic outlook can also be linked to a form of cultural relativism which involves the refusal to canonise one's own tradition as the only true or valid perspective. Relativism is sometimes seen as a bogey – 'a new spectre haunting Europe', as Ernest Gellner rather portentously described it – associated not only with the tragic loss of traditional certainties but also with the post-Christian ethos in which, in the prophetic words of Ivan Karamazov, 'everything is permitted'. For Jung, relativism represented a serious philosophical and moral position, one which, as he himself noted, had already been formulated ten centuries ago in the East (see MM: 249).[7] He consistently maintained that there is no single correct view of the world, that 'there is no one single philosophy, but many' (MM: 207), and hence that the modern scientific rationalism of the West 'is not the only possible one and is not all-embracing, but is in many ways a prejudice and a bias' (SY: 95). This attitude of Jung's was not, it must be emphasised, a brand of world-weary scepticism, a form of nihilism in which everything becomes devalued, for the very plurality of outlooks, emphasised vividly as one turns Eastwards, is the foundation for a more ample conception of human reality, and the basis for the widening of sympathies and the enhancement of toleration between peoples and nations. The premises for this morality of sympathy and mutual understanding are summed up in the following passage:

> there is only *one* earth and *one* mankind, East and West cannot rend humanity into two different halves. Psychic reality still exists in its original oneness, and awaits man's advance to a level of consciousness where he no longer believes in the one part and denies the other, but recognizes both as constituent elements of one psyche.
>
> (CW8.682, Jung's emphases)

Such an attitude, far from raising the spectre of nihilism, may help, in however small a way, to encourage a deeper sense of shared humanity, and to stem the insane advance of inter-ethnic hatred which constitutes one of the most serious threats to the world-order at the present time.

In some respects Jung's relativistic outlook fits well with the postmodern atmosphere, too, where the 'grand narratives' of the modern era – the ideas of indefinite progress, of the never-ending development of the theories of science and the methods of modern technology, in other words of human domination of inner and outer worlds – have ceased to have universal appeal. The mood of postmodernism is one of disillusionment with the pretensions of imperialism in all its various guises, and a desire to deconstruct the sacred tablets of the laws of modernism. Its relativism and its pluralism, its emphasis on difference and heterogeneity, are evident, as are its attendant inclination towards the unsettled, the ambiguous, the indeterminate, and in this regard Jung may be seen as its ally. For the postmodern mind texts are viewed not as objects with stable meaning, backed by authorial voices that speak through the words of the text, and which can be deciphered through the application of the appropriate methodology, but as a 'polysemic' plurality in which the revelation of meaning is for ever deferred. Jung's hermeneutical parrying with Eastern texts, and his refusal to close off or to seek to empty out their meaning, manifests a similar spirit. So does his attitude to Eastern metaphysics – 'I quite deliberately bring everything that purports to be metaphysical into the daylight of psychological understanding' – for as one recent commentator has observed '[Jung] is in league with Heidegger and Derrida in their assiduous efforts to deconstruct metaphysics . . . a very characteristic postmodern enterprise' (Edward Casey, in Barnaby and D'Acierno, 1990: 320).[8]

Other facets of Jung's thinking, however, seem to place him in a different category. Thus, for example, his concern for personal meaning and spiritual values, his theory of universal archetypal inheritance underpinning human nature, and his devotion to the cause of the self as the 'world's pivot' and as 'the greatest of all cosmic wonders' all seem to run against the postmodern tide. In spite of his claims to empiricism, we can discern in Jung clear vestiges of nineteenth-century metaphysics. The notion of an objective psyche in whose cultivation lies the potential for making sense of life has for many contemporary thinkers the taint of over-ripe humanism and romanticism, and his tendency to universalise human nature on the basis of the collective unconscious has the all the appearances of another 'grand narrative'. But even here he can still be read with sympathy by the contemporary generation. In spite of the sceptical and reductionist strategies that have characterised the intellectual life of this century, in spite of all attempts to deconstruct the self and the over-arching symbolic structures that have in the past protected it, and in spite of the postmodern inclination to the ironical dismissal of all transcendent values, there clearly survives an ancient and deeply rooted need for meaning and for a philosophy which gives a special place to the human person in the natural order. Jung found in the modern era a tendency to depreciate everything psychic and to treat the mental as a mere epiphenomenon, and in his attempts to counteract this tendency he became, as we saw in the previous chapter, accused of 'psychologism'. But here again his challenge to the prevailing reductionism and materialism is echoed today by many thinkers who seek to go beyond the modernist programme without slipping into the nihilism that so often seems to attend postmodern discourse.

JUNG'S CONTEMPORARY RELEVANCE

It is in ways such as these that Jung is still relevant for the contemporary world, and where he can still be read with more than historical or nostalgic curiosity. The criticisms outlined in Chapter 9 must suggest that Jung, in spite of his warning against building 'false and treacherous bridges over yawning gaps' (CW11.111), may have overestimated the strength of the psychological materials with which he sought to build his bridge of understanding. And, as I have suggested, in reading Jung today we may need to strip away some of the historical prejudices which from our perspective seem to have clouded his thinking, just, indeed, as he sought to strip away the metaphysical assumptions overlaying the texts *he* was reading. But in spite of these reservations, it is my belief that his efforts at articulating a methodology for inter-cultural dialogue represent important foundation work on which a more secure bridge might be – indeed, is being – constructed. It is true that the attempt to move beyond a narrow Eurocentric outlook is fraught with philosophical and ideological difficulties. Whatever benefits Jung's hermeneutical approach may offer towards the resolution of the West's own problems, the sceptic may still argue that no open-minded dialogue with the East is possible as long as the West remains in control, with its dominant language and its dominant conceptual framework, dictating all the time the nature and direction of the exchange. Nevertheless, in spite of such arguments and qualifications it is beyond dispute that the need for such an exchange is as urgent in our own day as it was in Jung's. Here is but one recent expression of it:

> What is clearly needed in East and West is a creative surge of a new order. Such a surge will not be possible while humanity goes on with its current fragmentation, represented by the extremes of Eastern and Western cultures. . . . A genuine dialogue between the two cultures is clearly called for in which there is no holding to fixed points of view, so that a new free and fluid common mind could perhaps arise.
>
> (Bohm and Peat, 1989: 259)

It may be that 'genuine' dialogue must ever elude us, but, in spite of the very real problems posed by Said and other critics, the enterprise is one which must be undertaken, and indeed may be unavoidable if the human race is to live at peace with itself. Perhaps it may even, as Mircea Eliade suggests, 'constitute the point of departure for a new humanism, upon a world scale' (1960: 245).

No less urgent in many people's minds is the search for a renewed spirituality. Jung spotted early in this century that the growing tide of interest in the Orient represented symptoms of spiritual alienation, a warning sign of a deep cultural malaise within Christendom. These symptoms are even more apparent as the century draws to a close, when the search for personal authenticity and for a renewed sense of a religious dimension to life appears as strong and as urgent as ever. Some in the West return to the traditional fold of Christianity; the growth of fundamentalism in America is witness to this. But for many the Christian churches have failed to revitalise the religious traditions of the West, and for them the East continues to offer a way back to a sense of meaning and of inner worth and value. A similar point can be made about the scientific rationalism of the twentieth century. Its positivistic representatives have tried to teach us that the exploration and domination of the natural world is mankind's supreme task, but as the century draws to a close the attractions and benefits of this project have palled, and in its place has emerged an alternative project which is drawn more to spiritual goals that try to overcome the disastrous bifurcation between the mental and the physical, and between the human and the natural worlds.

There are, to be sure, many for whom such considerations remain completely alien, and who are content to leave the Orient and its champions, and indeed all things which seem to lead us back to the confusions and superstitions of the past, in obscurity. But equally there are many people for whom interaction with ideas from the ancient traditions of the East appears increasingly fruitful, not just as an activity of disinterested investigation but as the seeding of new growth. C.G. Jung still has words to inspire such people:

The philosophy of the East, although vastly different from ours, could be an inestimable treasure for us too; but in order to possess it, we must first earn it.

(CW11.961)

NOTES

1 INTRODUCTION

1 Jung's Eastern interests claim only a brief mention in, for example, Bennett (1961), Dry (1961), Homans (1979), Jacobi (1942), Mattoon (1981), and Stevens (1990), usually in the context of his theory of archetypes. One gains little sense of the importance of the East for Jung in Brome's biography (1980), and Stern (1976) refers to Jung's interest in the *I Ching* as 'an odd detour to the study of alchemy' (p. 189). Segal (1992) emphasises the role of alchemy and Gnosticism in prefiguring Jung's formative psychological experiences, but fails to mention Eastern thought. Wehr (1987) and von Franz (1975), though, give wider and more sympathetic attention to this subject. Coward, who has offered the most complete account to date of Jung's relationship with Western thought, surmises that the apparent attempt to hide or ignore the Eastern content of Jung's theories could be either an example of Western bias or a fear that to admit such a content would make his ideas 'even less acceptable to the mainstream of Western psychology' (1985: 98).
2 The association of Jung with the New Age persists. See, for example, Segaller and Berger (1989: 162–3), a work based on a television series.
3 Jung was acquainted with at least two other contemporary writers who were drawing analogies similar to his own between East and West: O.A.H. Schmitz, author of *Psychoanalyse und Yoga* (1923), (see CW10.188), and J.H. Schultz, author of *Das Autogene Training* (1932), (see CW11.874).
4 See Halbfass (1988: 152–9) for a discussion of the issue of the history of Western bias in histories of philosophy. He points out that, despite Hegel's attempt to construct a universal history of philosophy in the early nineteenth century, non-European thought was almost systematically excluded from histories of philosophy thereafter. There have been some attempts in recent years to write universal histories of philosophy – for example, J.C. Plott's *Global History of Philosophy*. During this century a number of American philosophers have shown interest in Eastern thought; the list includes such names as James, Royce, Santayana, Hocking, Northrop, Hartshorne, Danto, and, most recently, Nozik.
5 In a work such as the present study it is impossible to avoid the use of this fiction since, apart from its obvious convenience, it enters deeply into the discourse that is being examined, and it would be tedious to keep placing 'East' and 'West' in scare-quotes or repeatedly to add qualifying riders. Nevertheless I must emphasise at the outset that one of the aims of this work is to demythologise certain long-standing prejudices surrounding the use of these terms along with allied expressions such as 'our culture'.

As I shall argue in Chapter 9, these terms not only represent a dangerous over-simplification of historical and cutural reality, but also help to perpetuate illiberal prejudices. Similar considerations apply to my use of the word 'philosophy' as in 'Eastern philosophy', which is used here as a convenient label, but which should also be read as if in scare-quotes.

6 Heidegger felt a close affinity for Eastern philosophy, especially Taoism and Zen, and was convinced of the need for a dialogue between the various traditions. However, he maintained that a universal 'house of words' could not be built at the present time since it would inevitably be constructed in a Western tongue and with Western presuppositions. For a useful collection of papers on Heidegger's relationship to the East–West dialogue see Parkes (1987), especially the article by Poggeler who claims that 'Heidegger has more than any other European philsopher initiated dialogue between the West and the Far East' (p. 76). Another discussion of Heidegger's relation to Eastern thought may be found in Halbfass (1988: 167–70).

7 Fuller attention will be devoted to these important ideas of Said in the next chapter. In the meantime it should be noted that Said's concept of 'Orientalism' was intended to refer to the Middle East, and most specifically to Arab cultures. Nevertheless I believe that many of his arguments have relevance for Western attitudes to the cultures of East and South-East Asia. In this work I shall be using 'the Orient' as an alternative term for 'the East'.

8 A similar view is held by Peter Homans, though not specifically with regard to Jung's interest in Eastern thought (1979: 140). He offers a useful study of Jung and the question of modernity.

2 ORIENTALISM

1 The opposite of enclavism is *inclusivism*, a term coined by the German indologist Paul Hacker to denote the belief that all religions are are variants of a single underlying universal religion, the chief exemplar of which is Indian Vedānta. See Halbfass (1988: Ch. 22).

2 Such widely-held attitudes concerning the origins and identity of Western civilisation have been challenged recently by Martin Bernal (1987) who has argued that the Classical civilisation of Greece and Rome has deep roots in Afroasiatic cultures. The attitudes expressed in this paragraph are not being ascribed indiscriminately to historians, and it should be noted that in recent years there has been a conspicuous reaction against modernist as well as Eurocentric assumptions.

3 For an interesting development of this idea see David Wood: *Philosophy at the Limit*, p. xvi, where he suggests that 'philosophical thinking is often unconsciously, and often quite openly, determined by . . . topographical intuitions'. We shall come across the topographical metaphor again when discussing Gadadmer's notion of the 'horizons' of understanding. This metaphor is particularly apt, of course, when considering geographicaliy distinct domains such as East and West.

4 The idea of conceptual frameworks which in some way are mutually incommensurable has been discussed by, *inter alia*, Bernstein (1983), Davidson (1984), Feyerabend (1978), and Popper (in Lakatos and Musgrave, 1970). See Richard Bernstein's discussion of 'incommensurability' in the context of East–West communication in Deutsch (1991: 85ff): he argues that 'Incommensurable languages and traditions are not to be thought of as self-contained windowless monads that share nothing in common' (p. 92). In the same volume Richard Rorty criticises those 'essentialist' habits of thought which have a disastrous tendency to encapsulate the West and to contrast the West as a whole with the rest of the world as a whole (p. 4). Alasdair MacIntyre (1988) also addresses the question of the commensurability of different linguistic traditions (see Chs 18 and 19).

5 An interesting discussion of the prevailing historicist attitude can be found in Rée (1991: 962ff), where he argues that the 'historical turn' initiated by Kuhn has been followed by influential historians of ideas such Quentin Skinner, John Dunn, and J.G.A. Pocock, and can lead to a situation where inter-cultural comparison and criticism become impossible.

6 Harris (1982: 295) offers an interesting discussion of debates about the possible influence of Indian philosophy on Plotinus. He notes that terms like 'purity' and 'contamination' are widely used by Western scholars concerned to retain Plotinus firmly within the traditions of Western philosophy, unadulterated by Oriental influences.

7 It all depends on what you call an 'argument'. Are there any arguments in the writings of Wittgenstein or Nietzsche, for example? The sinologist A.C. Graham points out that recent scholarship has come to recognise a period of intense philosophical disputation in China c. 500–200 BCE, and due to the recovery of lost texts in recent years we can now see that 'most of the ancient Chinese thinkers are very much more rational than they used to look' on the basis of the *Analects* of Confucius, the *Tao Te Ching*, and the *I Ching*, in none of which is there any sign of an argument in Flew's sense (see Graham, 1989: ix and 7). In a similar vein B.K. Matilal has commented that 'too often the term "Indian Philosophy" is identified with a subject that is presented as mystical and non-argumentative. A corrective to this view is long overdue' (1986: 4–5).

8 Halbfass (1988) provides a detailed exposition of the history of the Indian response to Western culture and philosophies from the time of Rammohan Roy (1772–1833). Iyer argues that, for all its baneful consequences, the West's irruption into the East at least had the merit of transmitting to Asia the spirit of the European Renaissance, the Reformation, and the Enlightenment (1965: 16). In the context of recent postmodern debates this claim might not appear very convincing.

9 Dialogue between East and West has become a veritable academic industry in recent years, especially in the fields of theology, philosophy, and psychology. Here are some representative examples: Allinson (1989), Barnes (1991), Claxton (1986), Johnston (1981), Parkes (1991), and Welwood (1979).

10 The theme of self-understanding through encounter with the East is a central theme of Halbfass's book, *India and Europe*. He cites, amongst others, the example of Max Weber who felt it necessary to approach the question concerning the peculiar nature of modern European culture by comparing it with the cultures of East Asia (see 1988: 143).

11 Aspects of the East–West passage of ideas, in the modern as well as the ancient periods, are discussed in Edwardes (1971), Halbfass (1988), Lach (1970), Radhakrishnan (1939), Schwab (1984), Welbon (1968), and Willson (1964).

12 For an account of the work of the Jesuit missionaries in China, see Edwardes (1971) and Cronin (1955).

13 See Mungello (1977) for a comprehensive account of Leibniz's dealings with Oriental ideas. There is some dispute about the extent of Leibniz's indebtedness to Chinese philosophy. Joseph Needham claims that the theory of monads, in which all aspects of the universe mirror all other aspects, had its source in Taoist organicist metaphysics (1956: 496–505). Mungello, on the other hand takes the more cautious line that the Chinese influence was 'more corroborative than germinal' (1977: 15), and Ming-Wood Liu, while pointing to a general parallel between Leibnizian and Taoist worldviews, emphasises differences in methodology and context (1982: 61ff). In any case, Leibniz was certainly engaged in a wide-ranging dialogue in which he was finding support and inspiration in what he was learning from Chinese philosophy, and to this extent can be likened to Jung.

14 Some, such as A.O. Lovejoy, hold that the Enlightenment enthusiasm for China prepared the way for Romanticism, though this claim is based on the passage of aesthetic rather than philosophical factors.

15 In fact Voltaire had made this claim half a century earlier, but while for him it was little more than a provocative *bon mot*, for Herder it was a key to his whole outlook. Herder, incidentally, was not uncritical of Indian culture. He disapproved, for example, of its practice of suttee, its caste system, and what he perceived as its attitude of resignation (see Willson, 1964: 52).

16 Other Romantics caught up in the general enthusiasm for the Orient included Schleiermacher, Novalis, Tieck, and the von Humboldts. It should be noted that Goethe, though drawn to Indian pantheism, was less enthusiastic about its mythological profusions. There are many references to India and to Eastern ideas in general in the writings of the British Romantics, but they did not match the Germans in the depth of their interest.

17 For a fuller account of Nietzsche's relationship with Oriental philosophy, see Halbfass (1988) and Mistry (1981).

3 JUNG AND HERMENEUTICS

1 On the question of the assimilation of Western philosophical ideas into the discourse of Eastern thinkers, see Halbfass (1988) and Satchidananda (1985). Satchidananda argues that in principle it is no more difficult for a Westerner to understand, say, Sankara or Nāgārjuna, than it is for a modern Indian (see pp. 198ff).

2 G.E.R. Lloyd's *Demystifying Mentalities* (1990) makes an important contribution to this endeavour. He examines the whole notion of distinct mentalities, found in such fields as social anthropology, philosophy, history and psychology, and concludes that in its extreme form the belief that there are distinct mentalities to be discovered in different cultures is a mirage and is the product of distance and the lack of detailed knowledge of the cultures concerned.

3 For an interesting discussion of this issue, see John E. Smith: 'Interpreting across Boundaries' in Allinson (1989).

4 On the East–West dialogue, see for example: Barnes (1991), Cox (1988), Griffiths (1982), Hick (1985), Netland (1991), Panikkar (1978), and Smith (1981). A classic example of this genre is Rudolph Otto's *Mysticism East and West*, first published in Germany in 1926, which draws extensive comparisons between Meister Eckhart and the Hindu philosopher-saint Sankara; in it Otto insists on 'the deep-rooted kinship which unquestionably exists between the souls of the Oriental and the Occidental' (1957: xvii). For an overview of this issue, see Smart (1981) and Johnston (1981). Johnston comments that 'we are now entering a new religious era, an era in which the most important event will be the meeting between Christianity and the great religions of the East', and in which such a dialogue will yield new insight into the Christian tradition, its theology, and its spirituality (p. 70). Likewise R.C. Zaehner argues that an understanding of Eastern religions 'can help us to see our own religion in a new way, and can shake us out of the "habit" of religion' (1970: 19).

5 W. Johnston, a leading exponent of Christian dialogue with Eastern religions, comes close to a hermeneutical account of dialogue, though he does not relate it explicitly to the hermeneutical tradition (see 1981: 10ff). W. Halbfass (1988: Ch. 10) discusses the possibility of using the hermeneutical theory of Gadamer in East–West dialogue. J.L. Mehta (1985, *passim*) also explores in some depth the relevance of hermeneutics, especially that of Gadamer, to questions of inter-cultural understanding.

6 The sense in which Gadamer uses the term 'hermeneutics', as well as thinkers such as Heidegger and Ricoeur, must be distinguished from the more traditional sense, still in currency, in which it is construed as a method or set of principles for the retrieval of meaning, especially from texts. In this latter sense it can be applied to the study of Oriental texts, as for example in *Buddhist Hermeneutics* (Lopez, 1988) which examines issues and traditions in the interpretation of the Buddhist suttras.

7 To describe Gadamer as a 'relativist' is over-simple and a matter of some debate. The issue of relativism in general and of Gadamer's position in relation to it are discussed in Bernstein (1983, *passim*). See also Clarke (1992: 42ff) for a discussion of historicism and relativism in relation to Jung, where a general case is put forward for construing Jung's method in hermeneutical terms.

8 For this account of Jung's hermeneutical approach I am particularly indebted to Steele (1982), especially Chapter 11. For other approaches to Jung via hermeneutics, see Brooke (1991), Brown (1981), Hogenson (1983), and Jarrett (1992).

9 The question of Jung's relation to the 'other' is the subject of a wide-ranging discussion in Papadopoulos (1984). The question of engaging with the 'other' in the context of the East–West dialogue was discussed by Richard Bernstein in his paper 'Incommensurability and Otherness – Revisited' at the Sixth East–West Philosophers' Conference in Hawaii in 1989 where he commented that 'only through an engaged encounter with the Other, with the otherness of the Other . . . [does] one come to a more informed, textured understanding of the traditions in which "we" belong. It is our genuine encounters with what is other and alien that we can further our self-understanding' (in Deutsch, 1991: 93). For a wide-ranging discussion of the importance of the issue of the 'other' in twentieth-century continental philosophy, see Theunissen (1984).

10 This is an approach recognised by some contemporary Buddhists, such as Lama Anagorika Govinda who writes that 'it is not our task either to imitate the forms of past ages or to take over without question thought patterns that were once valid . . . [but rather] we should try to extract from a doctrine everything that is relevant to our own time' (1989: 1). He goes on to claim that Buddhism, because of its very capacity to adapt, can play an important part in the process of global fusion 'so that all people will feel themselves to be citizens of this one world' (p. 11).

11 Emilio Betti, for example, in offering an alternative hermeneutical model to that of Gadamer, has objected that the latter's analysis 'opens the door and gate to subjective arbitrariness and threatens to cloud and distort and, be it only unconsciously, to disfigure historical truth' (quoted in Warnke, 1987: 98).

4 JUNG'S DIALOGUE WITH THE EAST

1 Radmila Moacanin also suggests that in his formative period Jung's pseudo-Gnostic work, *Septem Sermones ad Mortuos*, written in 1916 as a purely private and personal exercise, shows evidence of Buddhist influence (1986: 76–7). We shall return later to the link between Gnosticism and Eastern philosophies.

2 For fuller details concerning Jung's relationship with Keyserling, see Stern (1976: 202–9) and Hardy (1987: 163).

3 Jung speculated that on his return to Europe after many years in China, and with the assumption of teaching duties at the China Institute in Frankfürt, the conflict between his love of Chinese culture and his Christian faith became acutely painful for Wilhelm, and may have helped to precipitate his terminal illness (see MDR: 407). This conjecture may have been significant in convincing Jung of the dangers for a Westerner in becoming too closely identified with a non-European culture, a question which will be taken up in Chapter 9.

4 For an account of the *Eranos* seminars and Jung's role in their development, see Wehr (1987: Ch. 16). For an analysis of their role in the evolution of comparative religion, see Sharpe (1975: 210ff).

5 For fuller accounts of his journey to India and Ceylon (now Sri Lanka), see Jung (MDR: 304–14, CW10.981–1013, CW11.950–3) and Wehr (1987: Ch. 17). Wehr discusses the Maharshi 'episode', and notes with some surprise the fact that Jung

failed to mention either Mahatma Gandhi, or Sri Aurobindo Ghose who strove to bring about a spiritual synthesis of East and West.

6 This might appear to run counter to Jung's view, outlined earlier, that the psyche constitutes a kind of cosmos in its own right. There runs through his work a tension between a dualistic and a monistic point of view on the mind–body question, a tension which I do not think he ever resolved, though he clearly saw the need to do so, and lamented that he never had the opportunity to subject his theories to adequate philosophical analysis. Thus at times the material world appears to confront the mind as something ontologically distinct; at others it appears as a manifestation or projection of mind. I have argued that in *Synchronicity* he does in fact offer an outline of a position that seeks to reconcile the two positions, making use of something like Schopenhauer's 'double-aspect' theory in which the mental and the physical are viewed as two aspects of one and the same unified reality (see Clarke, 1992: Ch. 13).

5 TAOISM

1 Modern scholarship obliges us to modify this long-held view of Confucianism since, in the course of its long and variegated history, it did in fact develop forms of spirituality and sought the cultivation of the inner life. It is important, too, to bear in mind that there is no clear-cut distinction between Taoism and Confucianism (nor indeed are they monolithic doctrinal systems), and many of the ideas attributed by Jung to the former could in certain respects be seen as applying to the latter; for example, they shared to a large extent a common set of metaphysical terms and cosmological premises. The *I Ching* is a case in point; by including it in a chapter headed 'Taoism' I do not want to suggest that it was not also an important text for the Confucian tradition; nevertheless from Jung's standpoint it is more natural to view it in a Taoist light.

2 This account is drawn from Wilhelm's Introduction to his edition of *The Secret of the Golden Flower*. Not everyone agrees with the interpretation of this and other Eastern texts in psychological terms. See, for example, Grison, where the author, a disciple of Henri Guénon, castigates Jung's bridge-building as 'a total confusing of values' (1968: 141). This criticism depends on the possibility of a clear distinction being made between the psychological and the spiritual.

3 Jung's insight into the affinity between the role of the imaginal life in the psyche's economy in general and the way of thinking lying behind this Taoist text receives some recent confirmation from Roger T. Ames (1991) who argues for the central importance of the image in Chinese thinking.

4 For a rather different interpretation of the question of unrepeatability, see Aziz (1990: 146). Contrary to my own view, Aziz believes that Jung was convinced of the divinatory effectiveness of the *I Ching*. Marie-Louise von Franz, a close colleague of Jung, argues that the unconscious has knowledge of the past and future not available to the conscious intellect and that this is the source of the success of mediums, though she maintains that their insight is limited to general trends and probabilities rather than to precise certainties (1980, *passim*).

5 Jung's response here has something in common with the famous 'Turing test' which seeks to determine whether an entity, such as a computer, can be said to be 'thinking' by dint of the intelligibility of its responses rather than by reference to its physical structure.

6 For an account of a further experiment of this kind conducted by Jung, see Progoff (1973: 24ff).

7 Jung never adequately defined what he means by the term 'meaningful' in this context, though we might deduce from his writing on this subject that he is referring to that aspect of certain events which give the *appearance* of being intended for some

conscious purpose – it is *as if* they were intentional. He did not, of course, wish to infer the actual existence of a conscious being behind such an 'appearance'.

8 For this reason the term 'synchronicity' is not entirely well chosen since it was used to include a wider class of phenomena than simply that of synchronistic coincidence, and to embrace the whole notion of meaningful events.

9 Jung's closeness to Schopenhauer and to Leibniz on this point is especially interesting in the light of the former's fascination with Indian philosophy and the latter's with Chinese. As we noted in Chapter 2, Leibniz had a particular interest in the *I Ching*, and his metaphysical system bore a close resemblance to the metaphysical ideas that underlie the Chinese text.

10 The link with the new physics is an intriguing one, and invites comparison with more recent conjectures by Capra (1982), Bohm (1980), and others. Nevertheless, it must be pointed out that Jung's concern with *meaning*, as opposed to holistic inter-connectedness, is not one that is shared by physicists.

11 Compare this with the physicist David Bohm's idea of an 'implicate order', a concept of an unbroken wholeness that lies beneath the surface of the manifold phenomena. He remarks that 'In the East (especially in India) such views [of wholeness] still survive, in the sense that philosophy and religion emphasize wholeness and imply the futility of analysis of the world into parts' (1980: 19).

6 YOGA

1 I would wish to dispute Faber and Saayman's claim that 'Jung formulated his concepts in general ignorance of those of the East' (1984: 165). His close involvement with Eastern thought from about 1912 onwards coincided with the seminal period in the development of his most characteristic ideas, and although it is impossible to specify in detail the exact points and measure of influence, the two appear inextricably intertwined, as I hope my narrative here and elsewhere demonstrates.

7 BUDDHISM

1 For an account of this episode in cultural and intellectual history, see Almond (1988) and Welbon (1968).

2 Strictly speaking, Tibetan Buddhism comprises four schools, but neither in theory nor in practice are there fundamental differences between them, and Jung does not attempt to differentiate between them.

3 Late in life Jung appeared to take a more favourable view of the idea of reincarnation, largely as a result of a series of dreams, while still insisting on the need for more empirical evidence. His final judgement of the question of *karma* was that it remained 'obscure' (see MDR: 349–51).

4 For an account of Suzuki's background and influence, see Dumoulin (1979: 4–7). The author writes that '*Satori* and the *kōan* form the centre of Suzuki's teaching on Zen and are presented chiefly from the psychological angle in his early works', and notes that his appreciation of history was 'limited'.

5 In the light of the popularity of the work, it is of interest to note that Jung rather harshly dismissed Herrigel's *Zen in the Art of Archery* as 'superficial' and as having 'nothing to do with the inner life of man' (*Letters II*: 602)

6 The mandala, as used in the East for ritual and meditational purposes, is not confined to Buddhism, but is also characteristic of Hindu Tantra. However, Jung's detailed discussion is largely confined to its manifestation in the Tantric Buddhism of Tibet, and for that reason the present discussion is included in this chapter on Buddhism.

7 For a full account of the theory and practice of the mandala in Asian religions, see Tucci (1969).

8 RESERVATIONS AND QUALIFICATIONS

1 The idea that Jung was concerned with therapy in this sense has been argued by Murray Stein, though in my view he conceives it too narrowly in terms of Christianity (see Stein, 1985: 14–19).

2 Many similar sentiments were expressed by participants in the first East–West conference at Honolulu in 1939. See also Burtt (1967: 152ff). The somewhat utopian ideal of a world philosophy has been replaced in more recent years by the more modest ones of cross-fertilisation, of dialogue, and of comparative studies.

3 For a discussion of Jung's evolutionary theory of the psyche, see Clarke (1992: Ch. 7). Although Jung acknowledged the Darwinist factor of fitness for survival, a more important factor in shaping his ideas on this question was the nature philosophy of Schelling (1775–1854), for whom the Absolute is seen as the ultimate goal in which all opposites are reconciled and the universe achieves, finally, a state of complete self-knowledge. Although this appears on the face of it to be the reverse of the Upanishadic conception, in which plurality arises from an original One, it is interesting to note that Schelling was himself deeply interested in Indian ideas which, at that time, were beginning to penetrate European consciousness.

4 Jung seems to have been unaware of the part played by the Theosophical Society, especially under the inspiration of Colonel Olcott, in the revival of Hindu and Buddhist self-awareness in India and Sri Lanka.

5 Evans-Wentz, in his introduction to *The Tibetan Book of the Great Liberation*, gives an interesting example of the dangers for a Westerner who tries to make use of the powerful techniques developed by Tibetan Buddhists. Madame Alexandra David-Neel, one of the earliest explorers of Tibet from the West, succeeded in creating by psychological techniques the form of a monk who followed her about, but she lost control of it and it grew inimical, and only after six months of difficult psychic struggle was she able to dissipate it (1954: 29n). The psychoanalyst Medard Boss, who spent some time in India and was well disposed to its philosophy, describes how he came across patients 'who had to pay with a severe mental illness for their newly acquired acquaintance with the Indian tradition. Their attempts to sink into meditation in the Indian fashion and to yield themselves up to *Brahman* had unleashed in them a schizophrenic chaos' (1965: 186).

9 CRITICISMS AND SHORTCOMINGS

1 In spite of his deep reservations regarding certain aspects of Christian doctrine, Jung's imperative concerning the need to develop our own yoga must be seen alongside his attempts to heal the ailing Christian tradition. On this, see Stein (1985).

2 For more recent discussions of cross-cultural psychology, see Marsella *et al.* (1985) and Roland (1988). Roland points out that 'Freudian psychoanalysis has not been concerned with any cross-civilizational perspective' (p. 324), but omits to mention Jung's efforts.

3 A rather more acceptable version is offered by Robert E. Allinson, who speculates that 'the Chinese mind does not differ from the Western mind in terms of representing a different *kind* of mind but rather a different *degree* of emphasis upon a universal human potential of understanding' (1989: 11–12).

4 See G.E.R. Lloyd's attempt to demystify the whole notion of entirely distinct mentalities. He draws attention to the existence of clear parallels between the intellectual traditions of

ancient Greece and ancient China, and argues that cultures are too complex to be characterised in terms of simple psychological categories (1990: Ch. 4).
5 For discussion of this issue see, for example, Jaffé (1983), Masson (1989), Odajnyk
(1976), Samuels (1992), and Wehr (1987). In view of Jung's close association with a
number of Jews, both as friends and as colleagues, the accusation of anti-semitism
seems far-fetched. His general philosophy, too, with its concern for the individual as
against the collective, and its cosmopolitan, eclectic outlook, was diametrically
opposed to Nazi ideology. In a lecture delivered in 1933 in both Cologne and Essen,
he remarked that 'The great events of world history are, at bottom, profoundly
unimportant. In the last analysis the essential thing is the life of the individual'
(CW10.315). And in a Presidential Address delivered in Copenhagen in 1937 to the
International General Medical Society for Psychotherapy, he urged the need for
psychotherapy to transcend the narrow boundaries of nations, and spoke of the nations
of Europe as forming a single family (see CW10.1064).
6 Questions concerning the ideological implications of intellectual and cultural con-
stucts go back to Marx and beyond, of course, and were beginning to be discussed in
the inter-war period, but it is fair to say that it is only in the second half of the century
that they have become widely recognised and debated.

10 CONCLUSIONS

1 For a useful discussion of Jung's relationship with Arnold Toynbee and R.C. Zaehner,
see Ulanov (1992: 220–43). Zaehner's views concerning the misuse of Eastern
spiritual techniques can be found in his books *Zen, Drugs and Mysticism* and *Our
Savage God*.
2 For a fuller discussion of the importance of the *Eranos* conferences, and of Jung's
place in the history of comparative religion and in the study of the phenomenology of
religious experience, see Sharpe (1975: Ch. 9). See also Ulanov (1992: Chs 3–5) for a
discussion of Jung's influence on the study of religion and mythology.
3 Examples of Jung's role in the area of what I have loosely called 'alternative'
psychologies can be found in Ajaya (1984), Grof (1985), Rowan (1976), and Wilber
(1990). On Assagioli and psychosynthesis, see Hardy (1987); and see Ajaya (1984).
On the history of the techniques of visualisation, see Watkins (1986) where Jung's
influence is acknowledged along with that of Oriental techniques of inner exploration.
4 Writers drawing Jung and the East into these discussions include Capra (1982),
Sheldrake (1981), and Talbot (1981). For a discussion of Jung's relevance to 'green'
issues, see Bishop (1990).
5 Other distinguished psychoanalysts who have sought to build bridges with Eastern
philosophies include Karen Horney, Medard Boss, and R.D. Laing. The reader
interested in recent developments in this area should consult Claxton (1986), Crook
and Fontana (1990), and Welwood (1979).
6 For an interesting discussion of pluralism in relation to Jung's thought, see Samuels
(1989).
7 The reference here is oblique, but is presumably to certain ideas deriving from the
Mahāyāna tradition of Northern India and Tibet, especially from the *Mādhyamaka*
school. It is worth noting that relativism does not seem to have been the agonising
problem in India and China that it has been in the West, where the quest for epistemological certainty has been of more paramount importance.
8 Barnaby and D'Acierno (1990) contains several interesting discussions about the
relationship between Jung and both hermeneutics and postmodernism. A typical
remark is David Miller's claim that 'Jung was postmodern before the times' (p. 326).

BIBLIOGRAPHY

Abegg, L. (1952) *The Mind of East-Asia*, Thames & Hudson, London and New York.

Ajaya, Swami (1984) *Psychotherapy East and West: A Unifying Paradigm*, Himalayan International Institute, Homesdale, Pen.

Allinson, R. (ed.) (1989) *Understanding the Chinese Mind: Philosophical Roots*, Oxford University Press, Hong-Kong.

Almond, P. (1988) *The British Discovery of Buddhism*, Cambridge University Press, Cambridge.

Ames, R.T. (1991) 'Meaning as Imaging: Prolegomena to a Confucian Epistemology', in Deutsch, E. (1991).

Avens, R. (1980) *Imagination is Reality: Western Nirvana in Jung*, Spring Publications, Dallas.

Aziz, R. (1990) *C.G. Jung's Psychology of Religion and Synchronicity*, State University of New York Press, New York.

Barnaby, K, and D'Acierno, P. (eds) (1990) *C.G. Jung and the Humanities: Towards a Hermeneutical Culture*, Routledge, London.

Barnes, M. (1991) *God East and West*, SPCK, London.

Bennett, E.A. (1961) *C.G. Jung*, Bassie & Rockliff, London.

Bernal, M. (1987) *Black Athena: The Afroasiatic Roots of Classical Civilization*, Vintage, London.

Bernstein, R.J. (1983) *Beyond Objectivism and Relativism: Science, Hermeneutics and Praxis*, Basil Blackwell, Oxford.

Bishop, P. (1984) 'Jung, Eastern Religion and the Language of Imagination', *The Eastern Buddhist*, 17: 1.

—— (1990) *The Greening of Psychology: The Vegetable World in Myth, Dream, and Healing*, Spring Publications, Dallas.

Bleicher, J. (1982) *The Hermeneutic Imagination*, Routledge, London.

Bohm, D. (1980) *Wholeness and the Implicate Order*, Routledge, London.

Bohm, D. and Peat, F.D. (1989) *Science, Order and Creativity*, Routlege, London.

Boss, M. (1965) *A Psychiatrist Discovers India*, Oswald Wolf, London.

Brome, V. (1980) *Jung: Man and Myth*, Paladin Books, London.

Brooke, R. (1991) *Jung and Phenomenology*, Routledge, London.

Brown, C.A. (1981) *Jung's Hermeneutical Doctrine: Its Theological Significance*, Scholars Press, Chico, Calif.

Buber, M. (1957) *The Eclipse of God*, Harper, New York.

Burtt, E. (1967) *In Search of Philosophical Understanding*, Hacket, Indianapolis.

Capra, F. (1982) *The Tao of Physics*, Collins, London.

Clarke, J.J. (1992) *In Search of Jung: Historical and Philosophical Enquiries*, Routledge, London.

Claxton, G. (ed.) (1986) *Beyond Therapy: The Impact of Eastern Religions on Psychological Theory and Practice*, Wisdom Publications, London.

Cleary, T. (trans. and ed.) (1991) *The Secret of the Golden Flower*, Harper, San Francisco.

Coward, H. (1985) *Jung and Eastern Thought*, State University of New York Press, New York.

—— (1990) *Derrida and Indian Philosophy*, State University of New York Press, New York.

Cox, H. (1988) *Many Mansions: A Christian's Encounter with Other Faiths*, Beacon Press, Boston.

Cronin, V. (1955) *The Wise Man from the West*, Collins, London.

Crook, J. and Fontana, D. (1990) *Space in Mind: East–West Psychology and Contemporary Buddhism*, Element Books, Shaftesbury.

Davidson, D. (1984) *Inquiries into Truth and Interpretation*, Oxford University Press, London.

Deutsch, E. (ed.) (1991) *Culture and Modernity: East–West Philosophic Perspectives*, University of Hawaii Press, Honolulu.

Dry, A. (1961) *The Psychology of Jung*, Methuen, London.

Dumoulin, H. (1976) *Buddhism in the Modern World*, Collier Books, London.

—— (1979) *Zen Enlightenment: Origins and Meaning*, Weatherill, Tokyo.

Dyer, D.R. (1991) *Cross-Currents of Jungian Thought: An Annotated Bibliography*, Shambhala, Boston and London.

Eliade, M. (1960) *Myths, Dreams and Mysteries*, Harper, New York.

Edwardes, M. (1971) *East–West Passage: The Travel of Ideas, Arts and Inventions between Asia and the Western World*, Cassell, London.

Evans, R.I. (1979) *Jung on Elementary Psychology: A Discussion between C.G. Jung and Richard I. Evans*, Routledge, London.

Evans-Wentz, W.Y. (trans. and ed.) (1954) *The Tibetan Book of the Great Liberation*, Oxford University Press, London.

—— (trans. and ed.) (1960) *The Tibetan Book of the Dead*, Oxford University Press, London.

Faber, P.A. and Saayman, G.S. (1984) 'On the Relation of the Doctrines of Yoga to Jung's Psychology', in Papadopoulos, R.K. and Saayman, G.S. (1984).

Feyerabend, P. (1978) *Against Method*, Verso, London.

Fields, R. (1986) *How the Swans Came to the Lake: A Narrative History of Buddhism in America*, Shambhala, Boston.

Flew, A.G.N. (1971) *An Introduction to Western Philosophy: Ideas and Arguments from Plato to Sartre*, Thames & Hudson, London.

Fox, W. (1990) *Toward a Transpersonal Ecology: Developing New Foundations for Environmentalism*, Shambhala, Boston.

Frey-Rohn, L. (1974) *From Freud to Jung: A Comparative Study of the Psychology of the Unconscious*, Putnam, New York.

Fromm, E. (1956) *The Sane Society*, Routledge, London.

—— (1960) *The Fear of Freedom*, Routledge, London.

—— (1986) *Psychoanalysis and Zen Buddhism*, Unwin Hyman, London.

Gadamer, H-G. (1975) *Truth and Method*, Sheed & Ward, London.

Girardot, N. (1983) *Myth and Meaning in Early Taoism*, University of California Press, Berkeley.

Glover, E. (1950) *Freud or Jung*, George Allen & Unwin, London.

Govinda, A. (1989) *A Living Buddhism for the West*, Shambhala, Boston.

Graham, A.C. (1989) *Disputers of Tao: Philosophical Argument in Ancient China*, Open Court, La Salle, Ill.

Granet, M. (1934) *La Pensée Chinoise*, Albin Michel, Paris.

Griffiths, B. (1982) *The Marriage of East and West*, Collins, Glasgow.

Grison, P. (1968) 'The Golden Flower and its Fruit', *Studies in Comparative Religion*, 2: 3.

Grof, S. (1985) *Beyond the Brain: Birth, Death and Transcendence in Psychotherapy*, State University of New York Press, New York.

Guenther, H. (1975) *The Dawn of Tantra*, Shambhala, Berkeley.

—— (1989) *Tibetan Buddhism in Western Perspective*, Dharma Publishing, Berkeley.

Guthrie, W.K.C. (1971) *A History of Greek Philosophy Vol.II: The Presocratic Tradition from Parmenides to Democritus*, Cambridge University Press, London.

Halbfass, W. (1988) *India and Europe: An Essay in Understanding*, State University of New York Press, New York.

Hannah, B. (1976) *Jung: His Life and Work*, Pedigree Books, New York.

Hardy, J. (1987) *Psychology with a Soul: Psychosynthesis in Evolutionary Context*, Routledge, London.

Harris, N.D. (1928) *Europe and the East*, George Allen & Unwin, London.

Harris, R.B. (ed.) (1982) *Neoplatonism and Indian Thought*, International Society for Neoplatonist Studies, Norfolk.

Hearnshaw, L.S. (1987) *The Shaping of Modern Psychology*, Routledge, London.

Henderson, J.B. (1984) *The Development and Decline of Chinese Cosmology*, Columbia University Press, New York.

Hogenson, G.B. (1983) *Jung's Struggle with Freud*, University of Notre Dame Press, Notre Dame.

Homans, P. (1979) *Jung in Context: Modernity and the Making of a Psychology*, University of Chicago Press, Chicago and London.

Hick, J. (1985) *Problems of Religious Pluralism*, St Martin's Press, New York.

Hillman, J. (1975) *Revisioning Psychology*, Harper & Row, New York.

Iyer, R. (ed.) (1965) *The Glass Curtain Between Asia and Europe: A Symposium on the Historical Encounters and the Changing Attitudes of the Peoples of East and West*, Oxford University Press, London.

Jacobi, J. (1942) *The Psychology of C.G. Jung*, Routledge, London.

Jacobson, N.P. (1969) 'The Possibility of Oriental Influence on Hume's Philosophy', *Philosophy East and West*, 19: 1.

—— (1986) *Understanding Buddhism*, South Illinois University Press, Carbondale.

Jaffé, A. (1983) *The Myth of Meaning in the Work of C.G. Jung*, Daimon Verlag, Zürich.

—— (1989) *From the Life and Work of C.G. Jung*, Daimon Verlag, Zürich.

Jarrett, J.L. (1992) 'Jung and Hermeneutics', *Harvest*, 38.

Johnston, W. (1981) *The Mirror-Mind: Zen–Christian Dialogue*, Fordham University Press, New York.

Jones, R.H. (1979) 'Jung and Eastern Religious Traditions', *Religion*, 9: 2.

Jung, C.G. (1953–83) *The Collected Works of C.G. Jung* (edited by H. Read, M. Fordham and G. Adler; translated by R.F.C. Hull), Routledge, London, and Princeton University Press, Princeton.

—— (1961) *Modern Man in Search of a Soul*, Routledge, London.

—— (1973 and 1975) *Letters* (edited by G. Adler and A. Jaffé; translated by R.F.C. Hull), Vol. I: 1906–1950; Vol. II: 1951–1961. Routledge, London, and Princeton University Press, Princeton.

—— (1974) *The Undiscovered Self*, Routledge, London and New York.

—— (1975) 'Psychological Commentary on Kundalini Yoga, Part 1', *Spring: A Journal of Archetypal Psychology and Jungian Thought*.

—— (1976) 'Psychological Commentary on Kundalini Yoga, Part 2', *Spring: A Journal of Analytical Psychology and Jungian Thought*.

—— (1983) *Memories, Dreams, Reflections* (recorded and edited by A. Jaffé), Fontana, London.

—— (1985) *Synchronicity: An Acausal Connecting Principle*, Routledge, London.

Katz, N. (ed.) (1983) *Buddhist and Western Psychology*, Prajna Press, Boulder.

Kuhn, T.S. (1962) *The Structure of Scientific Revolutions*, University of Chicago Press, Chicago.

Lach, D. (1970) *Asia in the Making of Europe*, University of Chicago Press, Chicago.

Lakatos, I. and Musgrave, A. (eds) (1970) *Criticism and the Growth of Knowledge*, Cambridge University Press, Cambridge.

Larson, G.J. and Deutsch, E. (eds) (1988) *Interpreting Across Boundaries: New Essays in Comparative Philosophy*, Princeton University Press, Princeton.

Lévy-Bruhl, L. (1922) *La Mentalité Primitive*, Felix Alcan, Paris.

Liu, Ming-Wood (1982) 'The Harmonious Universe of Fa-tsang and Leibniz: A Comparative Study', *Philosophy East and West*, 32: 1.

Lloyd, G. (1990) *Demystifying Mentalities*, Cambridge University Press, Cambridge.

Lopez, D.S. (ed.) (1988) *Buddhist Hermeneutics*, University Press of Hawaii, Honolulu.

Lundquist, J.M. (1990) 'C.G. Jung and the Temple: Symbols of Wholeness', in Barnaby, K. and D'Acierno, P. (1990).

MacIntyre, A. (1988) *Whose Justice? Whose Rationality?*, University of Notre Dame Press, Notre Dame.

Marsella, A.J., de Vos, G. and Hsu, F.L.K. (eds) (1985) *Culture and Self: Asian and Western Perspectives*, Tavistock, London.

Masson, G. (1989) *Against Therapy*, Collins, London.

Matilal, B.K. (1986) *Perception*, Oxford University Press, Oxford.

Mattoon, M. (1981) *Jungian Psychology in Perspective*, Free Press, New York.

Mehta, J.L. (1967) *Martin Heidegger: The Way and the Vision*, University Press of Hawaii, Honolulu.

—— (1985) *India and the West: The Problem of Understanding*, Scholars Press, Chico, Calif.

—— (1989) 'Problems of Understanding', *Philosophy East and West*, 39: 1.

Mistry, F. (1981) *Nietzsche and Buddhism: A Prolegomena to a Comparative Study*, W. de Gruyter, Berlin.

Moacanin, R. (1986) *Jung's Psychology and Tibetan Buddhism: Western and Eastern Paths to the Heart*, Wisdom Publications, London.

Mungello, D. (1977) *Leibniz and Confucianism: The Search for Accord*, University Press of Hawaii, Honolulu.

Needham, J. (1956) *Science and Civilization in China*, Vol. 2, Cambridge University Press, Cambridge.

—— (1969) *Within Four Seas: Dialogue between East and West*, George Allen & Unwin, London.

Netland, H. (1991) *Dissonant Voices: Religious Pluralism and the Question of Truth*, Apollos, Leicester.

Nietzsche, F. (1986) *Human, all too Human*, Cambridge University Press, Cambridge.

Northrop, F.S.C. (1946) *The Meeting of East and West*, Macmillan, New York.

Odajnyk, V.W. (1976) *Jung and Politics: The Political and Social Ideas of C.G. Jung*, New York University Press, New York.

Otto, R. (1957) *Mysticism East and West: A Comparative Analysis of the Nature of Mysticism*, Meridian Books, New York.

Panikkar, R. (1978) *The Intrareligious Dialogue*, Paulist Press, New York.

—— (1979) *Myth, Faith and Hermeneutics*, Paulist Press, New York.

Papadopoulos, R.K. (1984) 'Jung and the Concept of the Other', in Papadopoulos, R.K. and Saayman, G.S. (1984).

Papadopoulos, R.K. and Saayman, G.S. (eds) (1984) *Jung in Modern Perspective*, Wildwood House, London.

Parkes, G. (ed.) (1987) *Heidegger and Asian Thought*, University Press of Hawaii, Honolulu.

205

—— (1991) *Nietzsche and Asian Thought*, University of Chicago Press, Chicago.

Plott, J. *et al.* (1979ff) *Global History of Philosophy*, 5 Vols, Motilal Banarsidas, Delhi.

Progoff, I. (1953) *Jung's Psychology and its Social Meaning*, Dialogue House Library, New York.

—— (1973) *Jung, Synchronicity, and Human Destiny*, Julian Press, New York.

Radhakrishnan, S. (1939) *Eastern Religions and Western Thought*, Oxford University Press, Delhi.

Rée, J. (1991) 'The Vanity of Historicism', *New Literary History: A Journal of Theory and Interpretation*, 22: 4.

Reynolds, J. (trans. and ed.) (1989) *Self-Liberation Through Seeing with Naked Awareness*, Station Hill Press, Barrytown, New York.

Roland, A. (1988) *In Search of Self in India and Japan: Towards a Cross-Cultural Psychology*, Princeton University Press, Princeton.

Rorty, R. (1979) *Philosophy and the Mirror of Nature*, Princeton University Press, Princeton.

Rowan, J. (1976) *Ordinary Ecstasy: Humanistic Psychology in Action*, Routledge, London.

Said, E. (1978) *Orientalism*, Penguin, Harmondsworth.

Samuels, A. (1985) *Jung and the Post-Jungians*, Routledge, London.

—— (1989) *The Plural Psyche: Personality, Morality, and the Father*, Routledge, London.

—— (1992) 'National Psychology, National Socialism, and Analytical Psychology', *Journal of Analytical Psychology*, 37: 1.

Satchidananda, K. (1985) *Philosophy in India: Traditions, Teaching and Research*, Motilal Banarsidas, Delhi.

Schmitz, O.A.H. (1923) *Psychoanalyse und Yoga*, Darmstadt.

Schultz, J.H. (1932) *Das Autogene Training*, Berlin.

Schweitzer, A. (1936) *Indian Thought and its Development*, Adam and Charles Black, London.

Schwab, R. (1984) *The Oriental Renaissance: Europe's Rediscovery of India and the East, 1680–1880*, Columbia University Press, New York.

Segal, R. (ed.) (1992) *The Gnostic Jung*, Princeton University Press, Princeton.

Segaller, S. and Berger, M. (1989) *Jung: The Wisdom of the Dream*, Weidenfeld and Nicolson, London.

Sharpe, E.J. (1975) *Comparative Religion: A History*, Duckworth, London.

Sheldrake, R. (1981) *A New Science of Life: The Hypothesis of Formative Causation*, Blond & Briggs, London.

Smart, N. (1981) *Beyond Ideology: Religion and the Future of Civilization*, Collins, London.

Smith, W.C. (1964) *The Meaning and End of Religion: A New Approach to the Religions of Mankind*, Macmillan, New York.

—— (1981) *Towards a World Theology: Faith and the Comparative History of Religion*, Macmillan, London.

Spiegelman, J.M. and Miyuki, M. (1985) *Buddhism and Jungian Psychology*, Falcon Press, Phoenix.

Steele, R.S. (1982) *Freud and Jung: Conflicts in Interpretation*, Routledge, London.

Stein, M. (1985) *Jung's Treatment of Christianity: The Psychotherapy of a Religious Tradition*, Chiron, Wilmette, Ill.

Stern, P. (1976) *C.G. Jung: The Haunted Prophet*, Brazillier, New York.

Stevens, A. (1982) *Archetype: A Natural History of the Self*, Routledge, London.

—— (1990) *On Jung*, Routledge, London.

Stuart-Hughes, H. (1979) *Consciousness and Society: The Reorientation of European Social Thought, 1890–1930*, Harvester, Brighton.

Talbot, M. (1981) *Mysticism and the New Physics*, Bantam Books, New York.

Teilhard de Chardin, P. (1959) *The Phenomenon of Man*, Collins, London.

Theunissen, M. (1984) *The Other*, MIT Press, Cambridge, Mass.

Tucci, G. (1969) *The Theory and Practice of the Mandala*, Rider, London.

Ulanov, B. (1992) *Jung and the Outside World*, Chiron Publications, Wilmette, Ill.

Verikatcher, C. (1965) 'The Historical Context of the Encounter between Asia and Europe', in Iyer, R. (1965).

von Franz, M.-L. (1975) *C.G. Jung: His Myth in our Time*, Putnam, New York.

—— (1980) *On Divination and Synchronicity: The Psychology of Meaningful Chance*, Inner City Books, Toronto.

Warnke, G. (1987) *Gadamer: Hermeneutics, Tradition and Reason*, Polity Press, Oxford.

Watkins, M. (1986) *Waking Dreams*, Spring Publictions, Dallas.

Watts, A. (1973) *Psychotherapy East and West*, Penguin, Harmondsworth.

Wehr, G. (1987) *Jung, A Biography*, Shambhala, Boston.

Welbon, G. (1968) *The Buddhist Nirvana and its Western Interpreters*, University of Chicago Press, Chicago.

Welwood, J. (ed.) (1979) *The Meeting of the Ways: Explorations in East–West Psychiatry*, Schocken Books, New York.

Whorf, B.L. (1956) *Language, Thought and Reality: Selected Writings*, MIT Press, Cambridge, Mass.

Wilber, K. (1990) *Eye to Eye: The Quest for the New Paradigm*, Shambhala, Boston.

Wilhelm, R. (trans. and ed.) (1962) *The Secret of the Golden Flower: A Chinese Book of Life*, Routledge, London.

—— (trans. and ed.) (1968) *I Ching or Book of Changes*, Arkana, Harmondsworth.

Willson, A.L. (1964) *A Mythical Image: The Ideal of India in German Romanticism*, Duke University Press, Durham, N.C.

Winch, P. (1958) *The Idea of a Social Science*, Routledge, London.

Wood, D. (1990) *Philosophy at the Limit*, Unwin Hyman, London.

Woodroffe, J.G. (a.k.a. Arthur Avalon) (1974) *The Serpent Power*, Dover, New York.

Zaehner, R.C. (1970) *Concordant Discord: The Interdependence of Faiths*, Clarendon Press, Oxford.

NAME INDEX

SUBJECT INDEX

fantasy 50–1, 85, 88, 134, 136, 157;
  world of 6, 83
Faust 132
feminism 4
Five Classics 89
Flower Sermon, the Buddha's 130, 131
fore-structures 43, 45

Gestalt 112
glass curtain 17–18
Gnosticism/gnostics 48, 52, 64–5, 71,
  83, 109, 135, 149, 156, 160, 175, 197
Golden Elixir of Life, Order of the 81
grand narratives 189–90
Greece, ancient 15, 20, 28, 32, 33
gymnosophists 28

harmony, pre-established 98
hegemony, cultural 18, 23, 27
hermeneutical circle 43, 45, 51, 85
hermeneutics 11–13, 42–7, 82, 95,
  112, 196; Jung and 47–54, 59, 62,
  67, 70, 88, 89, 94, 112, 126, 132–3,
  136–7, 144, 150, 152, 157, 161, 165,
  166–70, 177, 180, 182, 187, 190
hexagrams 90–4, 99
Higher Criticism 35
Hindu/Hinduism 33, 35, 70, 76–7, 79,
  103, 106, 159, 188
historicism 17, 37, 197
historicity, of human understanding
  42–5, 50
history, of ideas 7, 8, 9, 12, 17, 33, 78,
  179; intellectual 25, 28, 181; Jung's
  view of 153; theory of 18; Western
  15; universal/world 8, 21, 33
History of Greek Philosophy 21
History of Western Philosophy 21
holism/holistic 72–3, 112, 185; and
  quantum physics 98, 185; and
  Taoism 80
horizons, of understanding 43, 45–6
human nature, theory of 66, 190
humanism 190
humanities 8

I Ching 3, 7, 12, 31, 39, 49, 53, 60–1,
  63, 73, 79, 80, 89–102, 150, 156,
  172, 185, 186, 195, 198, 199
idealism, philosphical 128, 147
ideology 9
images, mental 69–70, 83, 84, 85, 86,
  128, 130, 135, 186, 198

imaginal, the 186
imagination 186, power of 88
Imitation of Christ, The 72
imperialism 190; cultural 17, 19, 165;
  Western 18
implicate order 199
In Search of Jung 4
inclusivism 194
incommensurability 21, 194, 197
India 3, 6, 11, 14, 15, 21, 23, 24, 25,
  26, 28, 29–35, 40, 57, 58, 65, 70, 75,
  78, 123, 127, 145, 154, 162, 181,
  200; Jung's visit to 61–3, 144, 158,
  179
Indian Thought and its Development 21
individuation 74–9, 104–6, 115, 121,
  137–9, 144, 160, 169, 186; and
  Buddhism 120, 122, 126, 129, 131,
  133; Jung's 78–9, 180; and Taoism
  80, 85–8; and yoga 112, 114, 167
inflation, psychic 146
instinct 113
International General Medical Society
  for Psychotherapy 163, 201
interpretation 42, 45, 47–8, 53, 95; of
  symptoms 47
Interpreting Across Boundaries 40
Introduction to Western Philosophy 21
Introduction to Zen Buddhism 130, 158
introspection 77, 86, 128, 149, 152
introvert/extravert 20, 167; cultures as
  66–7, 72, 109, 161
irrationalism 7
Islam 14, 23, 188

Japan 40, 75, 129, 130, 162
Jesuits 3, 24, 29–30, 35, 39
Jews 163–4, 188, 201
Judaeo-Christianity 15, 34

k'an 94
Kantianism, Jung's 65, 70
karma 107–8, 124, 125, 126, 150, 167, 199
Kendō 159
kleshas 117
kōan 130, 132–3, 177, 199
Konarak 62
kundalinī 110–11, 115, 134, 154

lamaism 123
language game 16–17
libido 75, 104, 105, 106–7, 172
Light of Asia, The 34, 58